Women of
Florida Fiction

Women of Florida Fiction

Essays on 12 Sunshine State Writers

Edited by TAMMY POWLEY
and APRIL VAN CAMP

McFarland & Company, Inc., Publishers
Jefferson, North Carolina

LIBRARY OF CONGRESS CATALOGUING-IN-PUBLICATION DATA

Women of Florida fiction : essays on 12 Sunshine State writers / edited by Tammy Powley and April Van Camp.
   p.   cm.
Includes bibliographical references and index.

ISBN 978-0-7864-7894-1 (softcover : acid free paper) ∞
ISBN 978-1-4766-1822-7 (ebook)

1. American fiction—Women authors—History and criticism. 2. American fiction—Florida—History and criticism. 3. Women in literature. 4. Florida—In literature. I. Powley, Tammy, editor. II. Van Camp, April, editor.
PS374.W6W68 2015
813.009'9287—dc23   2014041673

BRITISH LIBRARY CATALOGUING DATA ARE AVAILABLE

© 2015 Tammy Powley and April Van Camp. All rights reserved

No part of this book may be reproduced or transmitted in any form or by any means, electronic or mechanical, including photocopying or recording, or by any information storage and retrieval system, without permission in writing from the publisher.

Cover images © iStock/Thinkstock

Printed in the United States of America

McFarland & Company, Inc., Publishers
   Box 611, Jefferson, North Carolina 28640
   www.mcfarlandpub.com

Table of Contents

Preface (Tammy Powley) — 1

Introduction (April Van Camp) — 3

1. Karen Russell — 11
- Gators, Goggles and Giant Shells: Fantasy and Florida in the Short Stories (Tammy Powley) — 13
- Into the Swamp: An Examination of Folk Narrative Structures and Storylines in Karen Russell's *Swamplandia!* (Lori Cornelius) — 26

2. Elizabeth Stuckey-French — 39
- A Laughing Matter: Smiling Through the Pain in Elizabeth Stuckey-French's Novels (April Van Camp) — 41

3. Lynne Barrett — 51
- 'Canes, Critters and Criminals in Lynne Barrett's Storytelling (Claudia S. Slate) — 53

4. Jennine Capó Crucet — 63
- On Haunted Shores: Restriction and Resistance in Jennine Capó Crucet's *How to Leave Hialeah* (Camila Alvarez) — 66

5. Connie May Fowler — 77
- Cracker Redemption: Life, Death and Homecoming in *The Problem with Murmur Lee* (Jill C. Jones) — 79

Table of Contents

6. Janis Owens — 91
- A Summer to Pardon: Southern Gothic and the Family in Janis Owens's *Myra Sims* (Sarah M. Mallonee) — 93
- American Ghosts and American Realities: Past and Present of Race Relations in Janis Owens's *American Ghost* (Beate Rodewald) — 101

7. Heidi Boehringer — 109
- Walk on the Wild Side: Heidi Boehringer's Fiction and a Post-Feminist Landscape (Maxine Lavon Montgomery) — 111

8. Angela Hunt — 121
- Romance Fiction in Florida: The Crisscross of Jane Austen and Angela Hunt (Tammy Powley) — 123
- Angela Hunt's Uncanny Florida (Lisa K. Perdigao) — 133

9. Edna Buchanan — 145
- Florida's Femme Fatale (Wendy Dwyer) — 147

10. Ana Menéndez — 155
- Entrapment and Escape (Jane Anderson Jones) — 157

11. Vicki Hendricks — 169
- The Spectacle of the Body in *Florida Gothic Stories* (Angela Tenga) — 171

12. Mary Jane Ryals — 187
- Racial Progress, Not Movement, Is Evident as the Trees Slowly Walk in Mary Jane Ryals's *Cookie and Me* (Valerie E. Kasper) — 189

Appendix: Interviews (Lynne Barrett, Jennine Capó Crucet, Vicki Hendricks, Angela Hunt) — 201

About the Contributors — 219

Index — 223

Preface

TAMMY POWLEY

My thoughts turned to Florida female writers after I attended the 2011 Florida College English Association Conference (FCEA) in Melbourne, Florida. At the conference, I sat in on a number of presentations about the works of Florida author Karen Russell. The specific presentations included "For the Love of the Place: A Look at Karen Russell's Characterization and Setting in South Florida" by Lori Cornelius; "Telling Human Lies: Domesticating the Werewolf in Karen Russell's *St. Lucy's Home for Girls Raised by Wolves*" by Douglas Ford; and "Egdon Heath's Evil Cousin" by Rich McKee. So far, Russell has published two major works, the novel *Swamplandia!* and a collection of short stories, *St. Lucy's Home for Girls Raised by Wolves*. A basic explanation of her subject matter is fantasy, some of which is mixed with a dash of Florida style settings. At least, that is what I took away from the conference until I read some of her work. Though this genre seemed outside of my normal comfort zone for reading, which includes a mix of Southern literature and classic Victorian works, I was intrigued and a little surprised that I had not heard of her novel or this author before. I wanted to find out more about her work, and while I was at it, I became curious about other Florida writers who might be out there ready for me to discover and add to my ever-growing reading list.

After providing myself with some immediate gratification of Russell's works via Amazon's Kindle listings, I moved on to Google the key words "Florida fiction writers." I was directed to a list on Amazon.com of "Top Florida Novels." This list included 17 novels, all written by men, and most were detective or mystery novels. Almost a year later, I repeated this search, just out of curiosity, and this same search string brought up a similar list on Amazon.com. This time the list was entitled "Florida Fiction's best: some established authors and some new authors." This list includes seven books, all written by men. More than likely their names are familiar: Carl Hiaasen, Randy Wayne White, Robert Tacoma, Tom Corcoran, James O. Born, James W. Hall, and Dave Barry.

During my initial research, the more lists I checked and the more I drilled through Google links I wondered: Where were the women? I did find some who had written fiction pieces located in Florida, but the authors themselves were not Floridians. Additionally, I had to wade through a plethora of self-published authors who now are often merged in Amazon.com lists as well as other areas of the Internet, and I found it tricky to cull them. Of course, eventually, after much web searching, Zora Neale Hurston and Marjorie Kinnan Rawlings appeared, but I was still unable to find much as far as contemporary female writers from Florida. Plus, because of Russell's use of Florida-style settings, I was curious about female writers from Florida who actually placed their stories in the state. I moved onto Facebook and posted a simple question to my friends: Do you know of any female fiction writers who either are from Florida or live in Florida? My luck began to change, and a few of my bookish friends started answering. I also started finding more leads by searching through on-line library catalogs, and I read through Florida university and college writing program web sites for professors who are published authors, looking specifically for novelists versus poets and authors who are Florida residents and who are writing about Florida.

As I started compiling a preliminary list of my own, I wondered: Why are none of these women's works included on Amazon's "Florida Fiction's Best" list? Is there anything distinctive about being a Florida writer in the first place, let alone a female fiction writer from Florida? Is this list simply created because these books sell well, and if so, why are these books representative of Florida's best-selling fiction?

At this stage, I began to read Karen Russell's short story collection, *St. Lucy's Home for Girls Raised by Wolves*, and I also started talking about Russell and my research on female Florida fiction writers to my friend and colleague Dr. April Van Camp, which of course, produced more questions: What sort of relationships do we see between these authors and their works, especially those set in Florida? Do these works have any distinctly female elements to them? Where do the works and the authors belong in the general literary canon as well as in the Florida literary canon?

Our questions and my earlier research initiated a fairly comprehensive list. There did not seem to be a huge number of female Florida authors, so we just added everyone at first. We even included authors on this list who were merely part-time residents but were also established in Florida's canon, such as Marjorie Kinnan Rawlings and Elizabeth Bishop. However, while there is still plenty to discuss when it comes to these authors, we were more interested in writers whose works had acquired little or no critical research. An academic database search will invariably bring up plenty of secondary source material about Rawlings, but what about Russell? Even though Karen Russell has become the darling of the current literary world, giving interviews to various media such as the magazine *Poets & Writers* and even receiving an enthusiastic endorsement from Carl Hiaasen, there is still little academic source material about her work. Instead, databases include biographical information and book reviews. Of course, thanks to the three presenters at the 2011 FCEA conference, this has started to change, and that is what I wanted to continue to do, for Russell and other contemporary women writers from Florida.

Sorting through the list was our next step. We decided the scope of the project would include female Florida authors whose fiction, at least some of it, is set in Florida. A dozen authors made the final list for *Women of Florida Fiction: Essays on 12 Sunshine State Writers*.

Introduction

April Van Camp

The pursuit of Florida's feminine fiction is not a vain venture, and the question that initiated the search—In a collection of Florida literature, where are all the women?—is no longer difficult to answer. Florida's women writers are writing. Perhaps their anonymity or at least their dwarfed presence on the Internet and in critical work occurs because they are not solely writers, but they are also teachers, insurance underwriters, international travelers, conference speakers, wives, partners, moms, grandmothers, daughters, and mentors. In other words, Florida women writers are doing a whole lot of what all women do: multiple jobs! Like many women who have what my mother calls "too many irons in the fire," Florida writers use their busy lives, their colorful pasts, their hopeful futures, and their pressing deadlines as muses, including family, friends, and personal fantasies in their fiction. While this method may provide fodder for stories, it does not necessarily make time for writing or for self-promotion. Still, these women write. They write gritty/romantic, down home/up town, backwoods/big city, fiery/cold-blooded, kindhearted/mean-spirited, and sometimes downright dirty descriptions of Florida landscapes, its myriad of natives, neighbors, and transplants, and its beautiful, bizarre, allure to the retired, the reclusive, and the repugnant. Like Eve in *God's Garden*, Florida women writers point directly at the snake as well as the tree of life, reminding us of the peril in Paradise.

Since these women's works are so direct, so viable, so intriguing, why are there so few critical essays written about their fiction? Is there a prevailing arrogance among academia that dismisses popular fiction, and if so, what are the criteria for dismissal and admission? These questions also focused our work on *Women of Florida Fiction*, but many times, questions lead to more questions, more challenges, and—at the very least—some historical musing.

Book clubs were prolific in previous decades. When the Book-of-the-Month Club was in its heyday, 1930s through 1950s and fairly strong through the 1970s—it could create sales in the hundreds of thousands by selecting a book. Just mentioning a book in its news bulletin would often result in tens of thousands in sales. Something happened to book sales since the era of the clubs. Maybe it was the Internet—among other things. Did this club and others slight female authors, or were there just too few females writing? Men did sit on the selection committees in large numbers. Ironically, the feminist movement became prominent about the time that the book clubs were beginning their death march. Any connection? It is difficult to see any, but perhaps our vision is obstructed because the social changes are too big to be visible in small-scale things like books. Books ride on a social sea that is much bigger than individual works or authors.

Today, the clubs are gone in comparative influence although Oprah and others still maintain the tradition, as Connie May Fowler will attest. Reading habits in general change throughout the years. What are people reading today? Are women writing these popular, contemporary works, or are women writing other kinds of stories? Certainly, some women are feeding into the mainstream literary tastes. Still, if some critics and theorists are correct, women writers should—rather—be serving some more significant and exalted feminine tastes. Is there an audience with a desire for such literature large enough to support its writers? Jane Austen was one of the first great writers to face the wrath of more radical feminists because she seems to cater to backward—male—values and is too acquiescent to conventional social norms. Where do today's Florida women writers fall? Are they unique, overflowing with a specifically feminist critique of society, or do they simply happen to be female—like Austen? Scholars want to know. Floridians want to know. Students need to know. Hopefully, these questions throw down a gauntlet and provoke a larger, more intense conversation, one that can comprise another edition by other interesting and interested writers.

If Florida's women writers are doing something special, maybe they will need to develop a following like Zora Neale Hurston did after her death. Her disciples brought her back and into the literary canon. Without them, her unusual style would have kept her out of the mainstream—a painful, frightening thought—a loss too agonizing to consider—and, to belabor the medieval metaphor, a challenge that calls for a champion.

Zora Neale Hurston, Marjorie Kinnan Rawlings, and Elizabeth Bishop fit neatly into the category of Florida's literary elite, and clearly, their talent as well as their readership has made this so. When does a piece of fiction cross the arbitrary, imaginary line between interpretive and escape literature? Does it occur at its birth, or does it cross over to the holy land at the author's death? Hopefully not! This book addresses living authors, none of whom are willing to die to ensure canonization. I will pull a Jennine Capó Crucet switch in point of view here (albeit poorly done and with apologies, Jennine): I do not think so. I think a work's significance is more aligned with quantum physics. In an unashamed and over simplified explanation, I think a good work by a good writer becomes both literary and commercial at the moment we readers acknowledge the work. Paying attention has much to do with valuing and creating value. *Women of Florida Fiction* is a book of literary criticism and more. Literary criticism can devolve into gratuitous attacks and faultfinding; conversely, it can become hagiography, shameless glorification. Then, too, it can become theoretical analysis that forgets literature is a pleasure, a joy, an entertainment, not merely a text for scholars to deconstruct. Our literary critics approached our Florida authors' works with reverence, and their respect shows in the essays. A number of the writers find psychoanalytic insights and others use an expository approach, analyzing character and Florida settings. Other contributors discuss gender, race, and Florida's diaspora. Still others concentrate on Florida as symbol and myth. Everyone knows that there is a hype, something that draws tourists and retirees to Florida, but rarely does hype match the reality. Perhaps Florida illustrates this in the extreme. At least, some of our essayists suggest this is so. Together, these essays comprise the first critical anthology of current Florida female fiction writers.

Angela Tenga, Jill C. Jones, and Sarah M. Mallonee's essays examine connections between their Florida authors and the Southern Gothic tradition. Their tendency to make comparisons between Flannery O'Connor and their authors' works suggests something about the depth and significance of these Florida authors. Similarly, Tammy Powley uses Jane Austen as a jumping point for her comparison, demonstrating author Angela Hunt's successful use of Austen's formula for a romance novel. My own essay fits neatly into this grouping as well since I discuss the value of Aristotelian comedic relief in Elizabeth Stuckey-French's dark novels. This is

Introduction

high praise for our current authors and an indication of a hopeful literary future.

Although Valerie E. Kasper uses a Toni Morrison essay to launch her own analysis of Mary Jane Ryals's novel, a comparison does not drive her thesis. Like Camila Alvarez and Jane Anderson Jones, Kasper is more interested in racial tensions, ethnic roots, and the meaning of home. Alvarez and Jones's tendency to make biographical connections between text and author remind us that a body of work is the work of a body, a person. Their essays contend that being at home in Florida and feeling at home in Florida are not always the same.

Florida as symbol and myth is the subject of Claudia S. Slate, Lisa K. Perdigao, Lori Cornelius, Wendy Dwyer, and Beate Rodewald's essays. Their works suggest that Florida is a creation, a product of the stories told about the state, its history, and its people. Their comments remind of the serious implications that accompany storytelling, with its ability to liberate and bind those lives whose narratives are told by others. Maxine Lavon Montgomery and Tammy Powley also discuss the paradox of Florida, but they do so in terms of setting. For Montgomery, Florida provides Heidi Boehringer's protagonist the opportunity to "venture into the unexplored, uncharted margins of life—the forbidden wild side," while Powley's assessment of Karen Russell's Florida is like "a fun-house mirror that shows a distorted image which is unpleasant, even a little disturbing."

As co-editors of this volume, Tammy Powley and I shared the task of writing the chapter introductions to each author. Tammy introduces Karen Russell, Elizabeth Stuckey-French, Lynne Barrett, Janis Owens, Angela Hunt, and Ana Menéndez, while I introduce Jennine Capó Crucet, Connie May Fowler, Heidi Boehringer, Edna Buchanan, Vicki Hendricks, and Mary Jane Ryals. I had the pleasure of conducting all of the author interviews.

Women of Florida Fiction is about pausing for those people who are important in life, a genuine curtsy—rarely performed in this contentious world—to those in whom we see worth. It is a book about honoring women who write fiction, who write about fiction, and who read fiction. It is a book about sisterhood and scholarship that defies the vicious stereotypes of competition and the divisive verdicts between those who can and cannot write. It is a book about beginnings and foundations, for the essays in this book beg for those who agree, disagree, argue, and defy to continue writing and contributing to the body of critical work. It is also a call to Florida fiction writers—both published and unpublished—to keep writing.

Beyond all the relational reasons for *Women of Florida Fiction*, it is a book that provides a permanent record of critical data on current Florida women writers. Internet sources are useful, but they are mutable and fleeting. Online biographies, interviews, magazine, and newspaper articles frequently disappear or change before a critical piece can be published using such sources. This collection of critical work is a stable source, so Florida Studies teachers have a textbook that allows them to expand their syllabi. Literature teachers have an anthology that gives them options for assigning contemporary Florida novels. The public readership has a resource to explore thematic and theoretical underpinnings in their reading material. Equally important, we hope the book creates a relationship between the authors and critics that will give our Florida women writers as much attention and admiration as Florida male writers.

1

Karen Russell

A simple search on the Internet using the keywords "Karen Russell" turns up a plethora of blog posts, author interviews, and book reviews. Since publication of her first collection of short stories, *St. Lucy's Home for Girls Raised by Wolves* in 2006, author Karen Russell has been as popular with the press as she is with her readership and was included in *The New Yorker's* "20 under 40" list of fiction writers in 2010. She has also won the *Transatlantic Review*/Henfield Foundation Award in 2005; she was a National Book Foundation "5 Under 35" honoree in 2009; she won the Bard fiction prize in 2011; she was awarded the Mary Ellen von der Heyden Berlin Prize and Fellow, American Academy in Berlin in 2012; and in 2012 she also was a nominee for the Pulitzer Prize in fiction ("Karen Russell").

Russell attended Northwestern University where she studied Spanish and graduated with a BA in 2003. She went on to turn her attention to creative writing and earn her MFA at Columbia University in 2006. During her last year at Columbia, she submitted her first story for publication to *The New Yorker*, which accepted "Haunting Olivia" in 2005 (Loeb). This story later was republished in *St. Lucy's Home for Girls Raised by Wolves*. After that first story was published, she continued to write short fiction pieces and has since been published again in *The New Yorker* as well as in other literary magazines such as *Zoetrop, Conjunctions, The Best American Short Stories, Granta*, and *Oxford American* ("Karen Russell").

Following the publication of her short story collection, Karen Russell's next book-length work was a novel called *Swamplandia!* The basis of the narrative for this first novel came from her short story entitled "Ava Wrestles the Alligator," a story about a young girl who is left by her family to manage its theme park called Swamplandia! Like the stories in her first short story collection, this novel's protagonist, Ava, is an adolescent who is friendless and alone. The backdrop is the Florida swamp and the island where she lives with her mentally ill sister who elopes with a ghost.

In February of 2013, Russell published her second short story collection, *Vampires in the Lemon Groves*. Like her previous two book-length publications, this latest work garnered a great deal of attention and positive reviews. Lauren O'Neal explains that "the surreal phenomena in these stories break your heart but leave your suspension of disbelief completely intact."

Born in 1981 in Miami, Florida, Russell is known for her mix of the gothic, "magical narrative" (qtd. in Loed), and unique settings. In many of her interviews, the author discusses how the Florida environment where she was raised affects her narratives. Family outings to the Everglades and her childhood curiosity about early Florida settlers became her inspiration. Russell's stores have been described as "conduct[ing] a sort of marvelous flirtation with speculative fiction, placing her characters—mostly kids and teenagers—in bewildering, semi-magical situations perfectly calibrated to open the cocoon of adolescence and drag them into pain and knowledge and growth" (O'Neal).

Works Cited

"Karen Russell." *Books and Authors*. (2012). *Gale*. Web. 11 Apr 2012.

Loeb, Eryn. "The Strangeness Quotient." *Poets and Writers*. 39.2 (2011): 52–55. *EBSCO*. Web. 11 Apr 2012.

O'Neal, Lauren. "The Rumpus Interview with Karen Russell." *The Rumpus*. 4 April 2013. Web. 1 May 2012. http://therumpus.net/2013/04/the-rumpus-interview-with-karen-russell/.

Gators, Goggles and Giant Shells
Fantasy and Florida in the Short Stories

Tammy Powley

Magical swimming goggles, giant fiber glass conch shells, and alligator wrestling make up some of the strange circumstances that somehow become fantasy with a dash of reality in Karen Russell's short story collection *St. Lucy's Home for Girls Raised by Wolves.* The title of the book is also the title of the last story in this collection, and while this story does not have a connection to Florida, the theme of this story permeates the other stories in the book: loss and loneliness. Out of the ten stories in this collection, six of the stories have a subtropical setting; however, all include adolescent protagonists, who Mark Budman claims "talk and think like adults." Russell explains that she is "drawn to child narrators in part because ... they can shift fluidly between believing in animist or supernatural explanations and [have] a more analytical/conventional understanding of their situation" ("Ask Karen Russell").

In this collection, the child narrators have been abandoned, either physically, emotionally, or both, by the adults who are supposed to care for them, and they are "clueless about how to manage grief or fear or anger" ("Ask Karen Russell"). As a result, they look for love and acceptance in the world around them, a world that is reminiscent of Florida's past, reminiscent because there are glimpses of Florida from the past but also elements from the present; however, it is not a mirror image in anyway. A good comparison would be a fun-house mirror that shows a distorted image which

1. Karen Russell

is unpleasant, even a little disturbing. This sense of blurred reality is "the slippery border between the man-made and natural worlds that characterize the landscape of [Russell's] native state" (Leob).

Loss and loneliness are literary tropes, but in many works of classical literature after the protagonists endure much heartache and pain, they are rewarded with at least a sliver of happiness or at least the possibility of it. Taking an example from a Bronte story, an author whose novels Russell read while growing up (Leob), Cathy Linton and Hareton Earnshaw in Emily Bronte's *Wuthering Heights* are mistreated by family members and close relations (such as Heathcliff, of course) who should have protected and nurtured them, but in the end, they are the two who survive and find love and friendship with each other. This is where the story ends, but it is fairly certain the story will continue to be a happy one. In Russell's stories, there is no hope for the protagonists. Events start badly, and in some cases, end even worse. The setting may become an integral part of the protagonists' actions, but it does nothing to assist them, and sometimes, the setting works against them, leaving them isolated and abandoned, just as the adults have done.

Sad tales, like those written by the Bronte sisters or Thomas Harding, are tempered with the notion that at the end there is some tiny bit of hope. All the characters' sufferings are worthwhile. Russell's work does not offer any consolation or expectation of hope for the characters, but as Gillian Engberg explains, this collection of stories "stay[s] with readers." This feeling, one that is difficult to describe, may come from some of the stories' endings, which are "suspended in the air, failing to create a resolution" (Budman). Nonetheless, her characters capture the heart, and we wish for their redemption.

The Florida settings constructed by Russell are familiar to natives of the state who grow up in a world full of alligators, theme parks, giant fiberglass shells, and swimming goggles. In each story, there is "a world that feels emotionally true" ("The Cartography"). Russell describes South Florida as "virtually past-less, seasons are a question of degrees, and it's built on a primordial park full of monsters. So it already has that inbuilt ratio between liminal territories…. It's a really good place to ask questions like: what is reality? what is home?" (qtd. in McCormack). During a presentation given at a Tin House writers' workshop, Russell talked about how she concentrates on "set[ting] up a fantastic universe" and that Florida "ordered [her] way of looking at reality" ("The Cartography"). The author's perspective where she has created a fantasy Florida is evident in four of her short stories: "Ava Wrestles the Alligator," "Haunting Olivia," "The City of Shells," and "The Star-Gazer's Log of Summer-Time Crime." A comparison of real Florida versus Russell's fantasy Florida leads to the following questions: What elements of Russell's settings have some basis in the Florida the author grew up in as well as present day Florida? How does the subtropical environment in her stories affect the adolescent protagonists? Do the settings work as simply time and place, or do they have more relevance to the plot and characters? Do they somehow replace the paternal and maternal elements that are missing since these characters are alone and have no adult support or supervision?

In most areas of Florida, human residents have learned to share their surroundings with those who lived here before them: raccoons, possums, snakes, egrets, and of course, gators. Growing up, young Floridians are constantly warned that any form of freshwater, which includes lakes, ditches, canals, and retention ponds, more than likely have an alligator in it. An alligator may not be visible, but it is assuredly in there. Gators are iconic to Florida, and along with being the occasional neighborhood nuisance, they have also become an industry.

This gator industry becomes the backdrop for "Ava Wrestles the Alligator," the first story in Russell's collection, *St. Lucy's Home for Girls Raised by Wolves*, and later the author expanded the setting of this story into her novel entitled *Swamplandia!* At first, it seems like the adolescent protagonist is not alone. Ava and her sister Osceola have been told to stay at their grandfather's dilapidated house on the swampy island where their family's gator theme park, Swamplandia, is located. Osceola is 16 and Ava is 12, but the older sister is not left in charge by the father, Chief Bigtree, who leaves them so he can to go work on the mainland. Osceola is not mentally capable of keeping the family business going. She "has entire kingdoms inside of her" and becomes the lover of a ghost named Luscious ("Ava Wrestles"). It is up to Ava to maintain the park and the alligators, though there are no longer any tourists to entertain. Instead, Ava is basically left alone to feed the gators and chase her sister around the swamp when Osceola goes off to meet her ghost-lover at night.

Ava describes her life during Swamplandia's prime. She, along with her grandfather, aunt, mother, and father, entertained guests with an act that included alligator wrestling, music, and acrobatics. She feels at home in the swamp and almost fearless as she at one point attempts to tackle her sister in order to keep her from leaving. The dangers of the swamp are expected—darkness, alligators, and snakes mainly—but it is Ava's isolation that brings a more dangerous element to harm her, "a gypsy Bird Man" ("Ava Wrestles"); he seems to materialize out of the swamp. The bird man appears as if he is part of the swamp when he emerges out of the darkness right before dawn "covered in feathers and bird shit" ("Ava Wrestles"). The author points out that "when he first appears he is powerfully charismatic to Ava" and "the only adult on that island" ("Ask Karen Russell"). A mix of nature and man, this "bird man" seduces her with his bird calls and then rapes her. While Ava knows to be wary of him and "can tell right away that he is nobody's father," she needs human companionship and touch so much that she does nothing to protect herself from him and later imagines that she has "disappointed" her dead mother, who had a "beautiful scowl" when she was angry with Ava for doing something wrong. In Ava's mind, the rape is her fault ("Ava Wrestles"). The only adult in the story other than her father who leaves her, this man also leaves her after victimizing her.

Russell's Swamplandia theme park, developed around the iconic Florida alligator, is in many ways similar to Gatorland. Located off of highway 50, Gatorland is a family owned theme park and nature preserve that has been in operation since 1949. The tag line on the park's web site calls it "the gator capital of the world" (*Gatorland*). Just about anyone driving from Brevard County to Orlando will pass by the very visible entrance to the park, a huge gator, mouth open, white teeth gleaming and inviting tourist to come inside. Coincidentally, at Swamplandia one of Ava's chores is "brushing the plaster teeth inside the gator head" ("Ava Wrestles").

Almost every Florida child within a 60 mile radius attends at least one field trip to Gatorland. In the early 1970s, entertainment included watching gators jump up and grab dead chickens, which were tossed out by the park's employees, as well as snake handlers working the crowd urging children to touch the snake as they held the snake's head firmly with one hand and presented the body of the snake with the other. This experience, of course, was nothing like Ava's, who must feed live chickens to her theme park's gators.

Today's Gatorland looks a little bit more sophisticated. Birthday party packages are now an option and the web site boasts a podcast. There is a snack bar and restaurant, the latter of which not surprisingly offers gator nuggets on the menu. The park offers a chance (for a mere $125) to be a "trainer for a day," allowing visitors the opportunity to get a "glimpse into what it takes to be able to work with and around dangerous animals." A single day's admission to an adult visitor 13 years or older is $21.99 (*Gatorland*). This kitschy bit of Florida, while promoting the exploitation of wild animals, has a shiny coat of happiness painted on with a side of nostalgia, which represents the history that Russell weaves into her narratives, although, those who get the "trainer for a day" package do not see anything like Ava's dark and dangerous world.

When Emily Brennan asked Russell about her "inspiration" for creating Ava's home, Swamplandia, the author described an experience that is similar to the Gatorland field trip occurrence:

> There are so many places that resemble that ticky-tacky, mom-and-pop theme park. On some unannounced Wednesday in the fifth grade, you'd all pile into a bus and drive about an hour to the Miccosukee Indian Village, such a short commute to get to a place that felt so alien. It's a reservation with huts built out of palm fronds and saw grass, and a little like Colonial Williamsburg: you watch people doing daily tasks from the past, a woman making dolls, a sweaty man wrestling an alligator. And then you buy traditional dolls and bracelets. In Florida, we're very candid about the fact that we're selling you history or a fantasy. We're like, "This is our treasure, and you can have it for four bucks."

Another form of kitschy Florida borrowed by Karen Russell creates the setting for her story "The City of Shells." This story has another young girl as the main character, and as Christine Smallwood in a brief book review states about all of Russell's "childhood protagonists," this character has learned to live with "the weirdness of being a child in a world of bullies." While Lillith, most often referred to as Big Red, is not always physically isolated like Ava, she is also desperate for any crumb of positive acknowledgement or affectionate gesture. There are adults in her life, but they give her no love or attention: an unemployed mother who "is [frequently] away on business ... and often has to leave at a moment's notice" and an elderly step father, Mr. Pappadakis, who "grab[bed]" at her once "and pulled her onto his lap," but soon he "pushed her away, his lips curling in faint disgust." Momentarily, she makes a connection with Barnaby, the janitor at The City of Shells park who discovers Lillith has gotten trapped in one of the park's giant shells. For a moment, there is hope that this adult is going to rescue her from both the shell and her friendless existence. Barnaby is a likeable character who honestly attempts to save her on both counts. He goes so far as to imagine that he will "adopt her ... raise her as [his] sister-daughter ... [and] take her to magic shows on the Mainland" ("The City of Shells"). However, between Mother Nature and Lillith's resistance to trust him, this becomes impossible.

A sunny day, perfect for her class's field trip, changes as the last ferry leaves the island, the sun is starting to set, and a storm is rolling in. The rain first makes the sides of the shell too slippery for either Barnaby or Lillith to manage to crawl up. As the wind and rain intensify, "the whole conch rings like a tuning fork," and this sound gets so loud that the janitor must shout at her over it as he urges her to do whatever they can to escape before the shell fills up with water ("The City of Shells").

While Ava is able to give herself to a stranger just for the chance to be close to someone, anyone, Lillith's lack of security, "that unshucked, unsafe feeling" she has, is "with her all the time," and after she briefly attacks Barnaby in the dark shell, "she goes sliding away from him, cringing like a kicked dog" ("The City of Shells"). She just cannot allow herself to trust him even as he attempts to save her life. She goes so far as to move back into the water that is filling up the shell rather than to reach out for help.

The giant conchs in the park—a mix of fantasy and reality—are analogous to other Florida attractions. Before the downsizing of the orange industry, family weekend road trips in Florida unusually included stops at giant-sized structures incorporating natural symbols of Florida. Like the big gator of Gatorland, there were the huge orange-shaped houses which stood next to various citrus stands off the highway. These were round cement structures painted orange to resemble the fruit. They had walk-through pathways or sometimes just one entrance. Fruit stands offering bags of oranges for sale and free orange juice samples usually stood next to the giant oranges. Like the conch shells in Russell's story, they were much more exciting on the outside than on the inside.

Now that there are not as many citrus farms as there once were, there also are not that many giant cement oranges either. However, there is still a giant shell placed strategically off of US1 in Port St. Lucie, Florida that greets shoppers at The Shell Bazaar. According to its web site, The Shell Bazaar is one of the oldest businesses in the city and was opened by the Williams family in 1953 (*The Shell Bazaar*). The shop is full of shell related items, but much like the merchandise available at Wal-Mart (which, as it happens, is located just a few miles South on US1) the shell jewelry, coasters, wall hangings, and other shell knick knacks are imported, not made locally, and presumably they are not made with local shells either. This shell industry, like the gator industry, was built on a Florida icon, but closer inspection reveals this icon is polished on the outside but not on the inside, a fact Lillith discovers for herself during her school trip.

Shells show up again in the setting of the story "Haunting Olivia," when two boys, fourteen-year old Wallow and twelve-year old Timothy, search for the ghost of their dead sister who was accidently taken out to sea two years before while riding in a giant crab shell. Just as with Ava's story, "an otherworldiness [sic] [continues] to pervade ... the book" ("Karen Russell") as the boys try to search for Olivia's ghost by using magical goggles. The setting here is a barrier island, and again as in Ava's situation as well as Lillith's, this helps to physically isolate the characters. Karen Russell believes that islands in a setting help create "a visual metaphor for what grief looks like in a body" since they are "revised constantly by the tides" ("Ask Karen Russell").

There are few adults in the story, and those who are present do not help the boys. Gannon, the owner of the boat graveyard, is sympathetic to the boys' circumstances but chooses to ignore them. Like "all the other grown-ups on the island," ("Haunting Olivia") he knows the boys are searching for their sister, and he steps aside to let them search among the junk in the waters around his dock even though he at first tries to explain to them that they will not find their sister there, and if they had been anyone else, he would have told them to leave because they were trespassing on his property. Herb, of Herb's Crab Sledding Rentals, also turns away from the boys when they commandeer a sled to use on their search. As long as they pay him for the use of the sled, he is satisfied and does not interfere. Finally, there is Granana, the boys' 84-year-old grandmother. She is not a nurturing adult helping them deal with the death of their sister. In fact, her attitude is just the opposite of what is expected of a typical grandmother as she admonishes them for "still mooning over that old business" ("Haunting Olivia") and cooks nothing but food using bananas because she has no teeth. Her home is a shelter from the elements and nothing more. Their parents have left the boys in her care while they travel to third world countries and try to forget their grief, with no thought to the grief and guilt that their sons struggle with every day.

Timothy, the younger of the two boys, provides the point of view of the story, and though he and his brother are searching together, there is still a sense of isolation with this character because he is not able to tell his older brother how he feels. The fish ghosts move through him as he swims underwater looking for Olivia, and seaweed and trash viewed through the goggles become "a churning clump of ghost children" ("Haunting Olivia"). This terrifies him, but his brother dismisses his fears. Wallow is focused on finding Olivia, and he shuts down any attempt on Timothy's part to stop their search or even stop and think about what they are doing. In their world, her ghost exists, but once they find her, "what exactly are [they] going to do with her ... genie-in-a-bottle-her?" ("Haunting Olivia").

At the beginning of the story, the setting is not as hostile as alligator infested waters, but it is still not a safe place for children or anyone else to swim. Gannon's boat graveyard is full of abandoned and dilapidated boats. The boys salvage what they can from the boats, and except for the "diabolical goggles," most of what they find is worthless junk. The water is just as junkie, dark, and murky, "the liquid shadow of something truly awful" ("Haunting Olivia"). Later when they move onto travel around the island using one of the crab shells as a boat, the sea is not as murky as the water in the graveyard; however, it is still dark and full of ghost fish as they continue to search for Olivia each night. The ocean works as another character in the story since it kidnapped their sister, so this is where they must look for her ghost.

Water is everywhere in Florida, most notably the ocean, rivers, and canals. The haunted areas of the island explored by the boys are reminiscent of some of the family outings the author made when she was a child:

> My family would always camp in the Ten Thousand Islands. And [...] the mangrove tunnels felt just like the labyrinths [...] like portals to some other world. Such strangle-looking trees mangroves are, their roots like stilts in the water. There's something spidery and ominous about them. [...] As you go back toward Miami, it's a completely different ecosystem from the Gulf. My mother would take us biking on this trail in Shark Valley, a saw grass prairie lined with alligators. It's pretty severe looking, like an African savanna, just a few inches lower in elevation than the green mangroves, and this creates such a different landscape [Brennan].

Bird imagery is also a part of the fantastical Florida setting in "Haunting Olivia," which again makes a brief appearance in this story when Timothy remembers what his family was like before the tragedy occurred, and this is the only time and place that is not dark and full of ghosts. His parents met while bird watching. As a result, they give each of their children middle names related to birds: Waldo Swallow, Timothy Sparrow, and

Olivia Lark. The family spends time together enjoying the Florida outdoors, and Russell mentions familiar birds such as spoonbills and blue herons. Here Russell shows "the relationship between the realistic and the fantastic" as she references actual birds that do exist in Florida at the same time that the characters also ride crab sleds "in this particular universe." There is an attempt by the author "to maintain a stable ratio between the boys' supernatural explanations and a naturalistic explanation" ("Ask Karen Russell"). This short section in the story is more realistic than other parts of the story and is the only place that the environment is not working against the boys; however, the setting during Timothy's flashback does not provide any nurturing either since their parents are present at this time, a picture of a close and loving family.

In an interview with Carin Besser, Russell explains that since she is "from South Florida, where the lines between fantasy and reality have all melted together ... things like the goggles seem a lot less fantastical" (qtd. in. "Karen Russell"). Since her protagonists are adolescents, the existence of magical objects seems to fit given that children typically will use the environment and objects in it to create fantasy. Sometimes these fantasies are just part of everyday play while other times they become ways for children to deal with painful emotions and difficult situations. Russell explains that in her own childhood she found reading was a way to deal with solitude, and in an interview on the public radio show *All Things Considered*, the author discusses her view of how children perceive the world and learn to cope:

> I think kids are really alert to all kinds of darkness [...] and sorrow. I think that [...] it's like raw nerves in the world a lot of the time. And so, to find a way privately to reckon with some of the forces that you know exist but you're young, you don't maybe have the vocabulary to talk about them. Or, you know, [that] you're not going to be taken seriously if you try to bring them up, or those concerns get squelched.

Water once more plays a role, though a little smaller, in a story from this first collection of Russell's called "The Star-Gazer's Log of Summer-Time Crime" where the primary setting is a rundown resort called the Bowl-a-Bed Hotel. This story brings Russell's characters once more to the ocean and an island, making them physically isolated as the water becomes a barrier between the island and mainland. There is also a ghost, or the suggestion of one, in the character Petey, whose extremely pale complexion leads hotel patrons to believe he is a ghost. The adolescent narrator is a boy named Ollie. He is vacationing at the hotel with his father and sister, though they are actually residents and live on the other side of the island. According to Ollie's father, they are there so they can all get a better view of star constellations as a part of their family of three's astronomy hobby. There is no mother figure, and Ollie and his twin sister, Molly, barely remember her. Their father, a retired astronaut, is one of the few parents given dialogue in Russell's stories, but he makes only short appearances and does little parenting. He is shown each time with a drink in his hand, and he makes astronomical double entendres with his children, joking and making small talk but not really talking or communicating with either of them in any meaningful way. As Ollie spends night after night out later than his curfew and commits increasingly more disturbing crimes with two other preteens, he hopes for some attention from his father, even if it means getting disciplined. His father, though, "has gone somewhere pensive and inward" ("The Star-Gazer's Log"). The other parent shown is Marta's mother. Marta and Raffy have teamed up with Ollie to spend each night looking for trouble to get into from shop lifting to trying to buy alcohol. They occasionally run into her mother who spends all of her time drinking with strange men at the Crustaceous Cocktail Lounge.

Nature does not work as strongly in this story when compared to "Ava Wrestles the Alligator" or "Haunting Olivia." The beach and ocean are more of a backdrop to the seedy hotel and the characters vacationing there. The swamp and then the ocean become antagonists in the previous two stories to the point that the settings feel like they have as much weight as the characters, but here in this story, the characters drive the plot much more. Still Russell admits that "while some writers begin with characters" she "often started with settings" such as "the Bowl-a-Bed hotel," and therefore "the possibilities and constraints of these settings would then give shape to the characters" ("Ask Karen Russell"). The characters in "The Star-Gazer's Log of Summer-Time Crime" are on vacation and do not normally live in the hotel or this side of the island. This means their world changes a little since they are displaced in this environment, and we know little about their lives before their stay at the hotel. The vacation setting allows all the characters to be different people. Ollie befriends a boy he normally would avoid. The adults spend the day in the bar. Molly is estranged from her brother.

Ollie's world is not as magical as Ava's or Timothy's. It is much closer to Lillith's experience in "The City of Shells," as he is an outcast among his friends and barely acknowledged by his father. He does feel an emotional connection to his twin sister but resists it in exchange for a chance to experience what it is like to be part of what he sees as the popular crowd on the island: Raffy, a bully who normally torments him at school, and Marta, a girl he is sexually attracted to. The character of Petey, a 30-year-old mentally challenged albino, brings some of the "magical realism" (Loeb) Russell is known for as he dresses up to look like a "human disco ball" ("The Star-Gazer's Log").

The environment made up of the old hotel and bar, where his father spends most of his time, is inauthentic as far as being an enjoyable vacation destination. This lack of credibility is comparable to his relationship with Raffy and Marta and the group's escapades, which start off fairly innocuous, such as stowing away on a glass bottom boat, and escalate to a felony as they plot to disturb and possibly kill a group of newly hatched sea turtles. As his sister points out, Ollie is a "faker, a phony!" At school, Raffy is his enemy, but in this new vacation-land, they are buddies in crime. Inside, Ollie knows all of this and constantly thinks about stopping and walking away, but the peer pressure is too much for him ("The Star-Gazer's Log").

Other than references to the moon and constellations, the only other time nature becomes an important part of the story has to do with the children's horrible prank on the baby sea turtles. Just as Ollie feels lost while among his new friends, the turtles become "confused ... flip[ping] ... back and forth in a miniature of real agony." The turtles grow disoriented and cannot find the ocean, and Ollie cannot find his way back to the safety of his family, to "room 442 with [his] dad and Molly, clean linens, and buckets of ice" ("The Star-Gazer's Log"). By doing nothing, he participates in the sick joke.

Much like Ollie's family, residents and those who live outside of the state, frequently plan trips to the beach. This is one reason Florida is known as a vacation destination. A multitude of small beach front hotels ranging from deluxe accommodations to less glamorous quarters that the Bowl-a-Bed Hotel epitomizes are scattered up and down the Florida coast, so small hotel and local businesses briefly mentioned in the story are not uncommon in most coastal or island locations throughout Florida. Sanibel Island and Cedar Key, for example, are both islands off the West coast of Florida that are popular with tourists and natives looking for a place to unplug. There is almost nothing to do but spend all day at the beach, go fishing, and then go out to the local seafood restaurant during the evening.

While there is some exaggeration and tweaking of facts, Russell's stories have a sincerity about them that anyone who has spent significant time living in Florida will recognize. Children, especially, are able to rearrange their reality since they "have access to different ways of being in the world" (qtd. in Leob), and because Florida is a state that allows for year round outdoor living, the environment naturally has a greater influence on its residents.

Setting unmistakably is much more relevant than providing simply a time period and location for the action of Russell's characters. The author admits that she starts with the setting and characters emerge from it. As she puts it, she "tr[ies] to play with the Kansas-to-Oz ratio; learning to work the place between the literal and the dream space" ("Karen Russell"). The use of island settings in each story helps form the circumstances of her protagonists: Ava is left alone and vulnerable at Swamplandia; Lillith is not missed by anyone in her class as they leave her behind and take the last ferry home; Timothy is left to struggle with his brother to find Olivia's ghost as they travel around the outskirts of the island; and Ollie is marooned in a way at an old island hotel while his father drinks to forget his own troubles. They are left alone, cut off from the mainland and from any adult who should be caring for them. They are not orphans, but the adults in their lives who should be taking care and nurturing them choose not to do so—which is worse.

The natural landscape around these children is full of beauty: sandy beaches, blue oceans, sawgrass, birds, and alligators, and they all spend most of the time outside in their quests to find some kind of balance and reassurance. They are "on the verge, struggling to reconcile the facts of their lives with the allure and terror of the unknown" (Loeb). While nature sometimes steps in and is responsible for significant events in the stories, it does not provide support or sanctuary for these lost children. Even Mother Nature chooses not to care for them.

Works Cited

"Ask Karen Russell." *GoodReads*. 2011. Goodreads Inc. Web. 9 May 2012.
Brennan, Emily. "The Everglades As Inspiration." *New York Times* 18 Nov. 2012: 3(L). *Academic OneFile*. Web. 3 May 2013.

Budman, Mark. "The Ghosts of South Florida." *American Book Review*. 28.1 (2006): 29. *EBSCO*. Web. 11 Apr 2012.

Engberg, Gillian. "Karen Russell: St. Lucy's Home for Girls Raised by Wolves." *Booklist*. 103.2 (2006): 29. *Gale*. Web 11 May 2012.

"Karen Russell." *Books and Authors*. (2012). *Gale*. Web. 11 Apr 2012.

Loeb, Eryn. "The Strangeness Quotient." *Poets and Writers*. 39.2 (2011): 52–55. *EBSCO*. Web. 11 Apr 2012.

McCormack, JW. "PW Talks with Karen Russell: The Kansas to Oz Ratio." *Publishers Weekly*. (2010). n. pag. Web. 11 May 2012.

Russell, Karen. "Ava Wrestles the Alligator." In *St. Lucy's Home for Girls Raised by Wolves*. New York: Random House Digital. 2007. E-book.

_____. "Haunting Olivia." In *St. Lucy's Home for Girls Raised by Wolves*. New York: Random House Digital. 2007. E-book.

_____. "The City of Shells." In *St. Lucy's Home for Girls Raised by Wolves*. New York: Random House Digital. 2007. E-book.

_____. "The Star-Gazer's Log of Summer-Time Crime." In *St. Lucy's Home for Girls Raised by Wolves*. New York: Random House Digital. 2007. E-book.

_____. "The Cartography of Imaginary Places." *Tin House*. 18 March 2011. Web. 10 May 2012.

Shell Bazaar. Web. 1 May 2012.

Smallwood, Christine. "Short Takes." *The Nation*. 283.10 (2006): 34. *EBSCO*. Web. 10 May 2012.

"Wrestling Gators and Language in 'Swamplandia!'" *All Things Considered* 9 Feb. 2011. *Biography In Context*. Web. 3 May 2013.

Into the Swamp
An Examination of Folk Narrative Structures and Storylines in Karen Russell's Swamplandia!

Lori Cornelius

Karen Russell's first novel, *Swamplandia!*, tells the story of a family of self-proclaimed indigenous people known as the Bigtree tribe in the Ten Thousand Islands of Southwest Florida, not far from Cape Coral. The six-member Bigtree family lives on a hundred acres island, which is home to their alligator wrestling attraction Swamplandia!, a tourist trap of a bygone era where visitors are ferried in several times a day from the fictional town of Loomis on the mainland of Florida. When the headlining act, an alligator-pit diver named Hilola Bigtree, dies from cancer, it sets into motion the ultimate downfall of the park. Hilola's death, combined with the opening on the mainland of a Hell-based theme park called The World of Darkness, leaves her family with little hope of regaining their alligator park's popularity and saving their family home.

Hilola Bigtree leaves behind three adolescent children, none of whom have known life away from the island. As the island is located thirty miles from the mainland, the children have been homeschooled, raised by not only their mother, but also their Grandfather Sawtooth, and their father, Chief Bigtree. All family members participate in the running of the park's various attractions, which have been competing with "several enemy forces, natural and corporate," for some time (Russell 6). Now they face a new enemy: loss from within the family circle.

After their mother's death, each child attempts to cope with loss differently. Seventeen-year-old Kiwi, the oldest, begins to challenge his father and his methods of running the park and dreams of escaping permanently to Loomis where he can obtain a proper education and a job. Sixteen-year-old Osceola, or Ossie, as her family calls her, turns to a book that she has found called *The Spiritist's Telegraph* and begins to regularly consult a homemade Ouija board in order to communicate with (and date) the dead. Thirteen-year-old Ava strives to emulate her mother as the star of the show, forming and attempting to work her own plan for saving Swamplandia!

As the tourists finally stop coming to the attraction at all and the family's income disappears, each male family member ultimately departs for the mainland, leaving only ghost-infatuated Ossie and sensible Ava to care for the island. Alone, and working to eliminate an invasive species of tree from their land, they discover what appears to be a huge abandoned boat trapped in a canal but turns out to be a dredge from the campaign to drain and develop the Everglades in the late 1800's to early 1940s (Russell 78). It is here on the dredge that Ossie either meets or begins to concoct the ghost of Louis Thanksgiving, a 19-year-old swamp dredge worker who died during an explosion on the dredge.

Within a few of weeks of their father's leaving, Ossie boards the dredge to leave and marry Louis, and somehow manages to get the dredge moving again. Ava attempts to follow, aided by a stranger, a gypsy Bird Man who visits the island to remove unwanted birds. Through leaving the island and finding one another, the Bigtrees ultimately regain the family that has been scattered. In a modern retelling of an ages old story of loss and rebirth, Russell conveys what it means to claim identity in a world where nothing is stable, where total fabrications have become a part of the familial history. Russell's characters and the worlds they create for themselves, real or otherwise, demonstrate her ability to draw on core concepts of oral narratives and traditions of folk and fairy tales as they discover their true identities beyond the myth of the Bigtree family.

Oral narrative tradition is quite notable in the history of how the Bigtree family business became a well-known alligator wrestling theme park. Born Ernest Schedrach, the patriarch of the family who becomes Grandpa Sawtooth Bigtree "changed his name to outwit his old boss" when he leaves Ohio, in part because he owes his former employer money (Russell 24). Unlike many expatriates who try to recreate their previous homeland in their new one, the family that becomes known as the Bigtree tribe has a different methodology. Schedrach, aka Sawtooth, buys the Florida property sight unseen and resignedly works with the results. Billed as farmland, his new real estate purchase "turned out to be covered by six feet of crystal water. Stalks of nine-foot saw grass glittered in the wind, in every direction, the drowned sentinels of an eternal slough. The only real habitable 'property' in sight was the island he later named Swamplandia!: a hundred-acre waste" (Russell 24). Within moments of their arrival, Schedrach's wife interacts with a large alligator. The ruckus made by the alligator causes a surge of water to douse her dress with brackish water, and results in the printed dots of the fabric being washed away. Thus begins the family history of the tribe of Bigtree, with the dress that Schedrach's wife, Risa, wore that day becoming an artifact in the Bigtree Museum (Russell 24–25). It is the kind of story that improves and grows with telling, a storyteller's yarn.

In harmony with the fluidity associated with oral tradition, The Chief, son to the original self-proclaimed Bigtree, frequently creates an alternate history for the family, as needed. One way he does this is through family portraits, as noted by Ava: "Although there was not a drop of Seminole or Miccosukee blood in us, the Chief always costumed us in tribal apparel for the photographs he took. He said we were 'our own Indians'" (Russell 5). The Chief also makes careful selections of "an ever changing carousel of objects from [their] lives, accompanied by little explanatory cards that he typed up and framed himself" and places these in the Bigtree Family Museum (Russell 25). When some bit of their past no longer fits with the story being told, it is simply removed, rearranged, or rewritten:

> [The Chief] took down Grandpa's old army medallions, which did not fit with his image of our free and ancient swamp tribe.... Certain artifacts appeared or vanished, dates changed and old events appeared in fresh blue ink on new cards beneath the dusty exhibit, and you couldn't say one word about these changes in the morning. You had to pretend like the Bigtree story had always read that way [Russell 25].

Such re-creation of history often occurs in literary folk tales, and even more so in oral storytelling. In fact, the tradition of oral storytelling is the richest of all narrative forms as an oral story knows no precise date of inception, and even the presumed first version of every well-known story ever told is fluid and ever changeable. Stories are told and retold so that it becomes impossible (and really unnecessary) to locate the "original" version, unless, as is the case for the Bigtree children, such revision rewrites their very existence and prevents them from accessing their true heritage. This oral tradition, which allows for perpetual revision, typifies the underlying tension of the Bigtree family, resulting in feelings of isolation and confusion for the children. It is difficult for them to know who they really are when their history fluctuates from day to day. The handwritten cards become the literary proof of their (new) past, and whatever their identity yesterday, it may have changed overnight.

Other examples of oral narrative concepts are apparent throughout *Swamplandia!* and harmonize with oral narrative concepts and specific storytelling structures noted in Danish scholar and medievalist Axel Olrik's research in folklore theory. In *Principles for Oral Narrative Research*, Olrik details the use of the number three, the use of repetition and patterning, and the importance of final stress or final position, as some of the staples of oral storytelling structures. These structures are often referred to as Olrik's "Epic Laws" and according to one scholar, "[these laws] are based on the regularity observed in compositional style common to large areas. These are devices used to achieve an enduring narrative with suspense and a coherent plot" (Zeyrek).

Olrik's Epic Laws are clearly demonstrated in *Swamplandia!* with patterning and the use of three; this is especially notable in the number of characters and the manner in which they ultimately leave the island. Originally, three adults and three children inhabit the island. First to go is Grandpa Sawtooth, banished by the Chief to the Out to Sea Retirement Community, a month before the mother dies (Russell 9). Next Hilola leaves by dying not at home, but on the mainland in a hospital (Russell 7). Nine months later Kiwi leaves to try and improve the family fortunes. The Chief leaves shortly after Kiwi, purportedly to go to the mainland and obtain investors to rebuild their failing attraction. Only the two girls, Ossie and Ava, remain to fend for themselves. In three weeks' more time, Ossie leaves to marry her ghost, and what can Ava do besides try and follow? Ultimately, the island is completely abandoned by all in favor of the mainland.

The three Bigtree children leave the island in traditional folktale patterning with the eldest out of the door first, followed by the next oldest, and finally the youngest child. As they attempt to regain their emotional footing, the impact of losing their mother begins to reveal each child's strengths, weaknesses, and fears. Kiwi, the most financially savvy and their self-proclaimed "homeschool's valedictorian," (Russell 22) looks to the mainland and a college education as the means to move on. He suggests to his father that they sell everything and move (Russell 29). Unable to convince his father of the logic of his plan, Kiwi runs away to the mainland where he obtains a job working at the rival park, the World of Darkness.

Shortly after her sixteenth birthday party, a sad affair in which her family gives her presents from Swamplandia's gift shop, Ossie, the second oldest child, leaves home to wed to her fiancé, Louis Thanksgiving. Unfortunately, as Louis is either a real ghost or a fantastic creation of her own making, the relationship is doomed. Introverted and neglected, Ossie is neither a purported genius like her older brother nor a potential alligator wrestling star like her younger sister. She believes that she can find love through communication with the dead although she fails to make contact with her mother. Her vibrancy comes from her ability to tell the story of Louis Thanksgiving, an amazing biography spanning his birth and immediate orphaned state to his death at 19 on a dredge in the Everglades. Ossie relays his story to Ava shortly before embarking on her wedding travel plans with Louis.

Regarding the importance played by the character in the final position, in this case, Ava, Olrik states that "the epically important character is normally in the 'position of final stress'" (52). Many times the character in the final stress is the youngest male of a family, and as the youngest, the most likely to elicit the sympathy of the reader. Ava is the heir apparent to the mother's athletic endeavors in the alligator pit; she is the understudy to her mother's wrestling act, an ingénue. (Russell 14). While not the youngest *son*, Ava is the youngest of the children and she repeatedly earns the sympathy of the reader as the novel unfolds.

The only one who recognizes the dangers to the family structure, Ava tirelessly endeavors to keep the family together. She supports her father's plan to revive the park through what Russell calls "Carnival Darwinism" and secretly begins raising a rare red alligator (or "Seths" as alligators are referred to throughout the book) as part of the plan. She writes postcards to her brother, Kiwi, once he has left for the mainland, and says of the stack of postcards amassing on the dresser that she feels as though she "collected Time itself for [her] brother. Kiwi could just read these, come back to the swamp, and pick up where he left off" (Russell 122). Ava chases after her mentally unstable sister as Ossie becomes increasingly engrossed in communicating with ghosts and stays out nights in pursuit of their affections. Sometimes this requires that Ava follow her and keep watch to ensure her safe return home. The difficulty is increased when Ava must follow an eloped Ossie and Louis into the Underworld in the care of a stranger, known as the Bird Man, who claims to know the route to the Underworld when he tells her: "Nobody can get to hell without assistance, kid" (Russell 146). As the youngest and most vulnerable, Ava's trust in a stranger triggers alarm in the reader, especially as the reader begins to suspect long before Ava does that the Bird Man's intentions have nothing to do with showing her the way to find her sister and everything to do with taking advantage of her. It is this last test, though—that of her trip to save Ossie by going to the Underworld herself—that proves decisive for Ava. Having made that trip, she loses her innocence, and from that loss there is no real way back.

Many oral and literary folk tales incorporate the danger to a young female attempting to negotiate through the forest, in the company of a wolf. In such folk tales, often dubbed as "Red Riding Hood Tales," wooded areas are fearsome places. In the Medieval ages, woods became synonymous with a particular type of danger: "Little children were attacked and killed by animals and grown-ups in the woods and fields. Hunger often drove people to commit atrocious acts" (Zipes 23). In many cases, wolves became synonymous with evil. In her book *From the Forest: A Search for the Hidden Roots of our Fairytales,* Sara Maitland explains, "Wolves are the stuff of fairy stories—the name and shape of the terror of the wild" (ch. 8). Wolves were prevalent throughout Britain during the Middle Ages until a deliberate campaign of destruction brought about their complete eradication. Regardless, they live on in the "psychological embodiment of what the fairy stories knew and what we want to forget, or at least ignore: nature is indeed red in tooth and claw, and nowhere more so than in the terrible forests" (Maitland ch. 8). In the swamp though, instead of dark woods inhabited by crazed and starving animals, the invasive melaleuca trees appear to be the initial representation of the dangerous landscape to avoid. Appropriately, since it is Ava who must eventually negotiate the fearful landscape with a wolfish man, it is Ava who describes this particular forest during a melaleuca eradication campaign:

> *Melaleuca quinquenervia* was an exotic invasive, an Australian tree imported to suck the Florida swamp dry.... Exotic invasives, the "strangler species" threatened our family long before the World of Darkness. The Army Corps of Engineers had planted thousands of melaleuca trees in the 1950s as part of the Drainage Project, back when the government though it was possible to turn our tree islands into a pleated yellowland of crops [Russell 76].

Now, many years after the Army Corps of Engineers has given up on the drainage project, "the melaleucas were still root-committed to the old plan" and continue to spring up all over the island (Russell 76). Just as the woods in many folk tales hide or reveal dangers, so do the woods of their island. The relentless melaleucas with their ability to consume land at "fifty trees to an acre" (Russell 77) are a fierce enemy. Notably, it is during this particular passage where Ava describes the invasive species and the family's constant work to destroy them that the girls find the dredge, another danger with which to reckon.

The dangers in the figurative woods of folk tales are next embodied by the swamp itself during Ava's attempt to locate her sister before Ossie can be taken by the Underworld. After navigating by constellations of birds on water throughout the Ten Thousand Islands, Ava is raped by the Bird Man. When she flees afterward, she spends the better part of three days alone in "the most treacherous part of the swamp" (Russell 271) where she contends with varying difficult terrains and their inhabitants: snakes, mosquitoes, and alligators. Her great thirst and exhaustion eventually brings on a form of madness.

The storyline involving Ava and her descent with the Bird Man into the Underworld closely mimics patterns of various versions of Little Red Riding Hood from folk and fairy tales. At the outset, Ava both does and does not recognize the Bird Man, just as Little Red both believes the person in her grandmother's bed to be someone she knows and simultaneously recognizes that something is amiss with grandmother's appearance. Ava finds the Bird Man in a tree (Russell 128). They startle one another. "*I know what you are!*" thinks Ava upon realizing his occupation (Russell 129). Notably, she does not think *who you are* but *what you* are: a gypsy Bird Man. Ava knows "there are several such men who travel around Florida's parks and backwaters, following the seasonal migrations of various species of birds. These men are like avian pied pipers, or aerial fumigators," who lure the birds off one person's property and onto another's (Russell 129). Starved for adult attention and human companionship, Ava finds him a fascinating exotic guest, not realizing that she is being lured by him as well.

The Bird Man's initial way of entrapping her is quite simple; he catches her fancy with a unique bird call, one filled with sounds that are familiar, but others that are new to her:

> I tried to imagine what species of bird could make a sound like that. A single note, held in an amber suspension of time, like a charcoal drawing of Icarus falling. It was sad and fierce all at once, alive with a lonely purity. It went on and on, until my own lungs were burning.

"What bird are you calling?" I asked finally, when I couldn't stand it any longer.
The Bird Man stopped whistling. He grinned, so that I could see all his pebbly teeth.
"You" [Russell 129–130].

Within minutes of meeting this stranger in the swamp, an enthralled Ava invites him to stay in the family house, hoping that they are friends (Russell 130). With childlike candor, she demonstrates her alligator wrestling capabilities and performs a private show for him, her first actual dive into a pit of live alligators (Russell 131). He praises her abilities, smiling at her all the while, and gives her a type of standing ovation (Russell 132). Then, she shows him something she has not shared with anyone else yet, her red alligator, and awaits his reaction: "'Beautiful,' the Bird Man said. He said it exactly right, with the whistling wonder that I had dreamed the red Seth would elicit from a tourist" (Russell 133). The wolf has set the trap and sweet Ava bounds toward it.

That Ava would choose to share the information about her prized alligator with a stranger is indicative of Red Riding Hood story similarities. First, like Little Red Cap in the tale by the Brothers Grimm, she exhibits complete trust in him: "Little Red Cap did not know what a wicked sort of an animal he was and was not afraid of him" (Grimm 135). Second, there is a confusing attraction towards him that was awakened in her with the whistle. Ava says, "just the memory of that sound caused many bright fibers I had not known existed inside me to tighten" (Russell 151). The implication is that Ava has recently begun menstruation, which is hinted at very early in the novel when she superstitiously waits to tell her family about the existence of the red alligator (Russell 47). This stirring of confusing sexuality is countered in certain Red Riding Hood tales by a mother reminding her daughter to stay on the path, by a grandmother attempting to protect her granddaughter, or by a woodcutter who rescues her from the stomach of the beast (Grimm 135–138). But Ava has no maternal guidance, no adult protection, and no male rescuer. And, as is characteristic of a metaphorical wolf, the Bird Man's ultimate weapon turns out to be his ability to out-reason her.

His recognition of her innocence allows him to play on her ignorance. When Ava learns that Ossie has eloped with the ghost of Louis Thanksgiving and has somehow freed the dredge from the canal, she runs to the house where the Bird Man is making breakfast. He convinces Ava that contacting the authorities to locate her sister would prove useless: "The problem, Ava, is that if your sister has already crossed over to the underworld, they won't find her.... Park Services will be useless to your sister. None of their dogs and helicopters can track a ghost" (Russell 152). Ava mistakes the Bird Man's interest in assisting her for genuine concern over Ossie's safety and allows herself to be drawn off the path of sensibility. The same little girl who proclaims that she was "raised to be suspicious of the Army Corps of Engineers, with good reason" (Russell 76) is unable to recognize the ulterior motives of the Bird Man. Like Perrault's village girl in "Little Red Riding Hood," she converses with the wolf, unaware of the dangers (Perrault 91).

Ava has been tricked like Red Riding Hood and, believing that he can track a ghost, she gives the Bird Man her whole-hearted support. Like Red, she has in her naiveté not fought his advances that eventually lead to rape: "At no point had I tried to fight his person" (Russell 262–263). This is in great part due to her youth and innocence, a misguided trust that the Bird Man is a magical presence in her life, a surrogate woodcutter who can help her reach her goal of finding and saving her sister.

Many Red Riding Hood stories indicate that Red recognizes that the wolf is indeed not her grandmother, but by the time she recognizes his real shape, she is powerless to escape him. She has already made conversation with the wolf and lifted the figurative latch at the door that previously protected her childhood beliefs and trust. Before the Bird Man rapes her, Ava recognizes that the entire endeavor—the search for Ossie and the trip to the so-called Underworld—has been a lie. First, when she believes that she may have seen her sister on an island of trees, he refuses to stop; when she calls out for Ossie, the Bird Man slaps her (Russell 240). Then, when she sees two gator hunters in a boat and hears their radio, she begins to doubt that the men are actually dead as the Bird Man asserts (Russell 241). Finally, she recognizes that his feathered coat, which until now has fascinated her, is nothing more than a rag, a "crazy person's disguise" (Russell 246). When she faces him, much like Red facing the wolf posing as grandmother, she sees a stranger:

> He crouched low and his pale lips sprouted teeth and I couldn't remember how to see this face as friendly.
> *Who are you?*
> Somebody was grinning at me. I could hear the wind fluttering his empty sleeves [Russell 246].

When the Bird Man "crouched low" and "his pale lips sprouted teeth" Russell underscores the concept of a wolf impersonating a trusted individual: "What big teeth you have, grandmother!" (Perrault 93). Ava no longer wonders *what the Bird Man is* as she had during their initial meeting. Rather, she *knows who he is*: a wolf posing as a man, a liar. Having been tricked and recognizing the error of her trust, when the Bird Man approaches her after he has molested her, Ava hurls her prized red alligator at him. Unsure of whether the alligator "bit him or clawed at him," she flees through the swamp (Russell 264). As she had willingly and trustingly shown him the alligator a few days before, something she had not shared with anyone else, the significance of the red alligator is defined by the loss of her virginity.

Once on a course away from the Bird Man, the following of a typical Red Riding Hood plotline seems to give way to that of lost Snow White or Hansel and Gretel, as Ava is indeed lost and does not know her way home. Nearly out of her mind with thirst, Ava discovers a single house, deep in the swamp, on the second day of her escape. The language denotes a nearly fairy tale cottage, where at any moment seven little men, or an ancient crone, might welcome her in:

> I looked inside a begrimed window and I thought: *abandoned*. For sure nobody lived here. There was a straw pallet on the needle-covered floor and no furniture that I could see. Dishes on shelves, little cups. Outside its wooden walls had been completely overtaken by weeds and strangler fig, thick vines doing their weird tethered ballet when the wind blew [Russell 286].

It is difficult to tell whether such a place is even real, or if Ava has conjured it to combat the whirlwinds in her mind. But her relief at finding the little house is short-lived. She finds clothing of her sister's hanging on the line, and then a woman, presumably the resident of the house who appears to be wearing a dress that was her mother's. Ava envisions the woman as a monster and takes the clothes from the line while accusing the woman of having taken her mother from her and trying to take Ossie from her too (Russell 289–290). To the reader, plausible reasons for the clothing and the woman exist as she appears to try and help Ava: "What on God's earth are you talking about? Where's your mother girl? Are you here alone? You got a sister with you?" (Russell 290). But Ava won't be fooled again. Some people are not what they appear and having created a way to keep from being injured again—by recognizing this person as a monster regardless of the dress—Ava marks new territory for herself. Her ability to learn from her mistakes mirrors the second ending of Grimm's version of "Little Red Cap" in which "another wolf" tries to engage her, without success (Grimm 137).

Shortly thereafter Ava is rescued, and at the conclusion of the novel Russell allows readers to make their own decisions about the choices the characters made and the results of those choices. Liberated from the swamp and the Chief's histories, all of the children are free to retain what they want, selectively, from the canon of Bigtree lore. The Bigtree children are no longer defined by the histories of their swamp or by those imposed on them by their father. While they have regained the family itself, they struggle with what it means to write a new history, one in which they are allowed to create their own tales or dream their own dreams, ones in keeping with the futures that they are in control to make. For Kiwi, it means accepting who he is, a member of the Bigtree tribe, as he pursues his education free of the burden of Carnival Darwinism and from needing to define his manhood through saving the family park. He has become his own man, first by saving a drowning girl, and later by rescuing Ossie from the dredge. For Ossie, it means psychiatric treatment and being drawn back to reality through medication and the love of her family. Ava's future, because of her youth and lost childhood, is still the most unmapped, the most uncertain path. Happy to have her family united even on the mainland, she is still never far from Swamplandia! in her dreams, although when awake, she says that recalling elements of it "feels like trying to light a candle on a rainy night, your hands cupped and your cheeks puffed and the whole wet world conspiring to snatch the flame away from you"(Russell 316). She is surrounded by features of what she has left behind, but rather than becoming the functional matriarch of the alligator acts, some re-creation of her mother or a new creation of her father's choosing, Ava is now free to construct her identity as she chooses. Such possibilities comprise one of the most important aspects of oral tradition, that of the fluidity of the narrative, but now instead of revising their past, instead of re-creating their history, instead of blotting out their existence, the Bigtrees are indelibly writing their future.

Works Cited

Grimm, Jacob and Wilhelm. "Little Red Cap." In *The Trials and Tribulations of Little Red Riding Hood* J. Zipes, Ed., pp. 135–138. New York: Routledge, 1993.

Maitland, Sarah. *From the Forest: A Search for the Hidden Roots of our Fairytales.* Berkley: Counterpoint, 2012.
Olrik, Alex. *Principles for Oral Narrative Research.* Bloomington: Indiana University Press, 1992.
Perrault, Charles. "Little Red Riding Hood." In Jack Zipes (Ed.), *The Trials and Tribulations of Little Red Riding Hood* (pp. 91–93). New York: Routledge, 1993.
Russell, Karen. *Swamplandia!* New York: Knopf, 2011.
Zeyrek, Deniz. "Principles for Oral Narrative Research." *Asian Folklore Studies* 52.2 (1993): 401+. Literature Resource Center. Web. 22 Aug. 2013.
Zipes, Jack, ed. *The Trials and Tribulations of Little Red Riding Hood.* New York: Routledge, 1993.

2

Elizabeth Stuckey-French

Elizabeth Stuckey-French was born in Arkansas and grew up in Lafayette, Indiana. Considering that both her parents are writers and taught college English, it is not surprising that Stuckey-French also became an author and teacher. Though her roots are Midwestern, she relocated to Florida and now teaches as an associate professor at Florida State University in its Creative Writing Program. Stuckey-French earned her bachelor's in social work and masters in English at Purdue University and later became a 1992 graduate of the prestigious Iowa Writers Workshop, Masters of Fine Arts Program ("About Elizabeth"). The author's book-length publications include *The First Paper Girl in Red Oak, Iowa, and Other Stories*, published in 2000; *Mermaids on the Moon*, published in 2002; *Writing Fiction: A Guide to Narrative Craft*, published in 2007 and co-authored with Ned French (her husband) and Janet Burroway; and *The Revenge of the Radioactive Lady*, published in 2011 ("Elizabeth Stuckey-French." *Contemporary Authors Online*). Both of her novels have Florida settings.

Her short stories have been published in a variety of literary journals including *The Atlantic Monthly*, *The Gettysburg Review*, *Five Points*, and *The Southern Review*. She received the O. Henry Award in 2005, for her short story entitled "Mudlavia," and is also the recipient of literary grants from the Florida Arts Foundation, Howard Foundation, and Indiana Arts Commission. In 2008, the author won *Narrative Magazine's* Love Story Contest for her short fiction piece "Interview with a Moron" ("Elizabeth Stuckey-French." *The English Department*).

A mixture of dark humor and over the top plots, Elizabeth Stuckey-French's fiction has been described as "humor [that] comes from grim situations we know we shouldn't laugh at" (Reynolds). The author explains in an interview with Eileen Reynolds for *The New Yorker* that as a reader she is drawn to dark humor and that she looks at works by authors such as William Trevor as models for her own creative efforts. She also compares this type of fiction to the works of Flannery O'Connor. For example, in Stuckey-French's most recent novel, *The Revenge of the Radioactive Lady*, the female protagonist, Marylou Ahearn, travels to Tallahassee, Florida to take revenge on a now elderly doctor. More than fifty years previously, he had experimented with radioactive matter on Marylou, who was an unknowing participant in the experiment. In a twist of the well-known cliché "fact is stranger than fiction," the novel is based on actual events that took place in the 1950s ("Elizabeth Stuckey-French." *Contemporary Authors Online*). As a survivor of thyroid cancer, which the author believes was caused by exposure to radiation, she admits that "part of [her] motivation" for writing the book was to make sure more people knew about this once secret government activity that was later documented by Eileen Welsome in her book *The Plutonium Files: America's Secret Medical Experiments in the Cold War* (Reynolds).

When asked whether she sees herself as a Florida author, Elizabeth Stuckey-French proclaims that she is "honored" to be considered a part of the South, a place where she feels "very much at home." Both her parents were originally from the South, and her family "visited the Deep South often when [she] was growing up." While she had no specific plans for another novel based in Florida during the time of her interview with Eileen Reynolds, Stuckey-French explained "I love Florida and will no doubt set another book here" (Reynolds).

Works Cited

"About Elizabeth." *Elizabeth Stucky-French*. 2013. Web. 13 May 2013. http://elizabethstuckeyfrench.com/about/

"Elizabeth Stuckey-French." *Contemporary Authors Online*. Detroit: Gale, 2011. *Biography In Context*. Web. 11 May 2013.

"Elizabeth Stuckey-French." *The English Department at Florida State University*. Web. 12 May 2013. http://www.english.fsu.edu/faculty/estuckey-french.htm

Reynolds, Eileen. "The Exchange: Elizabeth Stuckey-French on *The Radioactive Lady*." *The New Yorker*. 2 March 2011. Web. 13 May 2013. http://www.newyorker.com/books/page-turner/the-exchange-elizabeth-stuckey-french-on-the-radioactive-lady

A Laughing Matter
Smiling Through the Pain in Elizabeth Stuckey-French's Novels

April Van Camp

In *Poetics,* Aristotle argues that tragedies' heroes are better people than we are, and comedies' protagonists are inferior, partly because tragedies employ the nobler, loftier hopes of humankind, while comedies demonstrate the impediments. While Aristotle admits to a variation in tragedy and comedy's components, he is firmly committed to tragedy's superiority, indicating that tragedy leads to more mature and profound insights. For Aristotle, no one experiences catharsis in comedy; instead, audiences laugh at those whose lives incur foolish, even ludicrous, circumstances, and watch those unfortunates fumble through life—merrily and/or married-ly. However, the great theatre was a competition between tragedies and comedies, with prizes for both, and somehow the balance has been lost. We now have dramas, which are existentialist tragedies and overt tragedies, and comedies have a lesser place in fiction and drama. The postmodern, existential obsession with meaninglessness and relativity places the tragedy above the comedy, too, and frequently the works heralded as *great* are mere reflections of the public's preference for—or regular diet of—the hopeless. Perhaps the twenty-first century reader has accepted too readily Aristotle's position, and perhaps Aristotle's position offers a particularly male point of view on the meaning of life or on life's purposes. Perhaps that is why those books that wrestle the bazaar complexities of human relationships apart from the anticipated malaise lack commentary, and perhaps there is little surprise that many of these comedic looks at life's tragedies are primarily written by women.

2. Elizabeth Stuckey-French

Many women's lives are defined and muddied by life's tragedies, and comedy provides a lens from which to view the complexities of human nature and their challenging lives. After all, the players in real life are not noble Othello or godlike Oedipus, but they are real people—sometimes bazaar and always fallible. The characters are often stereotypes because real, fallible people deal with the same worries and heartaches, all addressing the problems of love, virtue, knowledge, aging, and death. Comedy tends toward stereotypes for "if the characters seemed [too] real, it would be difficult to laugh at them," too painful (Raph 196). Comedy provides a safe distance from which to view our personal frailties, reminding us of our common humanity.

There are theorists and scholars from various disciplines who challenge Aristotle's definition of comedy's inferiority and who argue that comedy "is capable of dealing with all aspects of our lives, including those that are most important to us, and not merely an escapist genre or a literary mode focused on trifles and trivialities" (Diaz-Bild 20). Of course, an issue is only trifling or trivial when the pain it causes happens to someone else, and only then can we laugh, which is why Elizabeth Stuckey-French's novels *Mermaids on the Moon* (2002) and *The Revenge of the Radioactive Lady* (2011) shine among Florida's current novels. The books present bazaar, nearly fantastic scenarios concerning the plights of their female protagonists, who are, without a doubt, female Florida stereotypes: elderly, retired, northern transplants, who address painfully raw issues; however, familiar types do not keep Stuckey-French's characters from being believable or engaging. The stereotypes simply permit readers to experience Grendy, France, Marylou, and the Sprigg's family's heartaches mediated by the psychic relief of a smile.

Mermaids on the Moon's (*Mermaids*) topic is so overt that critics may shy from its naked, nearly bizarre set of circumstances and fearless, honest revelation: the wife of an adulterous Methodist minister goes missing in Mermaid Springs, Florida, where she was and continues to be on the mermaid performance roster—reminiscent of Weeki Wachee, Florida's mermaid shows—and her bastard daughter, France—possibly fathered by Elvis Presley—goes looking for her mother, while caring for her dead sister's son, Theo, who—to complicate the plot further—has a neurodevelopment disorder akin to Asperger's Syndrome. A domestic disaster! A familial fix! Too irrational to be real! Perhaps, but families experience and address spousal adultery, parental abandonment, absurd behavior, illegitimate children, and mental illness, and comedy's characters must be exaggerated or its viewers will not look—comedic characters must be distant enough to be funny lest they be offensive. However, one look at Weeki Wachee Springs's website will reveal year round mermaid shows, which feature current mermaid profiles—many of whom have dreamed their whole life of being a mermaid—and a picture of two lovely women posing with Elvis Presley. These odd occurrences are not particularly peculiar in Florida. The situations in Stuckey-French's novels are not so much the overactive imagination of an author, but the lack of imagination in some readers.

Grendy, a thirty-six year Mermaid Springs alumni, returns as a Merhag in the Mermaids of Yesteryear, surprising her eldest daughter, France, and irritating her Methodist minister husband, North. She submerges herself in mermaid land two years after their daughter Beauvais's death, hoping the diversion will "help her through the shock" (*Mermaids* 13), but *Mermaids'* central storyline focuses on Grendy's sudden disappearance from the show and from the family, her husband's indifference, her grandson's frailty, and her daughter France's desperate search for her mother. Although Grendy makes no physical appearance until the end of the novel when she rather miraculously reappears to star in the *Mermaids on the Moon* underwater extravaganza, her absence is so tangible, so painful, and she is so missed that her rather kitschy entrance is forgivable. The family confronts death, divorce, adultery, Asperger's, violations, forgiveness, feminism, love, religion, and show business. They challenge notions of fear, aspiration, disappointment, despair, loss, erotica, and mythology. Their plight is daunting, so the plot does not dismiss as old-fashioned an ethic of care nor does it belittle the family's problems by examining them via humor. In fact, "[i]nstead of allowing personal tragedies or dramatic circumstances to destroy [her], the comic spirit renews [France's] hope and courage and the will to live" (Diaz-Bild 22). France is invested in her mother's whereabouts, so much so that she actually learns the breathing techniques to participate in her mother's merhag show. Instead of building a traditional mystery scaffold for Grendy's vanishing, Stuckey-French hangs the story of Grendy's disappearing on relationships, all of which include eccentric, dysfunctional, broken people, and the comedic results vary in degrees of intensity.

Much of the comedic variation relies on identification. Stuckey-French's subject matter is serious, but comedy "is one way of appraising the serious, so the comic must be taken seriously if [the subject matter] is to be rated at its true value. No one understands a joke by laughing at it; he laughs at it because he understands it" (Wallis 343). While the parameters of sorrow and pain have been rightly delineated into stages and discussed in myriad self-help books, a grieving person cannot be relegated to five steps. People are not processes, and Stuckey-French's characters refuse neat categories.

Grendy's past as a mermaid at Mermaid Springs is, all by itself, amusing. Her return to the merhags at 60-years-old is even more amusing, but for Grendy, "[e]verything gets clearer under water" and she is "happier under water than [she has] ever been on land," so funny or no, she dons a bathing suit and returns to show business (*Mermaids* 14). At the root of Grendy's return is an element of courage in the face of social ridicule, and while the idea of her water frolicking may elicit snickers, it may just as easily evoke admiration. In spite of Grendy's unusual pastime, she is believable because she "acknowledges the need the human being has for dreams, hopes, grand imaginings, or in other words, for moments of escape" (Diaz-Bild 21). She is also believable because Weeki Wachee Springs State Park, which is open 365 days per year, adjusts its performance schedule for weeks when the former mermaids perform. Grendy's daughter's frantic search underwater and among the merhags is also a bit preposterous albeit equally believable and touching because France's looking for her mother helps France to see "how much happier [she] will be if [she] learn[s] to rejoice in the familiar, actual world which is [her] only home" (Diaz-Bild 21)—a home that includes underwater hoses, costumes, rocket ships, and Elvis Presley. Many people wish to experience again something that they lost in their adult lives, and few have the courage to revisit those experiences; however, real daring manifests in an engaged, enthusiastic effort to live in the here and now, which is the essence of comedy, and comedy keeps hope alive in a situation where the idea of death hovers.

While looking for her mother, France and Theo board a boat at Mermaid Springs, and six-year-old Theo asks the captain about Crystal River and the alligators. The captain's reply is disturbingly unsuitable for a six-year-old, which makes the conversation oddly amusing:

> Few years back I was taking a tour group out on a glass-bottom boat....
> We all looked down and there went a gator swimming by, and I said,
> 'Folks, he's got him a deer.' Then we realized it wasn't no deer. Found out
> later it was some college student [*Mermaids* 86].

The story, gruesome and inappropriate, infuriates France, and she makes no secret of her ire, so the captain responds jokingly with, "'A gator wouldn't eat your grandma, son, ... I know Grendy. She wouldn't taste good," and the response satisfies the boy (*Mermaids* 87). Wilson D. Wallis's 1922 article titled "Why Do We Laugh?" offers some explanation for the captain's even more inappropriate, joking response to Theo's questions:

> Laughter is not always elicited by the pleasurable, nor is it always the expression of pleasure. It may be a means of expressing displeasure at personal pretensions. We may laugh in spite of ourselves, though to the spite of another, and to our shame and remorse, ashamed and sorry even while we laugh [346].

If the captain is sorry, and he most likely is, he attempts more humor with poorer results to counteract his initially failed humor. Regardless, the second effort at humor is kind, and the captain's comment "creates a comic perspective that allows [Theo] to keep a distance and thus transcend a menacing reality" (Diaz-Bild 22). In this way, comedy is nurturing.

Notions of the feminine and comedy are evident in France and Theo's conversations with the cat, Sisterwoman. Theo loves animals and wails until he convinces France's mother's friends Donna and Rose to give him their cat, Sisterwoman—a cat that spent the better part of its life in Cassadaga, Florida, the Psychic Capital of the World. The chats between the cat, France, and Theo are often silly, but they produce solid, relational, and informational results: Theo hears stories about his mother—stories no one else will tell; Theo communicates information about his grandmother to and through the cat—information he otherwise cannot access; and Theo quits acting like a cat himself—a clear social relief to France. The cat truly becomes a medium, a conduit for comedic relief from the tensions between an emotionally/mentally challenged six-year-old and his emotionally overwrought aunt, and the cat serves as a vehicle by which Theo relays important information concerning his grandmother and grandfather's relationship. In this way, Stuckey-French's cat becomes the means for what Elizabeth J. Marsh calls "conversational retellings," or recallings that "are interesting because they reflect properties of memory and allow study of the flexibility with which people can use memoires in social contexts" (16). But Theo's memories of his grandfather and his grandfather's affair are traumatic. Comedy makes the retellings possible for the little boy because "[c]omedy does not lead to despair or futility over the tension and problems of our lives, but to the celebration of life and renewal of hope and faith" (Diaz-Bild 22).

In "Wit and Politics: An Essay on Power and Laughter," Hans Spier proposes that human laughter at the impediments, even deformities in other humans, "dispel[s] the terror that the monstrous inspires" (1373), and the family life here is truly monstrous. Humor provides a lens through which France can view and analyze her life, and the humor is selfless and redeeming. France's compulsion to find her mother supersedes her penchant for a comfortable, artsy life in Cedar Valley, and forsaking her contented existence leads to discovery, empathy, and forgiveness. France finds her personal narrative inside the stories of her mother's merhag friends, she resurrects Beauvais's memory as she allows herself to love her sister's son, and she confronts years of rejection when she finds the strength to challenge her abusive father.

Stuckey-French's use of comedy to reduce the family's tension offers a way out of the hopeless despair and dark holes of postmodern relativity. For France, Grendy, and Theo, there is an end to misery, and not a cheesy ending, too tightly wrapped and unbelievable, but it is nonetheless an ending that fits Aristotle's definition of the comedy genre. Grendy comes home to her daughter and her grandson, but she leaves her marriage of thirty-five years and begins a new life. Grendy takes Theo, which is good, but France grieves because she has let herself love the little boy who has many problems. France returns to a loving boyfriend and an awesome job, but she is not the same woman she was several months earlier. She has shared in the difficulties of others, born the sadness and burden of her family's dysfunction, faced her grief, and grown from the confrontations. The comedy of the family members' lives does not make for a happily ever after ending, but life is worth living. For France, Grendy, and Theo, life is not a tragedy; life is an adventure.

If *Mermaids on the Moon* is an adventure, then *The Revenge of the Radioactive Lady* (*Revenge*) is an exploit! *Revenge* offers outrageous, but well-developed characters, ludicrous, but oddly realistic situations, and an absurd, but deeply human plot. Stuckey-French's Marylou Ahern is likely the most lovable murderer to enter Florida's fiction world since Tim Dorsey's Serge Storms. At 77- years-old, she re-fires retired, and she single handedly deconstructs Tallahassee Panhandle's Witherspoon family by encouraging adultery: Dad's got a thing for his graduate school colleague; facilitating pornography: daughter Ava's Asperger's cannot cloak her beauty; inspiring abandonment: Mom plans to leave the whole family; encouraging treason: Otis's Asperger's cannot stop his building a nuclear reactor in the garage; and enabling pedophilia—Molly's infatuation with her youth group minister leads to her first sexual encounter. All the while, poor ol' grandpa, Dr. Wilson Spriggs, suffers with dementia and does not even know he is Marylou's intended murder victim. The novel evokes chuckles and simultaneous shame for laughing, but laughing is one way to face and transcend the evils of this world, and Marylou Ahern desperately needs transcendence (Diaz-Bild 20).

Marylou's vendetta is fifty years old. Doctor Wilson Spriggs gave her a radioactive cocktail while she was pregnant with her daughter, Helen, who she and her husband watched die slowly from bone cancer caused by the experiment. Her baby dead and her marriage destroyed, Marylou's grief is achingly present and scenes where she recalls her eight-year-old child's agonizing illness are tolerable only because Stuckey-French relieves the agony with humor as Marylou moves in and out of her past and present, frequently conflating the two. Chauncey B. Brewster's 1907 article called "Humor: Its Kinsfolk and Acquaintance" offers an explanation for this comic relief:

> Humor means far more than the laughter of a fool or at one. It goes often hand in hand with compassion. It is always sane and clear-eyed, and none the less so for its kindly smile and thrill of sympathy as it contemplates the follies, foibles, and faults of men. In the sympathy lies its kinship and acquaintance with pathos. But it is the sanity, the clear-sightedness, of humor that keeps the pathos from degenerating into bathos or anything that could be described as maudlin. Humor is on the best of terms with sentiment, so long as it is true and healthy [712].

In Marylou's first confrontation with the dementia-ridden Dr. Spriggs, she calls him Adolf Hitler. She retells the radioactive cocktail incident, reminding the doctor first of his involvement in her daughter's death and second that the plan is to kill him, too. However, Wilson Spriggs is unable to retrieve the memory, conflating Helen's death with his late wife's death. Marylou proceeds to remind him of the "February day in 1963" when she and her then husband, Teddy, watched their sick baby's face, which "had lost much of its Helenness" (*Radioactive* 129). Helen's deathbed scene is the single most heart wrenching paragraph in the book and left alone, the pain is too much to bear. Unfortunately for Marylou and fortunately for the reader, Wilson Spriggs cannot pay attention, and he puts the coffee "mug back down with a shaky hand, [asking her if she is] feeling all right" (130). Marylou's response is first honest: "I'm tired," she says, and then furious, "Don't be pulling that doctor crap with me" (131).

The truth is that both Dr. Spriggs and Marylou experience mental and emotional suffering and humor keeps the conversation—and Stuckey-French's novel, for that matter—from reducing a serious conversation to overly sentimental, manipulative dialogue. Marylou, herself, must use humor to survive the mental anguish that tortures her daily, and readers are offered the same reprieve from pain as an act of mercy. The humor does not reduce the impact of the deplorable situation—Alzheimer's disease and Cancer are not laughing matters. Helen's death is a pervasive presence. The injustices of science and medicine are painfully evident. But comedy does provide a more optimistic view of life, one that acknowledges the difficulties and pains of living while celebrating the wonders and joys of life. This philosophy of life allows for a moment of tender sympathy to exist between the mother of a murdered child and the child's murderer. Humanity makes way for the hard sciences' errors. For a moment, Marylou Ahearn's grief and Wilson Spriggs's guilt are ameliorated by an empathetic smile, and life—with all its pain and sorrow—is still worth living.

Still, Marylou is not dissuaded from killing Wilson Spriggs, and the plan unfolds with a diabolical, psychopathic, and methodical dissembling of his daughter's family—Wilson Spriggs will watch his family die the way Marylou watched her daughter die and her husband disappear. Marylou insinuates herself into the family, setting up situations that range from the dubious to the heinous: She arranges for Asperger son Otis to get radioactive material, gets Asperger daughter Ava to pose nude for a pornography peddler, gets youngest daughter Suzi involved with a pedophiliac youth minister who seduces her to perform oral sex, and kidnaps Wilson Spriggs. The events are deplorable, repulsive, unconscionable, but the family's response combines rage with humor, and the outcome is hopeful.

Marylou admits to the family about her murderous plan:

> Ava asks, "How were you going to kill him?"
> Suzi's thinks, "How Aspergery," but she is also intrigued by the method.
> Wilson asks Marylou, "Why would you want to [kill me]?"
> Marylou tells the family, "I've told him, many times ... but he always forgets" (*Radioactive* 277).

The family's conversation does not shy away from the mental, physical, and behavioral disorders that define them; instead, they use humor to cope, and their humor highlights the fundamental facts of life without minimizing their painful effects or glorifying those who are infirmed. The family is painfully aware of its inadequacies, its failures, and its missed opportunities, but the family is also aware of its love for one another, its common interest in each other's lives, and its future as a familial unit. Comedy then becomes a practical means for explaining the common, inferior, and ordinary people whose troubles could easily make them despair of life but whose humor provides opportunities for the awe-inspiring and even, sometimes, the miraculous.

In a final act of desperation, Marylou kidnaps Wilson and takes him to the Memphis hospital where he practiced his radioactive experiments, hoping to prod his memory concerning the project. Two of the doctors there recall his work, and he is treated like a celebrity—an event contrary to Marylou's hopes and expectations. Then, a miracle happens. In a moment of pure lucidity, Wilson performs the novel's most heroic act: Instead of "bask[ing] in false but gratifying praise," from the young doctors, he takes Marylou's hand and says, "Actually, gentlemen, my friend here is not doing well at all. She hasn't been doing well for a very long time," and then he leads her out of the hospital (*Radioactive* 322). This moment of empathy, of sympathy, of apology is deeply poignant and suggests that people who are in their right mind will perform acts of selflessness, suggesting also that selflessness is heroic. Wilson performs a simple act, a kind act, relieving his victim turned vigilante of her overwhelming burden, which is precisely the point of comedy. Aida Diaz-Bild asserts, "The comic hero, unlike the tragic one, does not believe that the world of the commonplace is dull, boring or trivial, and that in order to give meaning and direction to our lives we have to despise immediate circumstances and search for the marvelous and wondrous outside them" (21). In the end, *The Revenge of the Radioactive Lady* conforms to Aristotle's model of comedy: Marylou Ahern becomes Mrs. Wilson Spriggs.

If comedy is not a particularly feminine genre used primarily by women, then it is an expression of the feminine ideal. Unlike tragedy, comedy pays attention to the unlikely, the common, and the commonplace. Comedy is nurturing. Comedy, like Grendy, France, and Marylou, finds that "humor dwells with sanity and common sense and truth. Her sisters are sympathy and humanity" (Brewster 717). These women whose lives are ravaged by the unthinkable mishaps and misfortunes of day-to-day struggles do not aspire or pretend to be Hercules or Sampson. Their strength is not focused on bringing down walls of destruction on their enemies, but the heart of their efforts is to restore, to heal, to comfort, and to help. However misguided Stuckey-French's female protagonists may be, they are led by and eventually succumb to their desire for family wholeness, and they are willing to brave life's difficulties for the promise of a smile.

Works Cited

Brewster, Chauncy B. "Humor: Its Kinsfolk and Acquaintance." *The North American Review* 184.612 (1907): 710–717. *JSTOR.* Web. 11 May 2013.

Diaz-Bild, Aida. "*Paula Spencer* or *The* Miraculous Transformation of Misery to Joy." *Estudios Irlandeses* 7 (2012): 19–32. *Academic Search Complete.* Web. 15 May 2013.

Marsh, Elizabeth J. "Retelling Is Not the Same as Recalling: Implications for Memory." *Current Directions in Psychological Science* 16.1 (2007): 16–20. *JSTOR.* Web. 11 May 2013.

Rapf, Joanna E. "Comic Theory from a Feminist Perspective: A Look at Jerry Lewis." *Journal of Popular Culture* 27.1 (1993): 191–204. *JSTOR.* Web. 11 May 2013.

Spier, Hans. Trans. Robert Jackall. "Wit and Politics: An Essay on Laughter and Power." *American Journal of Sociology* 103.5 (1998): 1352–1401. *JSTOR.* Web. 11 May 2013.

Stuckey-French, Elizabeth. *Mermaids on the Moon.* Waterville, Maine: Thorndike, 2002. Print.

_____. *The Revenge of the Radioactive Lady.* New York: Doubleday, 2011. Print.

Wallis, Wilson D. "Why Do We Laugh?" *American Association for the Advancement of Science* 15.4 (1922): 343–347. *JSTOR.* Web. 11 May 2013.

3

Lynne Barrett

As both a creative writer and literary editor, Lynne Barrett has worked on each side of the publishing world, and in a viral web-based article published by *Glimmer Train* in 2011 entitled "What Editors Want; A Must-Read for Writers Submitting to Literary Magazines," she pointedly explains the facts about each side: "The editor is a gate-keeper" and the writer should "help the editor by sending work that is developed, complete, thoroughly revised, and—of great importance—appropriate for the magazine."

On the publishing side of her literary career, she was the founding editor of *Gulf Stream Magazine*, participated as an editor for *Tigertail, A South Florida Annual: Florida Flash*, and is currently the editor of *The Florida Book Review*, a web-based journal founded by Barrett. She has also co-edited *Birth: A Literary Companion* and *The James M. Cain Cookbook*. You can find her speaking and conducting writing workshops at various writing conferences and related writing events. Some of these events include the Sanibel Island Writers Conference, Gulf Coast Writers Conference, Grub Street's Muse and the Marketplace Conference, Gulf Coast Association of Creative Writing Teachers Annual Conference, and Florida Mystery Writers of America Luncheon ("Lynne Barrett").

Barrett is best known for her work as a short fiction author, and she has three short story collections published. Carnegie Mellon University Press published *The Land of Go*, which was her first collection, in 1988. *Secret Names of Women* was published again by Carnegie Mellon University ten years later in 1998 ("Lynne Barrett." *Contemporary Authors Online*), and her most recent short fiction collection, *Magpies*, was published in

2012. In her third short story collection, the author "draws on genres from mystery to magical realism to tell tales set against the past decade of booms and bust" ("'Magpies,' Published"). Many of the stories in *Magpies* have Florida settings.

Her short stories and collections have received encouraging reviews and awards. *Magpies* was awarded the gold medal for general fiction in the sixth annual Florida Book Awards in 2012. Barrett also was given a fellowship in 1991 from the National Endowment for the Arts, earned the Edgar Allan Poe Award from the Mystery Writers of America in 1991, and received the Best Short Story Award at the 2001 Moondance Film Festival ("Lynne Barrett." *Contemporary Authors Online*).

Currently, Lynne Barrett is a professor in the English Department at Florida International University (FIU) where she teaches fiction and creative nonfiction in the university's Creative Writing Program. She teaches writing workshops at both the graduate and undergraduate levels. Some of her seminars include Plot, Form and Theory, and Mystery and Suspense. In 2012, she was selected by FIU as one of its Top Scholars, and the year before in 2011, Barrett was given the FIU Award for Excellence in Graduate Mentorship ("Lynne Barrett").

Works Cited

Barrett, Lynne. "What Editors Want; A Must-Read for Writers Submitting to Literary Magazines." *Glimmer Train*. 1 Sep. 2011. Web. 16 May 2013.
"Lynne Barrett." *Contemporary Authors Online*. Detroit: Gale, 2011. *Biography In Context*. Web. 16 May 2013. http://www.thereviewreview.net/publishing-tips
"Lynne Barrett." Web. 16 May 2013. http://www.lynnebarrett.com/
"*Magpies*, Published by Carnegie Mellon University Press, Wins Gold Medal at Florida Book Awards." *States News Service* 9 Feb. 2012. *Biography in Context*. Web. 16 May 2013.

'Canes, Critters and Criminals in Lynne Barrett's Storytelling

Claudia S. Slate

Place features prominently in Lynne Barrett's fiction, and for seven of the eight stories in *Magpies*, Florida is that place. Thunderstorms and hurricanes, lizards and toads, scandal and seasonal estates form the background of these stories, but as Barrett remarks about setting, "I don't think of it as a backdrop—it's much more three-dimensional than that. I'm very aware of the space characters move through, what can be seen from where, and how the sensory elements of a place affect those who are in it" (Kelsey "On Magpies: Part Two"). In many of her stories, Barrett creates suspense by portraying home not as a place of refuge or stability but as a place that is venerable and in-flux. Barrett, like many of her characters, did not originate in Florida. She grew up in New Jersey and now lives in South Florida, so her characters yearn for a familiarity that would foster security.

Carlos and Jen in the relationship-based stories "One Hippopotamus" and "Cave of the Winds," Tally in the magical realism of "Gossip and Toad," and Ray in the detective story "The Noir Boudoir" exploit the threatening environments created by South Florida weather, critters, and criminals to their advantage. Using this instability, these characters employ storytelling as a means of "connection, betrayal, and survival" ("Magpies Lynne Barrett"). Sometimes the story- within-a-story is lengthy and other times it is a mere anecdote, but either way, characters use the stories to make their homes their castles, fortresses against what lurks outside. In the process, they reveal their character and clarify what they value, just as the discriminating magpie collects shiny objects.

In "One Hippopotamus," new lovers Jen and Carlos hunker down in Jen's small cottage during a Florida thunderstorm. The electricity goes out, and illuminated by lightning, they lie in bed drinking wine and talking. Jen describes the scene:

> The thunder follows fast, and the storm casts the first big drips, hard as pebbles against the roof.... The air conditioning is gone—a kind of death, the cessation of the house's usual cool damp wheezing. The rain roars, Florida rain—there should be a special word for it. There's no separation of drops. Not sheets of rain. Blocks of it [29].

Carlos remarks that "'Florida gets more lightning strikes of any state'" (29). Florida can claim Lightning Capital of the United States (Boas), and Central Florida is known as Lightning Alley because of its astonishing number of lightning strikes. For Carlos and Jen, the severe Florida weather serves a more poetic purpose. A common foe, it unites the two "inside the belly of a giant" (33) as does the sexual current that surges between them. They count the time between lightning flashes to measure the thunder. Carlos counts, "One Mississippi, two Mississippi" while Jen recites, "One hippopotamus, two hippopotamus," from whence comes the story's title. This title is reminiscent of that of Hemingway's short story "Hills Like White Elephants," and both stories share another common element: revelation of a couple's relationship through dialogue. Although Jen narrates in first person, after her initial reflection on how she and Carlos met and an anecdote about his Chilean background and his becoming an orphan in Florida (her only bit of storytelling), the remainder of the story consists, mostly, of dialogue between them.

Despite the united front of Jenny and Carlos and their obvious attraction, they do come from different backgrounds: Jenny is an American-born Anglo and Carlos was born in Chile and came to the U.S. as a child. In addition, the newness and uncertainty of their relationship is readily apparent through Jen's questions to Carlos, like "'Do you like me then?'" and her narrative asides, inserted in between Carlos's storytelling. For example, she reveals her vulnerability when she likens herself to the land: "I picture the peninsula, sprawled out like me, full of holes, defenseless. We're in light so bright I can see the whole of this room and the next, as if they were x-rayed" (29). Though the rooms are exposed, so is Jenny. When Carlos interrupts his story to go to the bathroom, Jenny pulls her shirt on: "I don't want to be naked and thinking of the ways men found to dump me, their evasions, and their transparent lies" (33).

When Jenny asks Carlos where he learned to count thunder (certainly not in Chili, she remarks), Carlos is prompted to tell the story of Marianne, the girlfriend who seventeen years ago (when he was only twenty) taught him "to count Mississippis" (29). Remarkably, this story of a past relationship "frames the budding relationship" (Olshan) and serves to cut through Jenny's insecurity and connect these new lovers. Carlos wins Jenny over with his disarming honesty, willingness to articulate his own vulnerability as a young man, and his insight into his past foolish behavior. He reveals that he used selfish means to avoid breaking up with an old girlfriend. Ultimately, he says that this experience taught him "not to say more than I meant" and "to wait for someone of my own species" (36). After Jenny pulls off her shirt, exposing herself, Carlos asks her, "What do you say, Jenny, might we be of the same species?" (36). Jenny hesitates:

> I hold my breath and feel the whole weight of him, his sad Chilean orphaning, the neatness with which he arranges his possessions, strong hands, furious driving, nice guy smile, passionate allegiance to the Baltimore Orioles, detailed knowledge of space-age countertop materials, cowardice in a crisis, honesty—anything might be a rift someday, but for some reason I have a crazy shred of hope that I've never felt before [36].

Apparently, despite their disparate backgrounds, Jenny considers the details of Carlos's present more important than those of his past. She finally breathes freely and expresses that hope in her answer to Carlos: "I might be" (36).

Their connection appears to have tamed the storm. The electricity comes back on: "the answering machine beeps, back on the job.... The clock has reverted to midnight, blinking. The rain is just a patter" [36]. They laugh and continue their lovemaking; however, then, as if to exert its supremacy, "lighting to the west again" flashes and Jen thinks, "takes our picture" [36]. As his last words in the story, Carlos indicates how the atmosphere of the storm and their conversation has changed him. He abandons Marianne's way of counting and adopts Jenny's: "'One hippopotamus,' says Carlos" [36]. Jenny is charmed by this, but she also appears to recall Carlos's desperate antics to free himself from Marianne. Jenny displays a sense of humor equal to Carlos's—the "wry, lucid optimism" that a New York Times review notes is emblematic of Barrett stories (McLane)—when she reacts to Carlos's last line, thinking to herself, "Oh, no.... I'm going to love him. I'll never get rid of him now" [36]. She does not seem to consider that a terrible fate.

In another *Magpie* story "Cave of the Winds," Florida weather again influences the "One Hippopotamus" couple about a decade later. Carlos and Jen (no longer referred to as Jenny) have married, are parents to eight-year-old Riley, and live in a small house six blocks from Biscayne Bay, Miami. The story is told in the third person from Carlos's viewpoint and allows Barrett to "explore new angles of his character and the relationship [between him and Jen]" (Pycior). In anticipation of a severe hurricane season, Carlos and several of his neighbors rent out warehouse spaces, "caves of metal" (105), which they furnish and stock like bomb shelters of the 50s.

Barrett remarks on writing "Cave of the Winds" about home as a dangerous place: "After going through a couple of very bad hurricane seasons, I felt all too aware of the conflict between wanting a house to be something that shelters you and learning that a house is something that is itself in danger and can endanger you" (Pycior). In "Cave of the Winds," instead of weather uniting Carlos and Jen against a common danger, as it did in "One Hippopotamus," Carlos's extreme reaction to the possibility of destruction endangers their relationship. Barrett's remarks that she "likes to combine characters who represent different relationships to the setting" ("Guest Blogger Lynne Barrett"). This difference in perception is what creates the tension in "Cave of the Winds." Carlos believes that "men need to take care of the family, didn't she [Jen] understand that, he thought" (107). Jen doesn't like what she considers camping out, and when Carlos stays at the warehouse on weekends and stops by on a few weekday nights, Jen begins to question him about the whole idea of the rental, which pushes Carlos further away. Carlos thinks that Jen seems "immune, not feeling the immensity of the world's powers the way he did" and unlike his friend Mike the dentist, "who understood what it was to respect the arbitrary" (109).

Storytelling in "One Hippopotamus" fosters connection for the couple, but in "Cave of the Winds," the storytelling of Carlos's aunt instead contributes to Carlos's rationale for insuring his family's survival. His aunt, who raised Carlos, told him that "though they were Chilean their ancestors were from Asturia and that El Nuberu, if he were angry, could send a rain of frogs" (107). El Nuberu is the god who "whistled up winds in his cave and sent them across the sky" (110). To Carlos, hurricanes take on mythic proportions, so the warehouse becomes the equivalent of sanctuary for his family, "a refuge dedicated to a healthy respect for the deities of destruction" (107–8). Jen does not share her husband's reverence for the metal box: though she visits the warehouse when they tested the generators and even stayed overnight, she rushes home the next morning to shower before work.

Towards the end of the story and the close of the hurricane season, Carlos uses Hurricane Logan, which has weakened to a Category One with only 35 mph wind gusts, as an excuse to go to the shooting range with his friend Mike and stay overnight in the warehouse space. As Carlos lies on his air mattress listening to a high pitched note produced by the winds, Jen shows up unexpectedly with an overnight bag, fearful that her husband is having an affair:

> She said, "I thought you might be having a private party," and he said, "you mean with a woman?" and she said, "The thought occurred," and he, pleased, said, "I haven't seen one as cute as you, Jenny," which led her to lie down beside him, and when he said thought she didn't like camping she replied, "But slumber parties, yes," and whether this proved she was braver than him or just as anxious but with different concerns, anyway, after a while the sound stopped bothering him and he slept [110].

Their dry sense of humor, also evident in "One Hippopotamus," reveals their rapport and their chemistry. Their actions show that they both value family but have different ways of preserving it. Carlos needs to provide safe shelter for Jen and Riley and wants Jen to appreciate his efforts. Jen needs Carlos to spend less time at the warehouse space and more time with his family. Jen feels more threatened by the solution to the problem (Carlos withdrawing from her) than she is about possibility of the hurricanes themselves. Regardless, her appearance at the warehouse indicates that she is willing to compromise and come to him. His response— flirtatiously complimenting her and calling her Jenny (the nickname he used when they first dated)—shows that he welcomes her overtures. Most importantly, Carlos entertains the possibility that Jen is also fearful, just about different concerns.

Ultimately, the extreme weather of Florida has tested their relationship. The story's ending remains open-ended with Carlos leaning back and looking up "into the plum-colored, deep, unreadable sky," knowing that "having been spared for now just meant they were that much closer to their turn" (111). The author reveals in an interview her opinion about Carlos and Jenny—"I like their tenacity" (Pycior), so there are signs that they will weather the storm, both literally and figuratively.

Unlike Carlos and Jen, Tally, the protagonist in "Gossip and Toad," is not endearing, nor does she inspire optimism. Like them, Tally lives in South Florida and deals with Florida wildlife but in the form of real bugs and toads instead of the mythical "rain of toads" ordered up by the wind god El Nuberu, cited in "Cave of the Winds." A gossip columnist, Tally is more intrigued by the people she observes from her eighth story condo balcony than she is by the natural environment: "The ocean was, though of course one shouldn't say this, so boringly natural. In Florida it wasn't that easy to get away from nature. This humid September night was full of buzzes and croaks from unseen creatures" (38).

Tally's people gazing gives her material for making up stories about the rich and famous in South Beach, the more scandalous and nasty, the better. She comes by her storytelling abilities naturally: "Gossip was in her blood. She'd grown up in Alabama, in a town where, among the many skilled practitioners of chat, the champion was her grandmother, a fat old lady who sat on her porch all day and served strong sweet tea to whoever came by and brought her some morsel of news ... she sang the lines of descent and mismarriages of anyone mentioned" (41). Though Tally admits that she conveniently left this morsel of information out of her bio, Alabama was where "she'd learned to gather shreds and twigs of information from which she could shape something" (42), regardless of the consequences for her victims.

Despite Tally's reluctance to engage with Florida critters, Tally suddenly finds that her poisonous words produce insects every time she says something hateful. With a touch of magical realism, spiders and millipedes pop out of Tally's mouth as she sits at her desk in her condo and gossips into her cellphone to her assistant, "I hear the mayor broke up with his blonde, so he'll be after a new one." At her words, a toad hops out and sticks around. Alarmed, of course, Tally considers stopping her scandalous banter but decides that is who she is. She must decide what she values, and she chooses her career, which, though unsavory, is what she does well. So she learns to accept the fact that grasshoppers and slugs fall from her lips as she weaves her tales. The toad, who sticks around, gobbles up the insects. Thus, the survival of the toad—part of natural Florida but also representing her—is dependent on her storytelling. She accepts the amphibian, names him Sapo (toad in Spanish), and even sets up an umbrella for him on the balcony, where he sits "rather grandly, his legs splayed" (47). She moves her laptop to the chaise lounge to sit near Sapo.

They co-exist in a mutual dependence because Sapo serves as her barometer for her smut: "Delicious stuff. Tally tried out each item upon the toad and he snapped up the juiciest results, looking at her with perfect trust" (48).

In "The Noir Boudoir," the longest story in *Magpies*, practically a novella, the narrator, Ray Stout, uses storytelling as an escape from the twentieth-first-century real estate boom in Miami. He believes that the boom seduces newcomers to buy their "own piece of sky" and results in grand old deco buildings, with stories of their own to tell, being "knocked down and replaced by glass towers that can't emulate their glamour" (49). Ray seems to identify with one of the deco buildings, the Delphi, which has been recently rehabilitated: "I gaze up at the building: twelve stories of curves and niches to break the wind and survive a hurricane. When the glass towers collapse, the Delphi will weather on" (51). A divorcee who has moved down from New Jersey several years before, Ray describes himself as a survivor as well: "Old, but not that old: 63, retired cop, good pension, bad arteries, but I keep going. I'm into paper ephemera. Books, magazines, letters. Photos, bills, matchbooks, anything like that interests me. There's history in paper" (51).

The history—the story—of the femme fatale Helena Dorsett, dead at 77, captures Ray's attention as he and several others clear out her apartment at the Delphi. Ray describes their scavenging: "These are my fellow members of the species Magpie. We are small-time antique dealers, which is to say we are collectors who sell to support our habit. We glean old things and send some on their journey up in price, which lets us make a buck and keep the treasures we cannot bear to part with. We'd be mere hoarders if we didn't sell" (51).

Ray's attraction to ephemera is not merely appreciation for the old items or a way to make money but is an obsession. Other than working with the other magpies and fishing off his boat, appropriately named Paper Boat, Ray doesn't date and dines alone in front of the television: "I haven't been looking at anyone much of late except pretty gals forever young on paper. Last week I was smitten with a Broadway actress from the early '20s and then I realized she would be 105 if she weren't already dead" (57). Helena's photo, which he finds in a Lucite frame in the "noir boudoir" where she died, transports him into a mysterious past: "I assume it's the dead lady in her youth: white skin, full lips, beautiful curve of nostril and brow, the eyes pale under carved eyelashes. She's a babe. Her hair lifts from a side part and cascades. She's vaguely familiar, like a minor movie star" (53). He has a romantic attraction to unattainable women.

When Ray finds a driver's license photo of gray-haired Helena in the 1980s, he realizes that she had visited his booth and bought old crossword puzzle books from him; this gives him the personal connection that he craves. His co-worker Sharon, who deals in vintage clothes, remembers that Helena became notorious in 1963, not as the singer she was before her first marriage but because of the murder of her second husband. The vet for her husband's race horse was convicted and jailed for the crime, but the media implicated Helena as either causing the murder or instigating it.

Ray has to know the full story. As he says, "Eight years retired, but you never stop being a cop" (49). He visits the local library and searches microfiche to read old newspaper accounts of the trial. The details of the death of Helena's first husband and the involvement of the vet in the death of her second husband heightens the mystery for Ray, as is apparent in his continued fascination with her photograph: "I've got the lovely Helena's picture on the sideboard where I can see my femme fatale. Her photo has that strong line between light and shadow they liked in the '40s. Call it noir or chiaroscuro, it's dramatic. She seems a hard, lovely woman" (61).

As involved as Ray has become, the story really becomes personal when the home of his co-worker Sharon is burglarized and Ray suspects that the burglar is another co-worker, Cash, a very old man, who Ray believes is the vet who killed Helena's husband and Helena herself. In order to solve the mystery and find out the rest of the story, Ray decides to compromise the security of his old cinder block and stucco home built in the '30s. He drops hints with his co-workers that his house is vulnerable and leaves the back door unbolted that night. Cash shows up to steal any of Helena's possessions that might be evidence against him. Ray is waiting for him and encourages him to confess. This rehashing of his past is reminiscent of Carlos's story in "One Hippopotamus" but with much higher stakes. Cash tells a story of betrayal, including his taking the blame for the murder of Helena's husband because he was so mesmerized by her, only to have her wanting him dead. As Ray has noted earlier in the story, "'If you want something too much, you will pay any price" (71). This theory applies to unbridled lust as well as to real estate acquisitions. In an interview, Barrett refers to this excess when she questions "how far people will go for things that beckon but may not be real" (Necee). Cash admits to murdering Helena in what he sees as self-defense and now in his old age just wants to avoid going back to jail.

Ray has an important decision to make. Will he defend *his* femme fatale and turn in her murderer or will he let Cash go? He says to the intruder, "Miami. The place is full of killers. Guys who work on your car may have been in death squads in Peru, dictators own steak houses, drug kingpins become developers. I can't fix every little thing. Go home. I know you did it and you know I know, but there's not a bit of evidence left, I promise you. She is ash and her things are scattered and scattered further everyday" (78). Cash's storytelling proves to be a cautionary tale for Ray, clarifying for Ray what is important, what he values, including connection with other live individuals. Sadly, Ray is not able to free Cash, whose guilt leads him to commit suicide two days after his talk with Ray. Cash leaves behind little of resale value, except for his old dog Archie, whom he bequeaths to Ray.

After Cash's death, Ray decides to make up for lost time. Earlier he noted that he didn't really know Sharon, though they have worked beside each other for three years. Now he decides to remedy that situation because, unlike the cold photos that he has obsessed over, "She's a warm woman, as I'm coming to appreciate" (79). He appears to be ready to open himself up to another individual.

At the end of the story, there is an air of possibility as Ray gets "spruced up" (79) to take Sharon out to dinner on Biscayne Boulevard. Still, as he and his dog Archie leave the house to walk to Sharon's, Ray stops in the dining room to give one last look at the portrait of Helena: "What is it that she had? Beauty enough to kill for, any way you look at it. I strain to recapture the woman I met. Quite a lady, I remember thinking. Her face is a pattern of shadow and light" (80). Then he concludes, "Now just paper" (80). That paper, ultimately, does not exert the pull of a one-on-one human connection.

Barrett, in a website blog, reveals her sensitivity about such a change in her characters: "I'm always conscious that a character's movements out into the world promise both adventure and loss"; she continues, "I like to plunge characters into some new territory ... and let them study its language and codes" ("Guest Blogger Lynne Barrett"). Storytelling has quite the power over Barrett's characters. Stories enable Carlos, Jen, Tally, and Ray to accept, and even appreciate, their Florida homes. They begin to see their homes as something beyond concrete and stucco, a roof over their heads, and they make decisions accordingly. This means being realistic, tolerating something less than perfection in others and in themselves, and relaxing about what they cannot, or do not choose to, control—whether that is the weather, a toad, a criminal, or condo development. Ultimately, these characters choose connection with others and survival within their Florida environment.

Works Cited

Barrett, Lynne. "Cave of the Winds." In *Magpies*. Pittsburgh: Carnegie Mellon University Press, 2011. 9–26.

_____. "Gift Wrap." In *Magpies*. Pittsburgh: Carnegie Mellon University Press, 2011. 81–90.

_____. "Gossip and Toad." In *Magpies*. Pittsburgh: Carnegie Mellon University Press, 2011. 37–48.

_____. "The Noir Boudoir." In *Magpies*. Pittsburgh: Carnegie Mellon University Press, 2011. 49–80.

_____. "One Hippopotamus." In *Magpies*. Pittsburgh: Carnegie Mellon University Press, 2011. 27–36.

Boas, Sherry. "What Newcomers Need to Know." *Orlando Sentinel*. 11 June 2006. Web. 10 April 2013. http://articles.orlandosentinel.com/2006-06-11/news/SWNEWCOMER11_1_lightning-strikes-lightning-safety-national-lightning.

"Guest Blogger Lynne Barrett: Angles of Belonging." *Lisa Romeo Writes*. 24 May 2012. Web. 10 April 2013. http://lisaromeo.blogspot.com/2012/05/guest-blogger-lynne-barrett-angles-of.html.

Kelsey, Angela. *Angela Kelsey Tell the Story*. "On Magpies: Part Two of a Four-Part Interview with Lynne Barrett." 15 November 2011. Web. 10 April 2013. http://www.angelakelsey.com/on-magpies-part-two-of-a-four-part-interview-with-lynne-barrett/.

McLane, Maureen. "Impersonating Themselves." *New York Times on the Web*. 23 January 2000. Web. 10 April 2013. http://www.nytimes.com/books/00/01/23/bib/000123.rv115405.html.

"Magpies Lynne Barrett." *Carnegie Mellon University Press*. 4 Mar 2013. Web. 10 April 2013.

Necee, Regis. *Beyond the Margins*. "Interview with Lynne Barrett: Magpies." Web. 25 October 2011. http://beyondthemargins.com/2011/10/interview-with-lynne-barrett-magpies/.

Olshan, Joseph. "One Hippopotamus and Magpies." *MFA Writing Program at Greensboro*. 5 June 2012. Web. 10 April 2013. http://therumpus.net/2012/01/one-hippopotamus-and-magpies/.

Pycior, Casey. "The Story is the Cure." 20 October 2011. Web. 10 April 2013. http://thestoryisthecure.blogspot.com/2011/10/lynne-barrett-interview.html.

4

Jennine Capó Crucet

Jennine Capó Crucet is a Cuban born, Miami raised woman, who has compiled an impressive resume since her MFA degree from University of Minnesota in 2006. Besides the commercial success of her first book *How to Leave Hialeah*, Capó Crucet has amassed a significant array of awards and honors, including the Iowa Short Fiction Award—a particularly prestigious honor since "she is the first Latina to win this prize in its forty-year history" ("Jennine Capó Crucet"). Between 2009 and 2011, Capó Crucet accumulated nine awards, and she published sixteen additional works!

Capó Crucet's work celebrates her own life as a Cuban-American woman, underlining the tension that exists "living within and without her community, ready to leave and ready to return, 'ready to mourn everything'" (qtd. in Rev. of *How to Leave Hialeah*). However, she also sees herself as a Miami writer, who celebrates the "working class immigrant experience, honoring that voice." She intends for her work to present "the voice of Miami from a bunch of different angles," offering a "sense of place and a sense of culture that isn't necessarily Latino culture but is very much American culture" (*Furious Fiction*).

A natural born wordsmith, one of Capó Crucet's first language discoveries was the *nine* in her name; thus, she adopted the moniker *J9*. In fact, much of Capó Crucet's work "explores the Americanization of things—of names, of people, of traditions—and [she draws] a lot from [her] experience of maneuvering between two languages" (*Jennine Capó Crucet*). *How to Leave Hialeah* brings the whole of Capó Crucet's blended vision to the anthology, and this compilation has received notable commendations from recognized writers. Julia Alvarez's comments on *How to Leave Hialeah* offer high praise:

> This is definitely a young writer to watch for, sassy, smart, with an unerring ear for a community's voices, its losses, its over-the-top telenovela extravagances, and its poignant struggles to understand itself in a new land. I was glad not to have to leave Hialeah right away, but to stay long enough to hear its many stories as told by a gifted writer [Jennine Capó Crucet].

Although Florida is critical to Capó Crucet's personal identity and fictional setting, she is a Florida State faculty member who spends time between multiple states and continents and has served as the Picador Guest Professor at the Institute for American Studies at the University of Leipzig, Germany (*Jennine Capó Crucet*); however, in an August 2011 interview, Capó Crucet admits her *real* home is Miami, the place where she can recharge her "familial batteries," the place where her mom lives, and the place where she feels "stronger," more herself— "or the version of [herself she] sometimes [thinks she] wants to be" (Young).

Jennine Capó Crucet is a genuine Florida writer. No matter where she lives, being away from her family makes her "desperately homesick for Florida," and she misses home for good reasons (Young). Her Miami community gave her a "strong sense of identity" and she felt "totally empowered in [her] culture" (*Jennine Capó Crucet: How to Leave Hialeah*). In an interview for *Women of Florida Fiction*, Capó Crucet responded with this answer to a question concerning the characteristics of Florida women writers: "I think there's a boldness in the prose and in the choice and approach to subject matter. There's a palpable energy and heat to the work. I'm not sure how I fit in—that's probably a question for a critic or a scholar—but I know that I sense it and that I hope to tap into that lineage with every sentence I craft." As much as any Florida writer, Capó Crucet meets the standards for "energy and heat." If she does not know this already, then in 2015 when her second book, *Magic City Relic*, hits the bookstores, she will certainly be assured of her place in Florida's literary canon.

Works Cited

Furious Fiction: Jennine Capó Crucet Interview. 14 Feb. 2012. YouTube. 14 Jan. 2014. http://www.youtube.com/watch?v=kdaU_oHqM_8.

"Jennine Capó Crucet." *The English Department at Florida State University.* Web. 14 Jan. 2014. http://www.english.fsu.edu/faculty/jcrucet.html.

Jennine Capó Crucet: How to Leave Hialeah. 03 Mar. 2011. YouTube. 14 Jan. 2014. http://video.mit.edu/watch/jennine-capo-crucet-how-to-leave-hialeah–7780/

Rev. of *How to Leave Hialeah*, by Jennine Capó Crucet. *Amazon.* Web. 14 Jan. 2014. http://www.amazon.com/Leave-Hialeah-Short-Fiction-Award/product-reviews/1587298163.

Young, Melissa Scholes. "How to Leave and Why You Stay: An Interview with Jennine Capó Crucet." *Fiction Writers Review.* 2014. Web. 14 Feb. 2014. http://fictionwritersreview.com/interview/how-to-leave-and-why-you-stay-an-interview-with-jennine-capo-crucet/.

On Haunted Shores
Restriction and Resistance in Jennine Capó Crucet's How to Leave Hialeah

CAMILA ALVAREZ

La Florida or the land of flowers is a place haunted by Spanish ancestors. Its people are a mixture of nationalities, 23 percent according to the United States Census Bureau are Hispanic ("Florida"), but in certain places like Miami that percentage goes up to 70 percent ("Miami"). Many of Florida's people are hybrids—beings existing in two different worlds, white and Hispanic—moving fluidly towards and away from unison. The dual nature of an identity formed by living within and between these cultures creates part of the conflict in Jennine Capó Crucet's *How to Leave Hialeah*. The ideological tension develops on three macro levels: cultural and theological (these two are closely intertwined for Hispanics), educational, and sexual. Culturally, Jennine Capó Crucet is a first generation Cuban-American writing for a largely American audience. Educationally, she is a well-known Hispanic-Floridian author teaching creative writing at Florida State University. Sexually, as a female author, she is working in a largely male dominated field and is writing within two gender biased societies: American and Hispanic. This study yields a new theory for literacy as a dynamic system of restriction and resistance. This thesis studies the literacy of the oppressed finding breaks in the dominant hegemony of both academia and literacy practices challenging American twenty-first century norms.

A connection between Capó Crucet as a woman and Floridian to *How to Leave Hialeah* reveals a fluid structure of influence, creativity, and restriction. The macro of Florida's Hispanic and American historical background influences and constrains the micro of Jennine Capó Crucet's personal life experience creating the mezzo of both the stories that she writes in *How to Leave Hialeah* and this academic discussion. Literacy, therefore, functions as a mezzo layer influenced by both the micro of personal experience and characteristics and restricted through the macro of cultural and societal pressures. The tension and interplay that can be found in Hispanic women's literacy practices as a reaction to the pressures put on them by both American and Hispanic society are readily found within Capó Crucet's work. The methodology of this paper fluctuates through the micro of Jennine Capó Crucet's personal reflections in her literature, the mezzo of the project functions as a literary criticism of *How to Leave Hialeah*, and the macro will look at the pressures in Florida from the Hispanic and American cultures that intermix historically and modernly. The theory behind this work will suggest a model of literacy where rivers of communication flow between the pressures of the individual (micro) and the global (macro). The theory will allow an exploration of pockets of tension that women experience in a male dominant society. Moving through the discussion of these historical, sexist, and theoretical sections will be a discussion of *How to Leave Hialeah* as a literary and ethnographic text. This argument creates a case for personal connections to literary criticism as means of exposing literacy practices that resist the dominant hegemonies of canonical literature, academic disciplines, masculine hierarchies, and "white America." Jennine Capó Crucet's literature is the site of ideological tension where moments of her individual resistance to a masculine dominated Americanization can be found. The final theoretical model suggests a tripartite system that is both interactive and affective. Two dominant goals seek to (1) look at literacy as a struggle against hegemony, and (2) identify a subtext within Crucet's work that struggles against the depersonalization of academic study revealing a dynamic concept of literacy as an object that is both influenced and influencing. The mezzo of literacy represents struggles against hegemony in that the mezzo layer includes a larger scope than the micro. The mezzo influences a larger group of people and holds some of its own peculiar practices. As such, it functions as a connection between the micro or personal level and the macro level, but it also represents a possible influence on the macro. Literacy as a mezzo layer is written/performed/created by an individual functioning within the micro, but has connections that span out between larger social issues and to other groups of people represented by the macro. In other words, the resistance represented within a hybrid art or literacy can change the hegemony. The micro creates the mezzo changing the macro influencing the micro. This is a system of influences where each of the parts both influences and is influenced by each other. However the influence of the literacy as the mezzo flows with two currents towards the macro and the micro. This makes literacy as a mezzo layer a site that challenges hegemonic structures and works within a system where agency encounters constraint and creativity intersects structure.

Part I: The Macro Influence or an Ocean of Society

National identity is formed through the illusory belief in a certain outcome: that our understanding of who we are as a country is a manifestation of a specific destiny and that there is only one possible outcome (Balibar and Wallerstein 133). This overwhelming institution creates the macro that impinges upon Capó Crucet. Academic; American national pride; Hispanic, Spanish, and Cuban nationalism; and Feminine standards are set by a similar process. National formation is influenced by a long prehistory. "Every modern nation is a product of colonization: It has always been to some degree either colonized or colonizing, and sometimes both at the same time" (135). Balibar and Wallerstein argue that a national people produce themselves continually as a national community (138). Language and race work together to create a national origin (141). These two forces create a sense of identity that seems natural. However, immigrants to America are faced with a sense of duality—hybridity (Collins and Blot 115). This hybridity has been presented by previous theorists as a mere survival technique: adapt or die. However, the assimilation of the American culture by immigrants is not a submission to a dominant hegemony but rather a process of resistance and influence in which the culture is being changed from within. This change creates a hybrid America—a great welling ocean.

Macro influences rain onto American literacy creating storm clouds that inevitably move trans continentally. American literacy influences and restricts behaviors. However this literacy is changing along with the changes in cultural climate. Vieira discusses immigrants' perceptions of their documents and literacy. Immigration documents create a type of active literacy. These structure social action "like a crystal which bends light as it passes through." One of Vieira's participants says, "Everything you want to do, you depend on a document you don't have" (qtd. in Vieira 437). This is an example of the sense of powerlessness that is common within some Hispanics in America. There is a great sense of fear in interactions with the government. It is no small wonder that Hispanic documented literacy often turns to religious expression. Vieira's essay is valuable in its focus of an underrepresented people and a literacy that is minimized and excluded. Hispanic women experiencing fear and repression often turn to a religious belief—one that is not always approved by the dominant hegemony.

In Capó Crucet's first work in her collection "Resurrection, or: The Story behind the Failure of the 2003 Radio Salsa 98.1 Semi-Annual Cuban and/or Puerto Rican Heritage Festival," the main character Jesenia is a radio intern trying to resurrect Celia Cruz in order to ensure a successful 2003 Heritage Festival. The story begins "The church is quiet except for the nun's approaching footsteps" (1). Jesenia's first impulse is to go to church—to seek aid from God. This is further supported in Vieira's study as Carmem states, "It's not our country.... You have to know your place." Carmem's silence at the school suggests her marginalization in the academic environment; however, at church she was "always in the middle" (qtd. in Vieira 445). Hispanics have a strong belief in the supernatural, religious, and magical often living in a sacred space which is different from the common American belief in scientific reasoning. So when Jesenia attempts to garner aid in resurrecting Celia Cruz, the nun doesn't get upset; instead, she recommends a santera to get the job done: "This isn't *God's* work." The nun responds and scribbles onto a piece of paper the address of a santera, "And tell her hi from Marcela her sister—her *Sister* sister" ("Resurrection" 5). Here, the religious connections between Christianity and Santeria are exposed. For many Hispanics, these belief systems are not mutually exclusive. Although Santeria is considered evil witchcraft on the whole, many Christians also follow the Santeria gods. You just choose the right one for the job as evidenced by "Resurrection." The continued Hispanic worship of Santeria in America is a place of resistance against American and Hispanic norms as Christianity is the dominant religious view for both Americans and Hispanics—thanks largely in part to the Inquisition that spread across Europe.

4. Jennine Capó Crucet

Just as nationalism is impressed within the consciousness of a people so is gender: "Gender takes shape in and as thinking and forms of rationality.... [T]he material life of gender comprises multiple elements, is only intermittently palpable, and is constituted as much by culture, psyche, and language as by the sexual division of labor or the circulation of capital" (Brown 4). Women in America are not equal to men: when one group in a society has to modify its behavior not to get attacked or raped by another group, there is no equality. A woman "is less an agent than a marker of aporia, less a subject of emancipation than a figuration of nonidentity and abstract potentiality" (Marasco 89). Women are often looked at historically through "various forms of masochism: she enters civilization the only way she knows how, through submission to male dominance.... [W]oman [is seen] as the repository of an unreconciled utopian image and as the creature of complete submission to the totality of bourgeois life—represent[ing] two sides of a single coin, an either/or that functions to recenter man as the dynamic subject and object of history" (90). In Jennine Capó Crucet's "Men Who Punched Me in the Face," the stark reality of physical abuse represents gender and sexual differences. This story transcends American and Hispanic cultures, acknowledging the pervasiveness of physical abuse and the sexual dominance that still exists today. Focusing on a series of four vignettes, the story summarizes relationships in which the female narrator was punched in the face by a man. It is the first scene in which the narrator is punched that disturbs and creates as visceral a reaction in the reader's gut as she had: "By our five month anniversary, I was making myself vomit before every date for fear of throwing up on him when he'd come, which is what happened the first time, in the back seat of his car, and what made him hit me" (103). The narrator here is a young teenage girl performing oral sex for her boyfriend for the first time. The perspective of the narrator allows us to enter the mind of an abused woman and the type of thought process that accepts this abuse: "To be honest, it was closer to a slap than a punch, and I only stayed with him afterward because that's what I kept telling myself: it was a slap, not a punch, and every time I pictured it, his fingers opened more, my memory making it into something I could allow" (102). But what drove her to accept this? What compelled her to believe that she needed a man? The culture. Her family. Her mother. The answers are as simple as they are damaging. Women are indoctrinated into the fantasy from birth. As girls, bedtime stories suggest that a prince will come to save all good little princesses. But what happens when the prince is abusive? Women adapt and condemn themselves. This fantasy permeates the American and Hispanic cultures—soaking into minds, echoing from the mouths of those loved and trusted:

> Do not tell your mother you broke things off [with your Spanish boyfriend]; she loves Spaniards, and you are twenty and not married and refuse to settle down.
> —We are not sending you so far away [to a university] to come back with nothing, she says ["How to Leave Hialeah" 158–59].

An education is nothing compared to a man? For women indoctrinated into the masculine hierarchy—yes. This belief begets a cycle of dependence on the very men who may abuse the women who love them.

Gender also affects literacy and literary practices in the home. Traditional male and female gendered roles suggest that the man will work with finances and public concerns while the woman will focus on maintaining personal relationships (Barton and Hamilton 171). Traditionally the man is more educated, more literate than the woman. In Hispanic cultures a woman is thought not to need a higher education as she should constrain her efforts towards getting a man. The Barton and Hamilton study found that gender patterns were shown by people when asked about paying bills, opening mail, reading certain types of books, sending greeting cards, reading newspapers, etc. More women reported reading for leisure than men.

Men's literacy leisure activities include playing video games, which might fall into the expanded definition of literacy which Barton and Hamilton and others believe is needed (149). This literacy was gendered into rough genres with the women preferring romance, relationships, history, and drama while the men preferred action-adventure, war, humor, thrillers, and nonfiction (171). It is interesting that one of the reasons given for women enjoying romantic fiction was escapism (172). Oppressed people as a whole often desire relief from subjugation and have been documented as turning to literacy activities. Happily, Barton and Hamilton did recognize individual cases where gender roles did not follow the stereotypical patterns. However, looking at writing complaint letters as a household chore and relegating that to a female gendered behavior is a biased idea, as stereotypically women are taught not to complain. Women taking over that role would be an example of resistance to an oppressive stereotypical paradigm; much as their preference for escapist literature also demonstrates resistance to the restrictions men and society place on women

(Wittmann 307). While there is a strong gender hegemony around literacy, individual practices vary at the micro-level (Barton and Hamilton 176).

Part II: The Micro as Influence or as the Streams Flow

Deborah Brandt in *Literacy in American Lives* states, "The vividness of early reading memories suggests their importance and their association with pleasure and family intimacy" (150). Contrastingly, memories of writing experiences are emotionally charged and negatively remembered (154). Just as literacy is equalizing it is also separating. The literate seem to get even more literate as the rich get richer (169). Brandt suggests that literacy then is also stratifying people. Ironically, reading is touted as such an important activity for children, but it appears as not as valued a leisure activity for adults—at least when women read it seems to be discounted ... perhaps this prejudice stems from a hatred of idleness: "Idle hands are the devil's playground." Since we live in a capitalistic society, could the stigma surrounding adult leisure literacy practices stem from a connection to value? Yet society exists in an age of information, where literacy is the main energy source (171–72). So perhaps all forms of literacy will become increasingly valued, yet that suggests that these forms will be increasingly controlled by sponsors. In a podcast by the University of Wisconsin-Madison Writing Center, Deborah Brandt spoke about her *Literacies in American Lives* book saying, "You cannot take literacy independently. It's always going to be deeply implicated in social processes, social structures, identity formation, politics, power, ideology. And when you look at it that way it can sort of just disappear into those processes of itself." Miami is well known to have a large Hispanic community. Signs are predominantly in Spanish in certain areas of Miami. The dominant language and culture are Hispanic. Orlando and New Jersey also have dominant Hispanic centers. Jennine Capó Crucet was born in Hialeah, Florida from Cuban immigrants. She was the first of her family to be Cuban-American by birth. Spanish was her first language, and she spoke it exclusively until she started school. Much of Capó Crucet's "writing explores the Americanization of things—of names, of people, of traditions—and [she] draw[s] a lot from [her] experience of maneuvering between two languages." Therefore, she is a Hybrid and discusses hybridization within her writing. This makes her literacy an ideal focal point for the Mezzo section within this theory of influence. She is a college professor, so she has been indoctrinated into the Macro of American education. She worked with "at-risk" youth throughout graduate school and today, "because she realizes that by definition, [she] was one (again, something [she] didn't know until [she] left home and learned the words others used to describe [her] experiences growing up)." Capó Crucet's writing was shaped by South Florida, both its landscape and its people, and her parents and grandparents influenced her through stories of Cuba. Jennine Capo- Crucet says of her own experience: "My own stories are informed by my experiences as a Cuban-American woman living within and without her community." This suggests that she also sees herself as a Hybrid and that she attempts to address this within her writing. As she states on her homepage, "I strive in my writing to give voice to the voiceless, to give stories over to characters not yet readily found in established literature, to give them a place there where they belong. I write for the teenage me out there now, looking for a way into the world, and I write for her future friends and lovers, Miami natives or not, that they be ready to meet her" (Capó Crucet, "Bio"). She is both an insider and an outsider within the Hispanic and the American communities. This places her in a unique position as both familiar with the practices of both the Hispanic and American communities and distanced from them.

Part III: The Mezzo as Resistance and Change or the Rivers Rush to the Ocean

Duffy's idea of rhetoric based off of Burke's definition informs this theory: rhetoric "is a kind of symbolic action, a means through which individuals may respond to and influence the institutional forces that work to define human possibilities" (Duffy 18). In this way, literacy functions as a set of personally and culturally connected communication practices with intermixed streams, where each mode potentially intermixes with another or with all of them—flowing within or without oral, graphic, literate, physical, and digital communication—functioning as a mezzo layer influenced by both the micro of personal experience and characteristics and the macro of cultural and societal pressures. This can be expanded and connected to Duffy's rhetoric and Street's resistance and ideological model. The ideological model understands the technical skills and cognitive aspects of literacy as "encapsulated within cultural wholes and within structures of power" (Street 161). Here ideology is "the site of tension between authority and power ... and individual resistance and creativity" (162). Literature and literacy present ideologies in tension. *How to Leave Hialeah* reveals a resistance to American literacies and masculine dominance. This resistance is represented by Capó Crucet's deviation from both the English language and from an expected narrative: third person point of view flows into first person narratives that address Jennine Capó Crucet's personal life and second person inclusion of the reader into the storyline. For example, the first short story, "Resurrection" begins in third person but then shifts into a mixture of third person storytelling, first person accounts by Capó Crucet, and second person acknowledgement of the reader:

> What happens next is up to you because it relies on your knowledge of Santeria ... the point is, barring your own attempts at research—and you know how lazy you can be, how else do you find the time to read stuff like this?—you need to be told, preferably by someone you'd consider an expert, an insider.... Maybe your narrator—me—then tells you about the santeros that lived across the street from my childhood home [9].

This resistance is present in her deviation from standard American English practices, her inclusion of Spanish words within her text through dialogue and narrative, and her direct confrontation of physical abuse and the mentality that feeds it. Academia does not recognize the value of the personal experience, too often preferring to discuss the pattern of the whole: how entire groups behave to the detriment of the singular. Focusing on the macro, the larger roles and influences negate the reality that all of the larger roles are created by individuals, moving into groups, and then into the macro structures. One person can create change by getting others involved and then influencing larger communities. The story most suggestive of this goal in *How to Leave Hialeah* is the identically titled short story "How to Leave Hialeah." In this story, the female narrator relates how she escaped from the traditional small town Hispanic fate of living in a day to day low paying job, married with children, and subservient to her man. Near the beginning of the story, the narrator's mother and her friends mothers "compare their husbands' demands—put my socks on for me before I get out of bed, I hate cold floors, or, you have to make me my lunch because only your sandwiches taste good to me" (154). Of course the women laugh and say that their men "are like babies." But the reality is that these complaints work and the women obey their men. The narrator telling the story speaks to "you." The story begins, "It is impossible to leave without an excuse—something must push you out, at least at first" (153). In this not so hypothetical story, it is a man, Michael. He breaks up with our narrator for not having sex with him which motivates her to apply to college. Even harder than getting accepted into one university is to convince the family to let "you" go:

> [Y]ou will sell your car, you will eat cat food to save money, you are their American Dream. Get their blessing to go to the one school that accepts you by promising to come back and live down the street from them forever. Be sure to cross your fingers behind your back while making this promise, otherwise you risk being struck by lightning [156].

Capó Crucet speaks directly to the Hispanic girls who number among her audience. She invites them to put themselves into her life experiences and into the experiences of other Hispanics: To experience a part of the potential realities that all people can face and to choose their reality liberated to some extent from the pressures of society, culture, and family. *How to Leave Hialeah* pushes back the invisible waters of the hegemonies that haunt our shores and invites all people to choose their own path through the waves.

Works Cited

Balibar, Etienne and Immanuel Wallerstein. *Race, Nation, Class: Ambiguous Identities*. London: Verso, 1991. Print.

Barton, David and Mary Hamilton. *Local Literacies: Reading and Writing in One Community*. London: Routledge, 1998.

Brandt, Deborah. "Deborah Brandt on *Literacies in American Lives.*" Interview Transcript. *The University of Wisconsin-Madison Writing Center*. 28 May 2008. Web. 11 October 2012. <http://writing.wisc.edu/podcasts/transcripts/wc_brandt3.pdf.

_____. "Bio." *Jennine Capó Crucet*. 2012. Web. 12 August 2012. http://www.jcapocrucet.com/.

_____. *Literacy in American Lives*. Cambridge University Press, 2001.

Brown, Wendy. "Feminist Theory and the Frankfurt School: Introduction." *Differences: A Journal of Feminist Cultural Studies* 17.1 (2006): 1–5. *Literary Reference Center Plus*. Web. 18 Nov. 2012.

Capó Crucet, Jennine. *How to Leave Hialeah*. Iowa City, University of Iowa Press, 2009. Print.

_____. "Bio." *Jennine Capó Crucet*. 2012. Web. 12 August 2012. http://www.jcapocrucet.com.

Collins, James, and Richard Blot. *Literacy and Literacies: Texts, Power, and Identity.* First ed. Cambridge University Press, 2003. Print.

Duffy, John. *Writing from these Roots: Literacy in a Hmong-American Community.* Honolulu: University of Hawaii Press, 2007. Rpt. 2011.

"Florida." *State and County Quickfacts.* U.S. Department of Commerce. United States Census Bureau. 27 June 2013. Web. 2 July 2013. http://quickfacts.census.gov/qfd/states/12/1245000.html.

Marasco, Robyn. "Already the Effect of the Whip: Critical Theory and the Feminine Ideal." *Differences: A Journal Of Feminist Cultural Studies* 17.1 (2006): 88–115.

"Miami." *State and County Quickfacts.* U.S. Department of Commerce. United States Census Bureau. 27 June 2013. Web. 2 July 2013. http://quickfacts.census.gov/qfd/states/12/1245000.html.

Street, Brian V. *Social Literacies: Critical Approaches to Literacy in Development, Ethnography and Education.* Longman, 1995. Print.

Vieira, Kate. "Undocumented in a Documentary Society: Textual Borders and Transnational Religious Literacies." *Written Communication* 28.4 (2011): 436–461. *Literary Reference Center Plus.* Web. 18 Nov. 2012.

Wittmann, Reinhard. "Was There a Reading Revolution?" *A History of Reading in the West.* Ed. Guglielmo Cavallo and Roger Chartier. Boston: University of Massachusetts Press, 1999. Print. 285–312.

5

Connie May Fowler

Connie May Fowler is a native Floridian whose novels are set in Florida, but whose personal work spans the eastern United States. From 2003 to 2007, she directed Rollins College's prestigious "Winter with the Writers" series and served as the Irving Bacheller Professor of Creative Writing. She currently directs the St. Augustine Writers Conference, which is held the first week in October and where she is joined by notable authors like Sascha Feinstein and Laura Van Den Berg. Fowler also directs Vermont College of Fine Art's Novel Retreat. She is a core faculty member of the Vermont College of Fine Arts low residency creative writing MFA program, and she formerly served on the faculty of The Afghan Women's Writing Project (*Connie May Fowler*).

Fowler's personal work is largely influenced by her social concerns. A survivor of a violent childhood and abusive marriage herself, Fowler's work explores the psychological effects of women who enable, endure, and escape emotional and physical cruelty. Fowler says she is "here today—writing, and teaching, and loving life—thanks to the abundant kindness bestowed by friends and strangers" (*Connie May Fowler*); consequently, she founded the Kindness Project, a web-based archive, where people post thoughtful acts that they have either given to or received from others. Many of Fowler's protagonists are impoverished, broken girls and women, whose lives are saved not only by others' kindnesses to them, but also by the victims' generosity to others. Fowler's work suggests the path toward healing and wholeness includes both giving and receiving, and she has certainly modeled this ideal in her own life.

Fowler has been applauded by various domestic violence shelters and organizations that advocate for family safety and in 2002, she was awarded the Excellence Award from the Florida Coalition Against Domestic Violence. Fowler's personal identification and concern with those suffering in abusive families were the impetus for a non-profit organization called Women with Wings Foundation, where she served as director from 1997 to 2003. The organization supported women and children as they attempted to leave abusive situations (Lyceum Agency). Her service also includes a performance with Jane Fonda and Rosie Perez in *The Vagina Monologues*, "a production that raised over $100,000 for charity" (*Connie May Fowler*). Along with her human social concerns, Fowler frets about the Florida landscape, and she is currently writing an "environmental memoir that explores the psychological and spiritual effects of the Gulf oil disaster on everyday life along the northern Gulf of Mexico coast" (*Connie May Fowler*).

The giving and receiving model certainly works for Fowler. She has written a total of six novels, along with a memoir and numerous essays, and she has received the 1996 Southern Book Critics Circle Award and the Francis Buck Award from the League of American Pen Women for her first novel, *Before Women Had Wings*, which Fowler also adapted to an Emmy award-winning film, starring Oprah Winfrey—a prestigious and enthusiastic Fowler fan. Additionally, Fowler was the recipient of the Chautauqua South Literary Award for her novel *Remembering Blue*, awarded the Florida Individual Artist Grant for *River of Hidden Dreams*, and three of her novels have been Dublin International Literary Award nominees.

The Chicago Tribune calls *The Problem with Murmur Lee* "A thing of heart-rending beauty, a moving exploration of love and loss, violence and grief, forgiveness and redemption," but this is a fair description of all Fowler's fiction (qtd. in Lyceum Agency). Her novels convey the agony and grief that accompanies loss and disappointment without oversimplifying or over sentimentalizing and without losing hope for the human condition. Fowler testifies to "the soul-saving power of literature" in her own life, and then she offers the same salvation to her readers (Lyceum Agency).

Works Cited

Connie May Fowler. Connie May Fowler. 2014. Web. 4 Mar. 2014. http://www.conniemayfowler.com/.

Lyceum Agency. "Connie May Fowler." *Lyceum*. 2011. Web. 4 Mar. 2014. http://www.lyceumagency.com/connie+may+fowler.aspx.

Cracker Redemption
Life, Death and Homecoming in *The Problem with Murmur Lee*

JILL C. JONES

> During the time ... which intervenes between a man's death and the final resurrection, the soul dwells in a hidden retreat, where it enjoys rest or suffers affliction just in proportion to the merit it has earned by the life which it led on earth."—St. Augustine, *Enchiridion*
>
> Somebody else may have my rapturous glance at the archangels. The springing of the yellow line of morning out of the misty deep of dawn, is glory enough for me. I know that nothing is destructible; things merely change forms. When the consciousness we know as life ceases, I know that I shall still be part and parcel of the world.—Zora Neale Hurston, *Dust Tracks on a Road*

The themes of grace and redemption in a southern novel are as unsurprising as a character serving up sweet tea on the front porch or eating grits in a diner, but as everybody knows, with grits, sweet tea, and redemption, the magic is in how they are prepared and how they're served up. In *The Problem with Murmur Lee,* Connie May Fowler serves up more than one version of grace and redemption, with a strong dose of Southern moxie and a distinctly Floridian version of sass.

Fowler is not only invested in portraying the South, but invested in that specific South that is Florida—the land of Zora Neale Hurston and Marjorie Kinnan Rawlings: Cracker country. Thus, while Fowler, like all Southerners who write about redemption, must deal with (and revise) Flannery O'Connor's harsh legacy of sin and redemption, she's also working within a Floridian tradition which—despite her references to crackers and rednecks and the all-white cast of her novel—pays homage to Hurston as well as Rawlings. While Hurston famously defined playing the dozens, Rawlings wrote extensively of the Florida Crackers whose name came from "the vanished driver of oxen, who cracked years of rawhide whip over his beasts" (28), defining them as a truly impoverished but fiercely proud and self-sufficient group of dialect-speaking, uncivilized, Floridians. (In her rush to ennoble the Crackers, Rawlings was willing to overlook and even embrace the disturbing racism of the Florida scrub culture. Nonetheless, she defined white Florida dialect and spirit in the same decade that Hurston was defining black Florida dialect and culture and Fowler appears to draw from both of them.)

In *The Problem with Murmur Lee,* characters come home, come to terms, or are thrown out of paradise, such as it is. In the tradition of the Southern gothic (we have a dead child, a drowned body, and an abusive spouse), the novel is centered on a death. Plus in the tradition of the southern woman's coming-of age-novel, it centers on another woman finding her voice, in this case a voice that can hurl southern invective "cracker style."

Murmur's death serves as the catalyst for her community to grapple with the meaning of life and death, faith and blame. However while the novel uses multiple narrative voices and consciousnesses, at its core is the journey and coming to grace of the two primary characters, Charlee and Murmur Lee, who are both on a journey home. The best friends around whom this novel revolves will have to claim their grace and come home—in opposite ways. Charlee must come home to Iris Haven, Florida, from her education in the North, and Murmur Lee must leave Iris Haven and all she loves behind.

While Murmur's own post-death journey owes much to St. Augustine of Hippo, Flannery O'Connor, and even Thoreau, Charlee's relationship with Murmur, her journey for truth, and her coming of age as an empowered Southern woman flat-out rejects the kind of grace that rests on absolutes and theoretical faith. Charlee's home-coming owes more to Zora Neale Hurston's idea of living your life fully, embracing your colorful Southern dialect, and giving as good as you get than to these more transcendental or theological theorists. In a sense, Murmur has to let go of her sassy Cracker self, "the child of the lost Florida, the Florida of swamps and piney woods and cypress hammocks" (Fowler 43) who Charlee tells us "could spit in a snake's eye and live to tell about it" (82), in order to move into the realm beyond human consciousness. Charlee, on the other hand, needs to quit posing as a Yankee from Chicago, give up her abstract ideas about theology, and reclaim the part of herself that Murmur has always kept alive for her—her inner Cracker.

The Problem with Murmur Lee traces the impact of Murmur's life and death on several characters and by the end of the novel, rather neatly wraps up the consequences for all of them and the double coming-to-terms and redemption of Murmur Lee and Charlee, southern style.

Murmur's Journey

The Problem with Murmur Lee is set near St. Augustine, Florida and Murmur's own journey occurs within the context of an Augustinian (St. Augustine of Hippo) Christian paradigm—she delivers most of her narrative from what St. Augustine defines as a temporary state between her death and her "final resurrection" (*Confessions and Enchiridion*).

For Murmur, grace requires letting go of this world and moving into the next state of consciousness—understanding, forgiveness, knowledge, and absolution. Although the novel rejects a strictly Christian rendering of the meaning of life (and certainly rejects both the zealous Catholicism of Murmur's mother and, implicitly, the brutal Catholic vision of that quintessential Southern woman writers' literary mother, Flannery O'Connor), the book ends in blessing and epiphany. The final song is *Amazing Grace*, Charlee's final words are "God bless you" (Fowler 204), and Murmur, who speaks to us from beyond death, finishes the book as a "blithe spirit" who "finally! Finally!" moves to her "final truth" (209).

The novel begins with Murmur Lee Harp's own voice—in a letter to her best friend, Charleston Rowena Mudd . The letter, written six months before Murmur's death, establishes both women solidly as Southerners. Murmur Lee is as Southern as her name suggests and unlike Charlee has never left Florida and never tried to pass as anything other than a "simple white girl from North Florida who loved grits and sea oats and, sans racism, most all things southern" (Fowler 16). Writing about a spell that she learned from a man from Jacksonville Beach and her view of dragonflies and the ocean off a dock near Crescent Beach, St. Augustine, Murmur establishes her voice and her locale as Florida, staking out the Southern-ness, the Florida-ness of this novel in the first two pages. She ends the letter also establishing Charlee's temporary Northern-ness, reminding Charlee that "God isn't up there. She left Boston ages ago" (3).

Amid the chatter of Murmur's love life, description of the beauty of Florida and its creatures, and discussion of spells, Murmur raises the issue of God more than once in this first letter and posits a question about theological issues and spiritual moments. After writing about watching sunset from her dock, she writes about the beauty of a flock of terns that she watches rise and fly, wondering aloud to Charlee if God called them home. She asks Charlee if she thinks that's possible and asks, half-joking, for the opinion of any of her Divinity school professors.

Murmur's question for her Harvard Divinity student friend is a real one. Clearly both Murmur *and* Fowler reject Murmur's mother's Catholicism: the first half of the novel sets up a false Christian paradigm; Murmur's visions will be explained by science; and she will reject her mother's fervent Catholicism for something that more closely resembles transcendentalism. Nonetheless, this question about God and birds sets up the conversation, the theological questioning, that these friends have across the states—from Iris Haven, Florida, the little island off St. Augustine where Murmur lived, to Boston—and from beyond death. By the end of the novel, the answer about God, and the answer about birds, will be clear.

The scaffolding on which the novel and all the moments of grace in it are built, the friendship between Murmur and Charlee, resembles the famous friendship between Zora Neale Hurston's Phoeby and Janie in *Their Eyes Were Watching God.* Like Janie and Phoeby, Murmur and Charlee have been "kissin'-friends for twenty years" or more—since childhood (Hurston 7). Like *Their Eyes Were Watching God* and Alice Walker's *The Color Purple*, the novel sets forth—in the very first pages— the paradigm of the "sister" who stayed home and the one who wandered out into the world in order to investigate the nature of home and the part it plays in redemption. However, unlike either of these novels, in *The Problem with Murmur Lee,* the main character, the one who stayed at home, is dead by the end of the first major chapter. Since the novel is narrated in the first person to this point and Murmur's is the only voice we hear, this is as unexpected as any violent death in Flannery O'Connor's fiction. Though she constructs it very differently, Fowler, like O'Connor, uses this sudden death to explore the notion of grace and redemption.

After the two page letter to Charlee that opens the novel, the novel skips forward to a section taking place six months later, narrated by Murmur Lee. A mere few pages in, as suddenly and unexpectedly in terms of the fiction as it is to the characters who inhabit that fiction, the narrator is dead. Even more unexpectedly, she continues to narrate.

In the midst of an explanation of her argument with Billy Speare about music, Murmur states: "I do not remember plunging into the green river. It was only after death consumed me that any sort of consciousness emerged" (Fowler 7). Murmur's own sudden and unexpected death is the catalyst for her own salvation, for the absolution of several characters, and for the novel itself. Murmur's death, then, is what Heinrich Zimmer calls a "redemptive catastrophe" (qtd. in Shinn 60). However, while in O'Connor's literature the catastrophe often redeems only the person upon whom it falls—Julian in "Everything that Rises must Converge," the grandmother in "A Good Man is Hard to Find," and Shepperd, perhaps, in "The Lame Shall Enter First"— in Fowler's novel, Murmur's death sets her soul literally afloat and leads her friends to their own epiphanies.

Thelma Shinn states that "the moment before [they die] ... is frequently a moment in which God's grace seems to enlighten Miss O'Connor's characters," a moment when they become aware of their displacement from God (68). Murmur is robbed of this critical moment known to all post-O'Connor Southern women writers. She complains about "dying with my eyes wide open and not possessing a single anticipatory breath that my demise was imminent" (Fowler 8). So rather than a fleeting moment of epiphany an instant before her death, like the grandmother in "A Good Man is Hard to Find" or Mrs. May in "Greenleaf," Murmur has to come to terms *after* death: to understand and forgive her ex-husband and mother, embrace her life and death, and move to the next state. Surprisingly, despite Murmur's essentially transcendental outlook, despite her embrace of folk and new age medicines and healings, her narrative draws from both St. Augustine, Florida, and St. Augustine of Hippo, so while O'Connor's Catholicism haunts the text, Murmur Lee's own grace has less of O'Connor's certainty than it does of the paradox, unknowability, and mystery of St. Augustine's theology.

St. Augustine of Hippo, who framed any number of modern Christian principles, believed that there was an interlude between the moment of a person's time of death and his/her "final resurrection" during which the "soul dwells in a hidden retreat" (*Confessions and Enchiridion*). On the one hand, Murmur Lee's post-death epiphany is hardly within a recognizable Christian paradigm given the references to re-incarnation and transcendentalism rather than to Jesus and heaven. On the other, her death in St. Augustine, Florida turns her into a floating body—*literally* embodying St. Augustine of Hippo's notion of the soul's brief hiatus before moving into the afterlife.

Fowler gives us Murmur Lee, a moment after death, as a body floating down the Iris Haven River. She states: "I tried to close my mouth, but it would not move. Tiny fish entered and exited. I looked foolish, floating along, my mouth wide open" (Fowler 7–8). St. Augustine states: "The Lord saith, 'the kingdom of Heaven as like to a sein cast into the sea';" Augustine then elaborates, explaining that the "good fishes" will find their way to God (*Exposition on the Psalms* 65:5).

In her brief journey down the river, Murmur Lee explores the memory of her ancestors, discovering the rape of her mother that brought about her own birth and the birth of her mother's intense brand of Catholicism. Her state as a floating soul grants her not only the vision of her mother's rape but also an understanding of her ex-husband's heretofore unrealized (by Murmur) grief over the death of their daughter. This omniscient knowledge, while painful, will allow Murmur to forgive, understand, and move on by the novel's end. By the end of the novel, Murmur Lee's state of grace appears, finally, absolute, and she moves lyrically out of this knowable world, away from "human consciousness ... voice, sorrow, guilt, grief, joy" (Fowler 209) into the inarticulable and the unknowable.

After her friends mourn her, cast her last spell, sing *Amazing Grace* and spread her ashes, she breaks free of the living white bird who had "carried" her for a bit and is swept "into the dunes ... through nettles and oats, eventually coming to rest betwixt the heart-shaped leaves of a railroad vine. That is where I stayed.... I felt myself becoming root and stem, seed and soil." Here she "finally" realizes where her ancestors and daughter have gone and where she is headed: "I would become a speck of energy pulsing inside the taproot of this vine. There was no choice. It's what the world demanded: death and birth—the process of becoming—bonded forever in a single eternal heartbeat" (Fowler 209).

Although Murmur's condition and understanding speaks more to reincarnation than to a heaven, it's hard to forget that her last name is Harp. We are led to believe that these are Murmur's last moments in her soul's Augustinian state of "hidden retreat," and like the service her friends have for her, it seems an odd mixture of personal, witchcraft, Christian, and transcendental. In her last paragraph, Murmur subtly references both Shelley and Emerson.

Murmur's journey and the novel end on her words:

> I did the only thing a blithe spirit could: I hunkered down among the tender leaves and listened to the surf song. And I watched the moon slowly arc across the sky. And the constellations spill into the sea. And the shooting stars pierce the night's infinite dome. I pushed with all my might, opening my spirit's eye wider and wider, celebrating what would be my final truth: I loved this world [Fowler 209].

Murmur's last words seem oddly like a blessing, ringing somehow of both Gerard Manley Hopkins and Thoreau—and perhaps Marjorie Kinnan Rawlings—another lover of Florida rivers. By the time we get to them, we are ready to believe them.

Charlee's Homecoming

Given that Murmur narrates most of her sections of the novel from beyond death, we rather expect her eventual epiphany, but the absolution and redemption of the still-living characters is, perhaps, more interesting. Fowler's view of redemption is not unlike O'Connor's in that flawed human vessels can (and do) bring that grace—ugly, angry Silas to Lucinda the edgy cigarette-smoking Yoga teacher, and grief-stricken, broken, messy Dr. Z to Charlee (or vice versa), and perhaps Charlee to Billy Speare.

For both Charlee and Murmur, part of the paradigm that informs their coming home or coming to grace is love and, above all, forgiveness. In *The Problem with Murmur Lee*, as in Flannery O'Connor's work, all humans can be forgiven, and only learning both to repent and forgive can lead to redemption. Forgiveness is the balm for all ills. However, while O'Connor's work always deals implicitly with Christ's forgiveness, in Fowler's novel, forgiveness is more necessary for she who forgives than for he who receives forgiveness.

Murmur leaves the earth understanding, forgiving, and letting go. For Charlee, who is living, home-coming and redemption will be of quite a different order. She too will have to embrace, love, and forgive, but her absolution will also require finding and claiming her Southern grit.

Though inextricably tied to Murmur Lee's story, Charlee's story of grace and homecoming is less ephemeral: more Mary Karr than Flannery O'Connor, more Zora Neale Hurston than St. Augustine. Less a theological journey than one of claiming her voice, Charlee's homecoming will require grabbing onto this world and embracing it, fully claiming her southern cracker voice. In order for Charlee to be both the conduit for absolution and penance and to find her own peace, she must literally and figuratively come home; she must embrace her Southern self and voice so that she can serve up absolution in two forms: to absolve Z, "I wanted communion, transfiguration, forgiveness, grace" and to "goddamn well force a reckoning" from Billy Speare. These two forces drive Charlee's narrative and much of the novel: the search for love and forgiveness as well as " a reckoning," redneck style (Fowler 179).

Murmur brings Charlee home, literally and figuratively. Throughout the novel, Fowler implies that Charlee's rejection of her Southern soul can never bring her peace and that Murmur knew this—well before her own death and "homecoming." In her will, she leaves Charlee both her business –Salty's bar, "a tacky testimonial to Old Florida, pre–Disney Florida, the Florida of coffee-stained, nicotine-sticky, dashboard-faded uncluttered road maps that led visitors to the underwater big-fish wonders of Marineland, the amazing gators at the Alligator Farm" (Fowler 117) and her house, "this ounce of paradise I call home, the house I built with my own hands ... I always said I was going to get you to come back home one way or another" (22). Murmur literally leaves Charlee her home. Just as Janie comes home from elsewhere –out there—to tell her story to Phoeby and create a home, Charlee comes home both because Murmur left her both house and business and to find what happened to Murmur Lee.

A "Self-Loathing Southerner" (Fowler 11), Charlee has been passing for a Northerner in Boston, pretending her grits are couscous, calling herself Charlotte (which, to be fair, is her name), and pretending to be from Chicago. In the very early pages of the book, she displays her multi-culturalism in one paragraph, cooking Thai soup for her Nigerian lover while listening to Yo-Yo Ma. When her lover confesses that he is married, her Southern-ness emerges unsought. After shocking him by shrieking with "anger, hurt, and disbelief fueling the elongation of my vowels—- Why, you no good lily-livered shit ass!" (14), her final revenge on her Northern-educated lover is to yell, "Yes, you fucking asshole, you have been sleeping with a Cracker!" (15).

This moment of Southern invective, both as revenge and a re-emergence of identity, is evocative of other Southern women writers (Hurston and Mary Karr come to mind), but while Fowler has her fun with this Cracker Gone Wild scene, it's just a passing moment. Not until Murmur's death two months later does Charlee leave Boston for Florida, come back home, and truly embrace her roots.

Lucinda MacKeithan writes that "prodigal daughters," Southern women writers who leave the South and come home, "journeyed away from home and then returned, not in order to reconstruct the world they had left but to see it and create it anew from changed angles and visions" (38). In *"Their Eyes Were Watching God* and the (Wo)Man of Words," John Lowe states, "a woman's quest for identity ... like most quests, ends with the heroine's returning to the community for reintegration; she thereby achieves wholeness while enriching the community with her newfound insights" (73). He argues (as others have) that Janie's quest for identity is bound up with her quest for a voice. Charlee, like Janie, is a prodigal southern daughter, and after claiming Murmur's bar (her heritage, literally) and her home (both the town and the house left to her by Murmur), finds her voice—with a vengeance.

In many ways, Charlee's story is the inverse of Murmur's. Murmur moves away from the particular, from the messy, from the human. As Murmur leaves her friends and Iris Haven and her Southern identity to become "root and stem, seed and soil" (Fowler 209), Charlee exacts a penance, grants an absolution, and gives a blessing. Her homecoming will require the integration and acceptance of her whole self: while the blessing might owe something to her Harvard Divinity School training, it may also speak to Charlee finding the faith at home that she says she lost in Boston, and the reckoning certainly requires her to embrace her inner redneck.

While Murmur's language becomes more and more lyric as she nears the end of her narrative (and her Augustinian journey), Charlee's becomes more and more driven by sass and dialect. Indeed, by the end of the novel, Charlee is a champion signifier.

Fowler's homage to Zora Neale Hurston is twofold, extending not only to the explicit mention of Hurston (in her will, in the very early pages of the book, Murmur leaves her "Zora Neale Hurston collection" to "some deserving child"), but also to her embrace of Southern invective or playing the dozens, and even to the humor and structure of the novel (19).

It becomes clear that Murmur has left not just her house but her gift of cracker signifying to Charlee, and Charlee's re-claiming of her Southern tongue is a critical component of her journey home, necessary to banish Billy Speare from Iris Haven, the last act of retribution before the final Amazing Grace. This loosening (both setting loose and loosening up) of her tongue is as critical to her own absolution as that of Billy Speares.

In *Dust Tracks on a Road*, Hurston famously states:

5. Connie May Fowler

> I was a Southerner, and had the map of Dixie on my tongue ... northerners ... did not know of the way an average southern child, white and black, is raised on simile and invective. They know how to call names. It is an every day affair to hear somebody called a mullet-headed, mule-eared, wall-eyed, hog-nosed, gater-faced, shad-mouthed, screw-necked, goat-bellied, puzzle-gutted, camel-backed, butt-sprung, battle-hammed, knock-kneed, razor-legged, box-ankled, shovel-footed, unmated so and so! Eyes looking like skint-ginny nuts, and mouth looking like a dish-pan full of broke-up crockery! [98].

In *The Problem with Murmur Lee*, the ability to discharge Southern invective, to signify, is an unambiguous triumph for Fowler's Florida women—and a strength for both Murmur and Charlee. In the last pages of the novel, Charlee confronts Billy to find out the truth and "force a reckoning." When she learns that Billy didn't kill but did not go out of his way to save Murmur, she struggles:

> The white bird watched, and I wondered what was moral. What was vengeful? What was just? Where did compassion and forgiveness and settling the score fall? ... what should happen to Billy Speare? What would be a just punishment for an unintentional murderer whose selfishness was so bloated it smelled evil? ... Did the people who loved Murmur need ... retribution? [Fowler 201].

Charlee almost gives up. "Forget about a reckoning" she tells herself, "I need out of here" (Fowler 203). She goes on: "And right then, a single white feather curled its way from the bird to me" (203). The white feather, reminiscent of the first pages of this novel appears to come from the bird that Charlee has named "the Murmur bird" (202) and that, in fact, we are led to believe from Murmur's narrative—and who wants to impeach the testimony of the dead?—does indeed carry Murmur's spirit for the time. The omen of the bird pushes Charlee to carry on a "rosary of words" (203) in her head and to work towards the proper actions—for Billy, for the community, for Murmur.

Charlee's Harvard Divinity School-enlightened and new age self, apparently inspired by the single white feather that drifts her way a la Forrest Gump, engages in an inward monologue of love and forgiveness, a long litany towards all the characters in her life and the novel. It is the moment where Charlee proclaims her love and her sorrow for the Iris Haven group in her heart and mind, even stating "I will try to love [Billy Speare], in the way of compassion" (Fowler 203).

When the litany of forgiveness and love is finished, she tells Billy, "with the conviction usually reserved for people of faith" that "No one can absolve you" (Fowler 203). This seems very much an echo of Murmur's statement to her ex-husband that although she has forgiven his treatment of his daughter and herself, she will "never absolve [him] of the consequences" (19). However if Charlee cannot absolve Billy, she can do what is necessary for Murmur, her memory, for herself and for Iris Haven: she can banish him.

Charlee tells Billy Speare, with authority, with invective, with both a remembrance of Murmur Lee and love for her home and community, to pack up and leave Iris Haven immediately. When he hesitates, Charlee invokes her Cracker self, and in one sentence puts the "simile and invective" praised by Hurston to good use: to banish Billy Speare. She states: "I mean it, Speare. Hell hath no fury like a Harvard-educated redneck woman who's just been jilted and who knows how to handle a knife and all the places to bury a body" (Fowler 204).

Just as Hurston's Janie silences Jody Starks, just as Hurston's Delia takes all the fight out of Sykes, just as Walker's Celie transforms Mr.—, Charlee's redneck threat (albeit with a Shakespeare reference) silences Billy Speare. When he opens his mouth, as though to apologize, Charlee silences him again. He turns and walks silently away from Charlee and out of Iris Haven.

It's an odd kind of redemption and owes more to Zora Neale Hurston's southern women than to anything O'Connor. Billy is thrown out of Iris Haven, the place that Edith Piaf calls a "piece of paradise," Charlee has found her voice and (we suspect) a home, and Murmur is leaving the world as she has known it. Her final words and vision are very much like Hurston's in *Dust Tracks on a Road*: "When the consciousness we know as life ceases, I know that I shall still be part and parcel of the world" (226). On multiple levels, *The Problem with Murmur Lee*'s final vision and final words are both positive and powerful, finally embracing life, death, and home in every sense, from the unnamed spiritual realm to Florida.

Works Cited

Augustine, Saint, Bishop of Hippo. *Confessions & Enchiridion*. Trans. and ed. Albert C. Outler. 1955. Dallas, TX: Southern Methodist University. Digitized 1993. Web. 1 July 2013.

5. Connie May Fowler

Augustin [sic], Saint. "Psalm 65:5" *Exposition on the Book of Psalms.* Trans. A. Cleveland Coxe. Vol. 8 of *Nicene and Post-Nicene Fathers,* 1st Ser. Philip Schaff, ed. New York: Christian Literature, 1886. *Christian Classics Ethereal Library.* Calvin College. Web. 24 June 2008.

Fowler, Connie May. *The Problem with Murmur Lee.* New York: Doubleday, 2005. Print.

Hurston, Zora Neale. *Dust Tracks on a Road.* New York: Harper Perennial, 1995. Print.

Lowe, John. "*Their Eyes Were Watching God* and the (Wo)Man of Words" *IBloom's Modern Critical Interpretations*: Their Eyes Were Watching God—New Edition, Harold Bloom, Ed. Infobase Publishing, 2008. Print.

MacKethan, H. Lucinda. *Daughters of Time: Creating Woman's Voice in Southern Story.* Athens: University of Georga Press, 1990. Print.

Rawlings, Majorie Kinnan. *Cross Creek.* New York: Scribners, 1942. Print.

Shinn, Thelma. "Flannery O'Connor and the Violence of Grace." *Contemporary Literature*, 9.1 (1968): 58–73. Web. 17 Dec. 2013.

6

Janis Owens

According to Florida author Janis Owens, she inherited her inclination for storytelling from her family, especially her grandmother and father. Roy Junior Johnson, Owens' father, spent years as a Pentecostal preacher before changing careers and becoming an insurance salesman. Though she was a very young child, Owens remembers sitting with the congregation and listening to her father's passionate preaching. Her grandmother also entertained and taught Owens by recounting stories from the Bible as well as from mythology. The author describes her grandmother as "the greatest influence on [her] writing" because as "a poet herself, [her grandmother was] one of those wonderful, magical, southern grannies, the kind who put you to bed every night with a story" ("Janis E[llen] Owens").

Janis Owens was born in Marianna, Florida in 1960, and though her family moved to other parts of the Deep South while the author was growing up, eventually they moved back to an area of the state referred to as the Florida Panhandle, the northernmost part of Florida. In 1980, she married Wendel Ray Owens, and they had three daughters together ("Janis E[llen] Owens"). Not long after her marriage, Owens graduated in 1983 from the University of Florida "where she was a student of Harry Crews' Creative Writing Workshop and earned a degree in English with a minor in Southern history" (*Janis Owens*).

As a longtime resident with family from Florida, Janis Owens is part of the Florida Cracker tradition, and her novels' plots and characters are embedded in this as well. In three of her novels, *My Brother Michael* (1997), *Myra Sims* (1999), and *The Schooling of Claybird Catts* (2003), she spins the tale of a Florida family's secrets, pain, and grief through multiple generations and points of view. In her fourth novel *American Ghost*, which was published in 2012, the story is again set in Florida, this time in the northern part of the state where the author grew up. In 2000, Owens was awarded the Chautauqua South Fiction Award for best novel for her first novel, *My Brother Michael*. She also sold the film rights of *My Brother Michael* and *Myra Sims* to Citadel Films. Along with four novels, she has also published a southern cookbook entitled *The Cracker Kitchen* (2009), a unique book that is "part memoir, part family album, dedicated to the celebration of the Old Florida Rural Culture lovingly referred to as Cracker Florida" (*Janis Owens*).

Not surprisingly, this author has set all her fiction as well as nonfiction works around the unique traditions of this state and continues to make Florida her home. On her website, she describes herself as "a novelist, memoirist, folklorist and storyteller" who "is active in Florida conservation, oral history, historic preservation and dedicated to the celebration and preservation of small town Florida life" (*Janis Owens*).

Works Cited

"Janis E(llen) Owens." *Contemporary Authors Online*. Detroit: Gale, 2003. *Gale Biography In Context*. Web. 30 May 2012.
Janis Owens. Web 29 May 2013. http://janisowens.com/.

A Summer to Pardon
Southern Gothic and the Family in Janis Owens's Myra Sims

SARAH M. MALLONEE

When Myra Sims Catts comes across the proverb "There is nothing hidden that shall not be revealed" in her nightly Bible reading, she finds a key to unlocking some of her madness and taking control over some parts of her life, but even more importantly her family's. Because Myra suffers with deeply-rooted mental illness issues, she becomes more of a burden to her husband and thus Myra is never aware of his "work troubles," which circle around integration and the racial tensions in the mid–1970s in the most southern of all Florida places, a deep south panhandle milltown full of rednecks and small town insularity. Myra's existence—clinging to a fragile sanity—heretofore mirrors that of the iconic madwoman in the attic from the rich British Gothic tradition of works such as *Jane Eyre*, but by throwing herself into the fray at City Café, she gathers the courage to reveal the truly gothic nature of the Sims-Catts family drama. Myra's freedom from her personal demons becomes inextricably linked to the burgeoning social and civil rights freedoms, even though she readily admits "the lessons I learned in the twilight were accurate, it was just so hard to apply them to the lighted world" (Owens 279).

The novel *Myra Sims* is the second in the trilogy of the Catts family, encircled by *My Brother Michael* and *Claybird*. Each with a different first person narrator, these novels twist around the same dysfunctional family's stories as they deepen our understanding of the dynamic layers of mystery, hidden truths, and self-exploration. *My Brother Michael* is narrated by

Gabriel Catts, Myra's childhood friend, first crush, brother-in-law, lover, then finally husband, and *Claybird* is narrated by Clayton Catts, Myra's youngest son and the product of her affair with her brother-in-law Gabe. While this situation alone is enough dysfunction to evince head-shaking and tongue clicking reproach, Myra's story helps to further reveal just how deeply disturbing a life of violence and shame can be. The Sims-Catts family story shocks the reader, like a good Gothic text, as it "engage[s] 'the unspoken' and drag[s] into the light the grotesque truths about the most romanticized of institutions and societies" (Bailey). Like the Freudian uncanny, this familiar unfamiliar disorients and yet implicates the reader's involvement.

The familial and familiar violence, monstrosities, and degraded experiences threaded throughout this narrative of self-disclosure link this contemporary text with how Peggy Dunn Bailey describes Gothic roots: "The Gothic has from its inception included grotesque characters that, despite their mere humanity (or because of it), are able to generate real horror." The British progenitors of the Gothic mode Horace Walpole and Anne Radcliffe sent shivers down the spines of their eighteenth and nineteenth century readers; today, these same shivers pass down the spines of those inhabiting the contemporary American landscape. The American branch of this terror comes from elements that "suggest the inescapability of the past and of inheritance (via both blood and culture), the workings of obsession and monomania, and the naïveté or outright falsehood of foundational tenets of American society: freedom from persecution based on difference, original equality and opportunity, the possibility of self-determinism" (Bailey). The gothic mode then, becomes "an apt one for telling the truth about the quality of our life," as Leslie Fiedler describes in his evaluation of the realistic elements of American Gothic in his 1966 edition of *In Love and Death in the American Novel* (qtd. in Bailey).

Myra Sims, the novel, has all the trappings of the Southern gothic style, full of what Bridget Marshall identifies: "creepy buildings, mysterious landscapes, unhealthy obsessions with the past, revelations of dark secrets, acts of violence, and troubled mental states" (15). Peggy Dunn Bailey also defines the amorphous Southern Gothic in her article "Female Gothic Fiction, Grotesque Realities, and *Bastard Out of Carolina*: Dorothy Allison Revises the Southern Gothic." Bailey traces the literary Gothic lineage and traditions in order to show how Dorothy Allison's text layers the Gothic, the Southern Gothic, and the Female Gothic. Bailey points to subtleties particular to Southern Gothic:

The Southern Gothic is fueled by the need to explain and/or understand foundational trauma, the violation or loss of that which is essential to identity and survival but often irretrievable. Southern Gothic literature is characterized by obsessive preoccupations—with blood, family, and inheritance; racial, gender, and/or class identities; the Christian religion (typically, in its most "fundamentalist" forms); and home—and a compulsion to talk (or write) about these preoccupations.

Perhaps most importantly for this narrative, there is the presence of deeply flawed and disorienting characters whom we love and hate and, most importantly, recognize from our own lives.

Owens uses both the first two novels in this trilogy to demonize domestic and sexual abuse through the horrifying consequences of it in Myra's mental and physical demise. Myra's childhood torments reappear; the skeletons come out of the closet, so to speak, and therefore throw her into an endless loop of manic-depressive states and several full-blown psychotic breakdowns. Having started this storyline with Gabe's external observations about the family in the first novel, *My Brother Michael*, the second novel shifts to Myra's interiority. This shift parallels what Bailey identifies as the central theme of what she terms Female Gothic literature: "the imprisonment and vulnerability of women within structures purportedly designed for or devoted to their safety, especially the family home. Within this domestic and supposedly sacred space, women may live with the omnipresent threat of violence, if not the reality of horrific abuse." Myra's suffering originates with her father's physical, sexual, and emotional abuse, and these childhood experiences haunt her whole adult life.

Janis Owens's Florida panhandle roots enrich the physical details in the novel as the story moves between Louisiana, Alabama, and North Florida. This infuses the narrative with rich sensory details and intensifies the verisimilitude. In other words, the novel's foray into a fictionalized West Florida mill-town born from turpentine camps, sustained through Baptist revivals, and still clinging to the traditions found on old tree-canopied streets, rings true for those familiar with the old South trappings of the Florida experience. All of this, again, highlights the grotesque nature of the novel's flawed characters and their situations: even though they are exaggerated, they are recognizable in our neighbors, our friends, and the stories we pass on through generations. Owens is a storyteller whose desire to write stems from her admiration towards her grandmother, whom she claims inspired her by being an avid storyteller and poet herself. The deep religiosity presented in the novels, also known and experienced first-hand by Owens, further fleshes out these deeply embedded gothic tropes. This novel has what Myra calls "the smell of Eden, the heart of hell" (Owens 28).

Myth and reality converge in Florida's weather; many claim Floridians live in a perpetual summer. By living through the tragic, violent, maddening, damaging, and redemptive events in five very intense summers, Myra is able to leave her twilight world behind. As the setting smolders, the conflicts deepen until Myra is no longer the madwoman in a dysfunctional mill-town family, but a full-fledged citizen of the world. Myra's self-discovery and breaking free of the monstrous, grotesque entrapments parallel the emergence of what Patricia Yaeger deems predictable in a Southern woman writer's gothic text: representing "a culture dealing with crisis, unable to handle changes in the course of everyday life—the growing demand (from the thirties into the nineties) for African American equality, for greater access to education, citizenship, and economic resources" (4). The sudden appearance and disruptions of the grotesque nature becomes for Yaeger a witnessing act. Southern women writers "employ the grotesque dynamically—to repersonify people and ideas who have disappeared" (231) where the sudden appearance of monstrosity becomes "a form of social protest steeped in local politics" (224). Myra's struggles coincide with the struggle for greater racial equality in small-town Florida and culminate in deliverance from these burdens.

In July 1959, the Sims family moves to Magnolia Hill and becomes neighbors to the delightful, Baptist, helpful yet judgmental Catts family. Simon Catts, the patriarch, and Gabe, the gregarious cherub who is the youngest son, show a simple kindness to these new neighbors and thus create a reprieve for Ira and Myra, whose violent father is always on the brink of beating them in wrath for disobeying. The imprint of the gentleness of Mr. Simon and the irrepressible Gabe makes Magnolia Hill the most wonderful of homes for Myra, even though this is where she will experience the most horrific abuse. It is here that Myra can remember her father's face; one of the only memories she keeps with her of this hurtful man. Myra can pardon her father for his sins because she can see him there as simply a man and because there was love in that moment—pure and innocent love. Myra narrates:

> This is one of the few memories I have of my father whose face I cannot bear to remember in the world of reason and control. It stands alone, a

persistent memorial to the unarguable fact that beyond all the evil he was later to become, he was just a man after all, merely human, with hopes and dreams of his own, and maybe a few for the child he lifted in his arms and introduced with such love [Owens 18].

The summer of finding out comes just a year later and exposes the hidden truths of the white trash rumors about the Sims family. A simple gesture of kindness by Cissie Catts (matriarch and Queen of Magnolia Hill) to put sunscreen on 12 year-old Ira's back reveals the scabbed-over cigarette burns that cover him. At this point, neighbors intervene enough to involve *the state* and all that that entails. This moment becomes a turning point for the Sims family as Myra calls it "the beginning of the end" (Owens 38). Owens uses Myra's child-like point of view to explore the horrific qualities of the abuse by showing the effects of this abuse as commonplace. Myra thinks "His back wasn't such a big deal to me. I was the one who patted cold towels on it when it was fresh and scratched it later, when the welts finally healed and the scabs itched him to distraction" (40). Owens furthers this monstrous distortion by pitching the family's reaction to a potential escape as a threat instead of a relief; the family goes down to the Department of Health with the "mean" lady from the state "knowing we were going into battle, a battle that was somehow connected to Ira, somehow a threat to him" (41). Here we learn the insidious quality of that abusive household; it turns our common moral compass upside down.

The man who alleviates this child's idea of a threat (the state's intervention) is the source of all their real pain and suffering. When Daddy comes waltzing into the downtown offices, the children are overjoyed, throw themselves at him, and reattach to him immediately. Daddy's entrance to the Health Department hallways shows the true monstrosity of everyday horror that becomes infused into the cycle of abuse. As he swoops into the scene, he sweeps up the fragile, scared children and offers them "everything we weren't" (Owens 43). Myra's vision of her knight in shining armor come to rescue them continues. The child describes her grotesque father with words of affection and endearment. His entrance shows him to be "confident, controlled, the very personification of power" (43). This sudden appearance of their father thrills the children as we learn how in that moment Myra feels relief: "I was never so glad to see anyone in my life" (43). She and Ira fly down the hall to find comfort in this atrocious man, and they both leap into him, "hitting him in a powerful embrace, yammering bits of explanation and accusations against the horror that had invaded our home" (43). The reader, seeing the tragic quality of this misplaced trust, adoration, and love, knows this scene to reek of the insidious quality of abuse; the presence of the Gothicized conflation of victim and victor sends shivers down our spine. Questions surface: How can freedom be a horror? How could an end to the pain be considered scary? Surely, Daddy is so much scarier. The child Myra does not have the answers to these deeply psychological problems, but the adult one begins to see the light.

All this leads to the summer of confinement where Ira and Myra's lives become even more circumscribed as they are alienated from outsiders, neighbors, love, and childhood play: "In the meanwhile, my brother and I had the dog days of summer to contend with inside a screenless house without so much as a fan to our name, and our father coming home every night sober as a judge, a virtue that sounds a lot healthier on paper than it did to us at the time" (Owens 47). Their father's reformed adaptation of normality troubles his children more than his common animality; a monster's masquerade as saintly disturbs the balance of the embedded other.

As married adults with children, Myra and Michael Catts move from the Catts family home on Magnolia Hill into the most quintessentially Southern Gothic house buried as it is ten miles from town, isolated under the lush canopy of oaks and pines, overgrown foliage, and hiding amazing treasures like an Italian marble pool, stained glass windows, and an aristocratic air. As Myra's psychological edges truly begin to fray, she fills this house with ghosts, "*stairwalkers*" (Owens 195), and the anxieties of woman losing control over her realities. The first summer in the new house, Myra works day and night in a full blown manic state to make the house perfect. She has her first of three affairs in this first summer. The psychological torment Myra experiences in this summer shows how Myra loses herself into a deep darkness. Her emotional torment pulls at the reader's heartstrings as she seems both aware enough to recognize the trouble of her situation but not aware enough to have a clear voice in it. Myra wonders:

> Why was everyone so mad at me these days? I could hear Daddy's boots on the porch every night, could tell he was mad, I couldn't imagine why. I tried so hard to please him, ironing and cleaning and never spending a penny, never telling a soul, but it was never enough. That was the thing about men: they always wanted more. Tommy, on the phone, begging me to let him stay the night; Gabriel on the porch: *I did find me a wife; problem is, she married my brother.* They were never satisfied, and it was so confusing, my head hurting so much, never any relief [Owens 188].

The confusions in this non-linear narration of Myra's interior fight with her demons—her past and present struggles—reinforces the trouble with trauma that her x-rays already revealed: our bones never forget.

Michael tries everything he can—discretely and with an eye to their growing importance at Sanger the furniture manufacturer he now manages—to set Myra to right, including the psych ward at the hospital, medications, exorcisms, and lastly, inviting his brother into their home and charging him with the careful watch of Myra and their children. Gabe, always in love with Myra and driven by his own demons, entangles himself with Myra in the summer of 1974. Ira plays the role of the whistle-blower, again, calling Michael and exposing what's been happening right under his nose, but by then, Myra is already pregnant with Gabe's child. This twist firmly plants this family into the dysfunction of the Southern Gothic distortions—incest and intrigue, violence and sadness abound.

Like the hero he is, however, Michael remains a stalwart husband and father to all Myra's children, claiming them all as his own, trying to help Myra reclaim herself. In order to return this great favor of returning life to Myra, she finds a way to quiet the bullies and racists who begin tormenting Michael, strangling the Sanger company, trying to choke Michael out for making Sam McRae, a black man, the foreman and manager. The Klan is involved, as well as all the vitriol of the Southern prejudices and fears. With the law turning a blind eye and Michael feeling more and more threatened, Myra instigates the turning point by drawing on courage she doesn't even know to have, driving into town, nursing her baby, and throwing the dead, bagged-up, family dog into the congregated trouble-makers at the City Café. What Myra comes to realize that summer is "That was the thing with the darkness; it needed light, a witness" (Owens 297). So, Myra and her sister-in-law take to having their daily lunch at the City Café, showing these small-town rednecks that fear, intimidation, and a little racial tension are nothing compared to a woman who has been through the depths of darkness that few know and live to tell about.

Myra lives with unexorcised demons her entire life. This madwoman in the Southern Gothic mansion lives with the "murky waters of restored memory" (Owens 77). Having found comfort as a child in her own punishment chambers, a three-by-six closet, Myra found herself loving this confined space more than life; she returned to it over and over again even after her father officially freed her from it. This self-imposed imprisonment became an obsession that kept her in the dark, harder to overcome than the beatings. Through her many traumatic encounters, Myra experiences the dizzying effects of the "carousel of rage and regret" (57) from her abuser and suffers thoroughly for it. During a tremendous personal fight, both with herself and the external threats, Myra finds a life, an empowerment, a connectivity to her children, her beloved Michael, and she embraces the "lessons ... learned in the twilight" and does find a way to bring them to the light. This brings her freedom, love, acceptance, and a future in the light, under the canopy of the Southern Gothic still full of the deep flaws and macabre events. In her article "Making a Spectacle: Welty, Faulkner, and Southern Gothic," Susan Donaldson argues that bearing witness to and watching the grotesque unfold is part of the power in gothic narratives. She claims, "reading a gothic novel often takes on strikingly voyeuristic connotations" and as voyeurs, then, we are able to quiet our own demons and bask in the light of our new-found freedoms. In other words, as we witness the novel's portrayal of the rage and regret, the abuse, the suffering, and the recuperation, we are finally able to get off the carousel in an effort to embrace balance instead of the exaggerated. The deep sympathies elicited from the gothic, macabre events befalling the lovely Myra Sims Catts and her family help us come to terms with the real-world demons and deeply flawed characters we recognize and must deal with in our own families, neighbors, and communities.

Works Cited

Bailey, Peggy Dunn. "Female Gothic Fiction, Grotesque Realities, and *Bastard Out of Carolina*: Dorothy Allison Revises the Southern Gothic." *The Mississippi Quarterly*. 63.1/2 (2010): 269–281. *Literature Online*. Web. 1 July 2013.

Donaldson, Susan V. "Making a Spectacle: Welty, Faulkner, and Southern Gothic." *The Mississippi Quarterly*. 50.4 (1997): 567–585. *Literature Online*. Web. 1 July 2013.

Marshall, Bridget M. "Defining Southern Gothic." *Critical Insights: Southern Gothic Literature* (2013): 3–18. *Literary Reference Center Plus*. Web. 1 July 2013.

Owens, Janis. *Myra Sims*. Sarasota: Pineapple Press, 1999. Print.

Yaeger, Patricia. *Dirt and Desire: Reconstructing Southern Women's Writing, 1930–1990*. Chicago: University of Chicago Press, 2000. *eBook Collection (EBSCOhost)*. Web. 1 July 2013.

American Ghosts and American Realities
Past and Present of Race Relations in Janis Owens's American Ghost

BEATE RODEWALD

Janis Owens's novel *American Ghost*, published in 2012, is replete with ingredients for alluring popular storytelling; the paperback front cover quotes *People Magazine's* assessment of the novel: "Part thriller, part romance, and based on an actual event in the author's hometown, this novel is a fine example of Southern storytelling." Mystery, love, history, and biography all connected in a good story is what the magazine's reviewer identified as the essence of the book. But the more subtle nods towards an "actual event in the author's hometown" and the praise of the novel as "a fine example of Southern storytelling" point to other issues that are not explicitly discussed in the novel but that form an implicit parallel story for anyone who has been following recent discussions of the history of race relations in the United States.

Set in the fictional town of Hendrix in the Florida Panhandle, the story follows Jolie Hoyt, a preacher's daughter, and the consequences of her encounter with Sam Lense, a Jewish anthropology student from Miami, who comes to town for a semester, ostensibly to study the history of Florida Indians. Jolie's secretive extended family quickly become suspicious of the outsider's motives in visiting the town, especially since he is inquisitive about an event in local history that everyone in town knows about but nobody talks about, namely, a lynching that took place in the 1930s.

In "The Indian Study," the first part of the novel, set in 1996, Sam and

Jolie's intense relationship is abruptly terminated when Sam is invited to accompany the Hoyt family men on a trip to their fishing camp in the swamp; Sam gets shot in what is officially called a hunting accident, and through interventions from both his family as well as Jolie's family and other towns people, Sam and Jolie lose all contact with each other. In a way, their respective community's suspicions about each other pull Sam and Jolie back to where, those communities might say, they "belong."

In "When the Chickens Came Home to Roost," the second part of the novel, set approximately 12 years after the first part, Jolie and Sam meet again. The decade separating their encounters saw Jolie's spirited ventures to get out of Hendrix, culminating in her becoming mayor of another small town near Hendrix: Cleary. Sam, who in the meantime had been married and divorced, has become an officer in economic development; his excursion into the ghosts of Hendrix and the Hoyt family is part of a past he seems to have left behind until Hollis Frazier and his brother Charley track down Sam after Hollis, while doing genealogical searches on the Internet, finds Sam's article on the history of Hendrix. The Fraziers are sons of one of the men who were lynched in the 1930s.

The paperback edition of 2012 includes as an appendix to the novel a brief commentary by the author: "Janis Owens on the Story Behind *American Ghost*" (Owens 282–283). Referring to her own ancestry, Owen's describes it as not "of the typical Anglo-Southerner stock, but tri-racial Southerners of a sort only studied in rare corners of anthropological literature" (282). In her conclusion to the commentary, Owens writes about her motives for writing this particular work. In her view, her own father exemplified the complicated legacy her family carried through generations, and then Owens explicitly states that she "sought to write a story that would go outside the usual black-and-white theories of race relations in the South" (283). Owens then elaborates in a paragraph worth quoting in its entirety:

> I wanted to delve into the complexities of a culture touched by the long shadow of slavery, even today. Only such a brutal institution could produce this sort of extreme accomodation: a widespread faux race of Americans who were a study in contradiction—so fierce and loyal, so devout in their spirituality and so unthinkingly racist, with such particular longing to be (as the turn-of-the-century literature describes it) 'Pure White.' To my mind, these two extremes—fake ethnicity and stark violence—seemed to get to the roots of my own family's contradictions, which are nuanced and warped by ten generations of American values, both wonderfully good and almost incomprehensibly bad [283].

Given the explicit concern, expressed in Owens's own commentary, about a more nuanced approach to discussions of race relations in the United States, it seems odd that *American Ghost* does not really engage the difficult questions. The characters come from a variety of backgrounds; after Jolie gets involved with Sam, for example, Jolie's family and friends wonder about her having caught a "rich Jew" (Owens 66) as a potential husband. Each group of characters has its own cultural inheritance concerning other "cultures." The idiosyncrasies of families, groups, or just like-minded communities appear coincidentally as the narrative unfolds, but they do not become part of the story.

Also, Owens's narration is inconsistent in using (and trying to reproduce in written form) the language of the various characters, and so the voices of the narration and the characters appearing—and speaking—become blurred. Admittedly, no one is observing from the outside, i.e. the reporter is part of the picture, but the novel itself supplies hardly any scenes that give any indication of the narrator's stance toward the customs observed. One of the few scenes that seem to draw some attention to inherited customs worthy of examination is a Hoyt family dinner party. The narrator describes the event as follows:

> In a tradition as old as the river, the men ate first, with the women serving, and the children sometimes not eating till a third or fourth seating.... The only modern concession to this ancient custom was that female outsiders—girlfriends and miscellaneous pickups—were allowed to eat with their dates, though this was a relatively new twist, and if any of the men needed something not in immediate view ... they had no compunction in sending any available woman to the kitchen to fetch it, even if they didn't know her name (*sweetheart* and *baby girl* would suffice) [Owens 73].

The parenthetical note seems to point to the obvious sexism of the interactions among the people at the same time that the opening phrase, somewhat cliché, reinforces how deeply ingrained these behavioral patterns are. Other phrases in the novel that hover between oral story-telling conventions and clichés include the "childlike devotion" attributed, several times, to Lena, Jolie's best friend, who marries Jolie's brother, Carl. The dinner party example illustrates the perpetuation of patriarchal practices with, supposedly, everyone playing—willingly—along. The instances in the novel where the history of race relations is the context are equally uneven in providing questions (let alone answers) that remain about how much change has occurred.

6. Janis Owens

The year 2013 saw many anniversaries, Martin Luther King, Jr.'s "I Have a Dream" speech at the march on Washington in 1963 being one of the most important ones, but the 1863 Emancipation Proclamation also was recognized in various forums of public discussion. The nationwide attention paid to these anniversaries and the debates they spurred shows that, as Kinder and Sanders put it, "Race has been and remains still our nation's most difficult subject" (11); remembering, individually as well as collectively, the history of race relations is a key component of America's self-image and identity.

The year 2013 also saw several events that seemed to perpetuate the continuing chasm between people who believe that race relations have improved and those who believe that little has changed—or, even worse, that relations have deteriorated. The controversy over Paula Deen's use of racist language and the acquittal of George Zimmerman in the fatal shooting case of Treyvon Martin are the most prominent examples of the continuing debate; the Supreme Court's ruling of a part of the Voting Rights Act of 1965 also caused heated debates. Race relations are so much at the front of public attention that President Obama appeared in the White House briefing room on July 19, 2013, to make a statement about the Martin case, which included the following remarks:

> You know, when Trayvon Martin was first shot I said that this could have been my son. Another way of saying that is Trayvon Martin could have been me 35 years ago. And when you think about why, in the African American community at least, there's a lot of pain around what happened here, I think it's important to recognize that the African American community is looking at this issue through a set of experiences and a history that doesn't go away.

On September 1, 2013, George Yancy, a professor of philosophy at Duquesne University, commented on the president's briefing in "The Stone," the *New York Times* online opinion pages, in a post titled "Walking While Black in the 'White Gaze.'" In the post, Yancy argues that "[e]ven with the unprecedented White House briefing, our national discourse regarding Trayvon Martin and questions of race have failed to produce a critical and historically conscious discourse that sheds light on what it means to be black in an anti-black America. If historical precedent says anything, this failure will only continue."

Americans dealing, individually as well as collectively, with race relations in this country continues to be a highly charged topic not just in academic exchanges, but in popular culture as well. Films such as *The Help* and *The Butler* ignite arguments about whether or not they are perpetuating racist ideas or contributing to less stereotypical representations of racial communities than audiences were used to in pre–Civil Rights era productions. Actors, actresses, directors, as well as individual viewers were being interviewed about their impressions about the presence (or absence) of racial stereotypes, and these discussions in the media—including everything from TV to blogs to Internet forums to taped video of public events—revealed that it is very difficult to change people's long-held assumptions, but also that it is almost impossible to change people's inherited beliefs about their identity in the context of a larger community.

American Ghost seems another example of the need for the kind of conversation about unspoken events of the past. While the novel's promotional blurb implies some tackling of crucial questions concerning racial relations and communal as well as individual identities, these themes simply provide the material for the plot and characters, but the novel does little to encourage a more complex processing of this history. The novel seems too eager to present its world as having left behind the old mutual suspicions.

An exchange between Hollis Frazier and Jolie Hoyt may illustrate the transformation the world has supposedly undergone since the old ways of prejudice. In addition to being mayor of Cleary, Jolie also runs a bed-and-breakfast, which the Fraziers choose as their lodging. When Hollis offers to rent a room for a whole month and pay in cash, Jolie wonders whether he might be a drug dealer and asks directly: "Well, you're not wanting to ... deal out of here, are you?" (Owens 156). When Hollis assures her that he is a successful businessman who owns a chain of restaurants, Jolie, supposedly embarrassed by her assumptions, apologizes and adds: "I'm really not as backward and swamp-running as it might now seem, but actually considered pretty cool and tolerant. You know—renovated old house, vegan menu. Very hip" (156). The narrator follows Jolie's remarks with this sentence: "Hollis barked a laugh, as it was precisely what he'd been thinking, making for one of those pleasant little moments of connection, when you realize you're in the presence of a kindred spirit, a potentially good friend" (156).

Given their identities and affiliations with their families' entangled histories, it is difficult to see the narrator's interpretation (and Owens's imagining of this scene) as the most likely scenario in such an encounter.

The narrator's explanation of the scene as "one of those pleasant little moments of connection" seems somewhat contrived. Throughout the novel, individual voices, including the narrator's, are not consistent in tone, which makes occasional editorializing comments such as this one appear more like Owens's explanation of her narrative rather than an integral part of the fiction. Jolie's declaration that she is not "backward and swamp-running," despite her automatic assumptions, shows her awareness that the past is very much present.

"Collective Memory" has become, by now, one of the trendiest subjects of scholarly activities. Owens's *American Ghost* does include the ingredients to contribute to the expanding articulation of issues concerning history as remembered and transmitted, both individually as well as collectively. However, the novel does little to encourage readers to engage with history; it merely uses the history as backdrop for a fairly conventional love story that, it seems, just imagines that conflicts will—somehow (magically) – disappear over time. Clearly, the first twelve years of the twenty-first century have demonstrated that ghosts continue haunting us until they are dismantled.

American Ghost is a work of fiction, admittedly, and doesn't lay any claim to providing answers to actual social ills. However, insisting on aesthetic distance seems, in a climate of the hotly debated public issues clearly at the core of a work's narrative, disingenuous.

In an essay concerning contemporary literary theory, Albrecht Koschorke expresses the connections between literary culture, memory, and history; his point about remembering the past seems particularly pertinent to a discussion of Owens's novel. Koschorke claims that "we do not even own the past as an unchangeable fact—it is continually refashioned and produced afresh in collective memory. This too is a creative process, one that paradoxically affects with particular intensity the very elements of a culture that are felt to be an immutable inheritance" (Koschorke). The ending of *American Ghost* raises the question whether Owens succeeds in her explicitly stated goal of wanting "to delve into the complexities of a culture touched by the long shadow of slavery, even today" (Owens 283). It seems that the complexities are simply set aside for a coexistence of the various characters that reflects avoidance rather than engagement with the very real presence of the past, for the individuals as well as for the various communities.

Much recent work in memory research suggests that it is important to consciously make present those pieces of the past that illuminate collective as well as subjective perceptions of historical contexts and continuities in efforts to replace deeply ingrained dynamics with more productive exchanges. Bringing these perceptions to the forefront of our public discussions seems to offer a viable response to the (previously quoted) statement by Kinder and Sanders that "Race has been and remains still our nation's most difficult subject" (11). Given that their statement was published in 1996, it is worth noting that almost eighteen years later, in 2013, The Aspen Symposium on the State of Race in America offers a nuanced description of the discussions; it states that the symposium "explores the issues and opportunities for people of color with a particular focus on the role of race and racism in the United States. It will touch on issues of institutional racism, personal responsibility, multi-racial and post-racial attitudes, and other related questions within the context of the home, workplace, school, politics and the media" ("Aspen Institute").

Collective as well as individual memory is inextricably linked to any person's sense of identity. This connection is one of the reasons heated exchanges take place after the release of films or books that depict race relations in America's past. Invariably, arguments arise over how plausibly the characters are portrayed or how accurate a depiction of the time period the film or story offers. But works of art—whether they are visual, verbal, written, oral or any other kind of production—are artistic artifacts of our collective life. Unless they explicitly *claim* to present a historically accurate representation of the world depicted in the work, it is beside the point to fact-check details.

However, works of fiction that so deliberately echo complicated and highly charged issues of public debate have some responsibility to contribute to critical engagement and serious thinking about these issues. Thomas McCarthy, professor of philosophy at Northwestern University, uses the phrase "Vergangenheitsbewältigung in the USA" to write about the "Politics of the Memory of Slavery" in a 2002 article published in the journal *Political Theory*. The German term refers to "efforts to deal publicly with the Nazi past" (McCarthy 643), but it has since been used to discuss other parts of the world and their efforts to work through complicated histories (for example, South African Apartheit and American Slavery).

If Koschorke's claim that "the past ... is continually refashioned and produced afresh in collective memory" has any validity, then it becomes especially important that artistic productions that invoke particular historical events receive the critical attention they need to go beyond overly simplistic debates over the accuracy of representation. Examining *American Ghost* in the context of collective memory studies and communal and individual identity issues may yield useful insights that can contribute to the evolving conversation.

Works Cited

"Aspen Institute Symposium on the State of Race in America." *The Aspen Institute*. 22 April 2013. Web. 23 Nov. 2013.
Kinder, Donald R., and Lynn M. Sanders. *Divided by Color: Racial Politics and Democratic Ideals*. Chicago, Il: University of Chicago Press, 1996. Print.
Koschorke, Albrecht. "Response" *JLT Articles*. 1.1 (2007): n. pag. Web. 10 Dec. 2013.
McCarthy, Thomas. "Vergangenheitsbewältigung in the USA: On the Politics of the Memory of Slavery." *Political Theory*. 30.5 (2002): 623–648. Print.
Rogan, Helen. "American Ghost." *People* 78.17 (2012): 55. *Academic Search Complete*. Web. 3 July 2013.
Obama, Barack. "President Obama's Remarks on Trayvon Martin Ruling." 1600 Pennsylvania Av, Washington, D.C. 19 July 2013. Web. Transcript. http://www.whitehouse.gov/the-press-office/2013/07/19/remarks-president-trayvon-martin
Owens, Janis. *American Ghost*. New York: Scribner, 2012. Print.
Yancy, George. "Walking While Black in the 'White Gaze.'" *Opinionator. The New York Times*, 1 Sept. 2013. Web. 10 Dec. 2013. http://opinionator.blogs.nytimes.com/2013/09/01/walking-while-black-in-the-white-gaze

7

Heidi Boehringer

Heidi W. Boehringer lives with her animals in Deerfield Beach, Florida, but she grew up in a rural setting outside of Valley Forge, Pennsylvania. She graduated from the University of Florida, which she attended on an honors scholarship and studied creative writing with Harry Crews. Boehringer has appeared on National Public Radio's *The Spoken Word* and has written essays for *The Tropic* of *The Miami Herald*. She is also a conference speaker, has appeared on TV, and teaches creative writing. She is the Director of Underwriting for the National Council on Compensation Insurance (NCCI), and she has worked for NCCI for twenty-five years. Boehringer is also part of various organizations related to both her writing and her insurance work: Writers Network of South Florida, Project Management Institute (PMI), Instructor for Center for the Book, Mystery Writers of America, PMI South Florida Chapter, and PMI ISSIG, International Institute of Business Analysis (IIBA).

Boehringer's work is frequently described with words like *raw, pitiless, honest, brutal,* and *blunt,* but the overwhelming and overarching impetus is *guilt.* Her first novel, *Chasing Jordan,* reveals a mother's misery as she tries to overcome the grief of accidentally killing her two-year-old son. The germ for the novel came from a quote her teacher and mentor, Harry Crews, had said twenty years prior: "A marriage cannot survive the death of a child" ("Heidi W. Boehringer"). In true Robert Frost "Home Burial" fashion—but without the civility—the O'Hara's marriage deteriorates. Grieving mother Meg wanders from strange restaurant bars to stranger men's beds, trying desperately to atone for her sin and to assuage her guilt. Boehringer's second novel, *Crossing the Dark,* offers no reprieve from guilt. Mother and police officer, Mona Schlagel, rescues her thirteen-year-old daughter from the clutches of a pimp, but she cannot escape the prison of her own past and her responsibility for her daughter's emotional destruction. Her characters are unforgettable—for good or for bad—but this makes sense because for Boehringer, "memorable characters—whether you love them or hate them—are more important than a memorable plot" ("Heidi W. Boehringer").

Although Boehringer admits her work is not based on true stories, she does say that her "personal experience has made [her] interested in exploring the themes of loss, isolation, abandonment, getting love right and trying to save others" ("Heidi W. Boehringer"). Her next book explores domestic abuse, but the novel is on the horizon. Clearly, trauma and suffering is at the heart of her next book as well. Boehringer has "a demanding job, so [she doesn't] always have the energy to write" ("Heidi W. Boehringer"). She is not willing to force the process, but those of us who have read and enjoyed her first two novels hope she will take a little vacation time: "go out, eat some food and sit at the bar and write" ("Heidi W. Boehringer"). Her next novel cannot come soon enough.

Work Cited

"Heidi W. Boehringer." *Heidi W. Boehringer*. 2014. Web. 13 Mar. 2014. http://www.midnitemysteries.com/.

Walk on the Wild Side
Heidi Boehringer's Fiction and a Post-Feminist Landscape

Maxine Lavon Montgomery

In a scene that could come only out of the pages of detective fiction, *Crossing the Dark's* Mona, a feisty, no-nonsense police officer, executes a daring, if not melodramatic rescue of her thirteen year-old daughter from the clutches of Cesar Solomiente, a sado-masochistic pimp. Mona solidifies her image as hard-edged female cop who lives by her own rules when she threatens to take the law into her own hands by disposing of Cesar's dismembered body in the Everglades. Mona fails to make good on that promise—at least at this point in the narrative—and transports Cesar to the local jail, ostensibly a kinder, gentler fate. But the image of one's being fed to alligators lingers in the reader's mind, creating a haunting picture of a gruesome, painfully slow death in the sub tropical wetlands. Perhaps this is why Boehringer chooses to situate narrative action against a South Florida backdrop: she is bent on painting a portrait of a multi-faceted landscape that lends itself to an expression of not only the pleasurable events among an international crowd of thrill-seeking emigrants, but also the dark side of human experience, the moments that threaten to undermine the orderly, comfortable existence residents seek to maintain. The Florida that she evokes throughout her fiction is, at its best, a place where one is free to step outside the bounds of objective reality and venture into the unexplored, uncharted margins of life—the forbidden wild side.

Throughout its history, Florida has maintained its stranglehold on the popular imagination, as the state has been a rich cultural mine for writers, filmmakers, and producers seeking a setting for their works. One recalls the moment when a somnolent Lakeland is thrust onto a national stage with the timeless fantasy "Edward Scissorhands" (1990), filmed on location on the south side of town. Connie May Fowler immortalizes the anonymous trailer parks of north Florida in her novel-turned-television movie *Before Women Had Wings* (1996), featuring Oprah Winfrey as Zora, a kindly elder wise woman residing at a home in the woods. Last, but certainly not least, one is reminded of Zora Neale Hurston's Polk County with its thriving saw mill camps, sprawling orange groves, lively juke joints, and bustling front porches.

But none of these spaces would attract the likes of Cesar and his ilk, lured by the promise of fast money, power, and sexual domination. Nor would they have produced someone like Mona, a woman who lives by her own rules in a willful defiance of traditional conceptions of woman's place. Life in Boehringer's high-speed South Florida is anything except stable, predictable, or routine. There is a close, symbiotic relationship between the Florida emerging from the pages of the author's fiction and the characters that seem as indigenous to the tropical scene as the swaying palm trees, sandy white beaches, and gentle sea breeze. Boehringer could have situated her narratives anywhere; she earned a degree in creative writing from the University of Florida and is no doubt thoroughly familiar with life in the agrarian setting that has nurtured countless residents. Indeed, Gainesville has more in common with rural Florida than with metropolitan Deerfield Beach where Boehringer currently resides. Nevertheless, it is Broward County—a place some individuals would refer to as the 'real' Florida—that engages the talented author's imagination as she recreates the conditions prompting her largely female cast of characters to step outside the narrow boundaries demarcating a socially-prescribed role and enter what feminist critics aptly describe as a "wild zone" (Showalter 200). At this point, it is worth mentioning that a vengeful Mona not only promises to feed Cesar to the alligators, she hints at the possibility of castrating him with her night stick, a phallic symbol that signifies a reversal of the masculine system that legitimizes Cesar's sinister behavior. The stereotypic Mexican gangster is arguably no better off with the outraged mother than he would be with a group of hungry alligators, rattlesnakes, and water moccasins. Elaine Showalter discusses feminist attempts to theorize and realize the experiences of women, a subjugated group, and the possible existence of a "wild zone" beyond patriarchal control:

> We can think of the "wild zone" of women's culture spatially, experientially, or metaphysically. Spatially it stands for an area which is literally no-man's land, a place forbidden to men.... Experientially it stands for the aspects of the female life-style which are outside of and unlike those of men; again, there is a corresponding zone of male experience alien to women. But if we think of the wild zone metaphysically, or in terms of consciousness, it has no corresponding male space since all of male consciousness is within the circle of the dominant structure and thus accessible to or structured by language. In this sense, the "wild" is always imaginary.... French feminist critics would like to make the wild zone the theoretical base of women's difference. In their texts, the wild zone becomes the place for the revolutionary women's language, the language of everything that is repressed, and for the revolutionary women's writing in "white ink." It is the Dark Continent in which Cixous's laughing Medusa and Wittig's guerilleres reside.... The concept of a women's text in the wild zone is a playful abstraction [200–01].

Boehringer's female characters experience the unique marks of womanhood within the perimeters of a space characterized by unbridled autonomy—one where women are free to explore aspects of gendered difference without fear of masculinist authority and control. That space is imaginary not only because it is almost entirely a product of women's defiance of social norms, but also because it is temporary, subject to end as the patriarchal system seeks to regain power.

South Florida, with its glitz, glamour, and international ambiance, serves as a particularly suitable locale for the female heroine's quest for self-identity. Here, outside the boundary of a more provincial setting, one can easily escape the social constraints confining women to a restrictive role and be free to explore the dark side of life. Much of narrative action in Boehringer's fiction evolves out of the tension arising from efforts on the part of the contemporary female heroine to reconcile time-honored notions of a gendered identity with the expanding positions open to women in a post-feminist setting. *Chasing Jordan* (2005), her first and arguably best novel, takes up this issue through the perspective of Meg, a young wife and mother who accidentally runs over her twenty seven- month old son while watching her husband Paul ogle Susie, the couple's well-intentioned, but promiscuous neighbor. Susie's penchant for wearing short shorts and flirting with married men puts her at odds with the image of the domesticated wife and mother popular in nineteenth-century southern fiction with its valorization of the Cult of True Womanhood—an image that the author holds up for scrutiny throughout her fiction. Meg's unintentional act not only calls into questions her own ability to live up to this idealized role, but it is also the source for the unfolding drama involving the mother's frustrating attempt to atone for the death of her child. Meg becomes frigid, unable to be intimate with her husband as the couple tries to sustain their marriage in the face of a seemingly overwhelming loss. Not only that, but the grieving mother endeavors to escape her pain through, among other practices, sexual liaisons with a man she picks up in a local bar.

Trauma looms large in Boehringer's fictional cosmology. Whether it is rape, addiction, or unexpected death, suffering assumes a central place in her writing. The author is quick to mention her narrative engagement with life's tragic events: "My personal experience has made me interested in themes of loss, isolation, abandonment, getting love right, and trying to save others, which find their way into the things I write" ("Q/A"). Although Boehringer focuses attention on catastrophic occurrences and their lingering emotional, psychological, and social consequences, it is the suffering that women endure that concerns her most. Here, again, her first novel is instructive. The revelation of Meg's horrific family history involving her mother's alcoholism and the elder woman's role in the death of Meg's father and brother, Jake, lends a gendered dimension to the generational calamity that the novel's heroine faces. Women in her family endure horrendous pain and fail miserably at finding acceptable ways of coping with the stresses of life. None of them fit into the domestic roles to which society would consign them. In the fictional world that Boehringer constructs, male characters assume a peripheral role as they are relegated to the margins of a poetic reality in which women must find creative ways to heal themselves. Meg makes a futile attempt at recovery when she takes her infant daughter, Madeline, to therapy sessions for cancer patients, despite the fact that her infant daughter is not ill. Being around others who are grieving is, in Meg's estimation, one way to come to terms with pain. Later, she takes Madeline with her to bars and gives the child liquor, as if to suggest a continuation of the alcoholism that has plagued the family for generations.

Meg is a complex character reminiscent of the vexed maternal figures that people the pages of Toni Morrison's fiction. One is reminded of *Sula's* Eva Peace, *Beloved's* Sethe, *Jazz's* Violet Trace, or, more recently, the nameless African mother in *A Mercy*. Much of the action in these texts takes place in the intermediate space between the guilty mother and the abandoned child. Like Morrison's larger-than-life female figures, Meg is a mother whose ambivalent relationship with the maternal role prompts her to behave in uncanny ways. In *Beloved,* Sethe's "too thick" love motivates her to murder her daughter rather than witness that child's subjection to the atrocities of slavery (Morrison 164). Sethe's excessive maternal devotion becomes the catalyst for Beloved's ghostly intervention. The ex-slave mother attempts to atone for the death of her "crawling already" baby girl by an extreme devotion to the ghost-child, an embodiment of the horrors associated with the transatlantic journey (159).

Boehringer's novel takes place in a setting that is bereft of the intense spirituality that pervades Morrison's fictional world. Nevertheless, in spite of the obvious cultural differences between the ex-slave mother and Meg, the past intrudes on the present in bizarre ways. Jordan, Meg's deceased son, though not nearly as tangible a presence as the ghost-child Beloved, becomes a phantasm that embodies all of the pain that the woman has experienced as she constantly replays the events leading up to his tragic death. The middle class, contemporary wife and mother tries to cope with Jordan's accidental death by aligning herself with others who are grieving. Aside from joining a cancer support group, she breaks into a neighbor's home when Cameron, a neighbor's husband, is killed in a car accident. Finally, at the novel's end, Meg gains the courage to return to her son's Boca Raton gravesite where she apologizes for her role in his death: "Jordan, I miss you, my little man. Mommy is so, so sorry." Tears are running down my face, but I feel a calmness wash over me" (*Chasing* 246). Meg's apology to her deceased son constitutes a cathartic moment that is designed to pave the way for recovery.

If the novel's South Florida setting allows an opportunity for Meg to venture outward, away from the domestic arena which is, in many respects, a locus for her problems, it also encourages her to indulge in the destructive practices that forestall the healing process. Nowhere is this ambiguity more evident than in the rendering of Meg's visits to Broward County's many open-air bars and beaches. Caught up in the throbbing rhythms of a tropical locale, tourists and residents alike abandon restraint in a hedonistic pursuit of pleasure. At one point, Meg attempts to escape the mounting tension at home by going to a bar: "I gotta get out of the house, but I don't know where to go" [...]. "Maybe an open-air bar where the smoke won't bother Madeline. Plenty of them in South Florida. Most of them are restaurant-bars, so it won't look like I'm a bad mother to have a baby with me" (*Chasing* 40). Meg is, therefore, able to escape the watchful gaze of a judgmental public that would censure her for taking her infant daughter around those engaging in questionable practices involving drinking and smoking.

Broward County serves as an evocative "wild zone" where the female heroine is able to chart her own course—one that takes her away from a domestic space and identity. It is within the confines of an airport bar that she meets Al, a handsome stranger who soon becomes a lover and confidant. As if to signify her appropriation of an alternate identity, Meg tells Al that her name is Emily. The beleaguered wife and mother therefore forms an alter ego or dark double that engages in the kind of behavior that most would consider unacceptable. Through Emily, Meg's dark double, not only does the heroine free herself from all inhibitions, she maintains the false image of the model wife and mother—the identity she once held prior to Jordan's accidental death.

With Al, Meg rediscovers her long-suppressed sexuality. No longer confined to a traditional role, she derives pleasure from wearing the skimpy bathing suits that reveal her curvaceous figure. The couple attends a Mozart concert on the beach in Hollywood, carrying out their affair against a backdrop of pulsating tropical rhythms that mirror their sexual passion. There is an international population of Jamaicans, Cubans, and Puerto Ricans—each of whom contributes to figurations of South Florida as a borderspace located outside fixed geographic and cultural limits. Meg points out regarding the sultry environment, "That's South Florida for you, everyone's from somewhere else, running here to leave their shitty lives behind. Problem is, your life follows you" (*Chasing* 98). Boehringer's rendering of the illicit relationship between Meg and Al brings to mind the superficial bond between the American and the girl in Hemingway's classic short story, "Hills Like White Elephants." But Meg and Al are no more successful at finding happiness than Hemingway's international travelers are. At the novel's end, Meg's decision to run into Al's arms, leaving Paul and Susie behind, is one that encourages the reader to question the practicality of her efforts to abandon a socially-prescribed role in favor of a hedonistic lifestyle in which she is able to do as she pleases.

Narrative emphasis on cosmopolitan Florida—the nightlife, beach scene, and international population—underscores the ease with which Meg can move outside the perimeters of a staid, predictable existence and indulge her passions with little fear of reprisal from an established social order. No ecclesiastical body intervenes in condemning her for her adultery; no ancestor or elder wise woman arrives to berate her for being a bad mother in her decision to take Madeline to a bar. In a more rural setting, church members would likely intrude in the lives of individuals who were in crisis. In an agrarian locale, where traditional values and extended family networks exist, there is a sense of community present that tended to override notions of individualism. Such networks functioned as mediating bodies that set the terms for acceptable behavior. One is again reminded of Morrison's *Beloved*.

The novel's climactic scene involves a gathering of outcast women who arrive at 124 Bluestone in order to exorcise the ghost-child bent on consuming Sethe, and Sethe's recovery is a direct consequence of this communal act of reclamation. Sadly, communities of women, which figure so prominently in literature and life, are noticeably absent in the fictional world that Boehringer constructs. Instead, Meg experiences an unprecedented level of autonomy that, ultimately, hinders her quest for wholeness. The independence that she enjoys allows her to reinvent herself as she becomes an embodiment of the amoral women she once condemned. In this regard, there is little difference between Meg, the novel's benighted wife and mother, and Susie, the hot pants–wearing neighbor who has affairs with other women's husbands. Established conceptions of morality embedded in designations of "good" and "bad" lose all relevance in a fast-paced, contemporary setting where the rules governing women's actions are constantly in flux. Both Meg and Susie share a peculiar oneness owing to their confinement within a gendered identity.

Boehringer's first novel enhances the complex image of the state in the popular imagination through a focus on the role of a feminist "wild zone" in the lives of contemporary women. She continues this emphasis in *Crossing the Dark* (2007) with its revealing portrait of another heroine in crisis. Whereas Meg is a stay-at-home mother, Mona is a high-ranking police officer in a field once dominated by men. Despite her reputation for being an aggressive, hard-hitting police woman who can hold her own on the mean streets of South Florida, Mona's failure to protect her teenage daughter from Cesar reveals the routine vulnerabilities of the working mother who is torn between a domestic role and life in a competitive work place. Mona's guilt over her daughter's kidnapping, which takes place while the mother is at work, revives a popular debate in a post-feminist era concerning what it means to be a first-rate mother.

Concerns with the demands imposed upon working women who often struggle to find a balance between their job, marriage, and family assume center stage in a novel that Carol Cooper rightly labels a "good noir thriller." After Mona rescues Perdita, the mother and daughter move in with Les, Mona's ex husband, laying the foundation for an exploration of the woman's sexual phobia as she attempts to comprehend her role in an era of unprecedented sexual freedom. The revelation that Mona was the victim of rape suggests a oneness between the mother-daughter pair. Like Meg, Mona attempts to escape the unrelenting guilt over perceived parental failure through one-night stands. In this second novel, however, the feminist "wild zone" assumes a more shadowy cast than in the author's debut work of fiction as Boehringer explores issues of women's sexual freedom in an era of AIDS-HIV. Once again, the beach figures prominently as a place of unrestricted freedom. Mona often retreats to the beach in an effort to find a release from the mounting emotional problems she faces at home. At one point, she tells the reader that she "[d]rove to the beach to clear [her] head" (*Crossing* 139). It is at a bar that Mona meets Justin, and in a scene that recalls a similar one in the author's first novel, the young woman assumes an alternative identity in telling her acquaintance that her name is Rachel. Rachel (*aka* Mona) goes home with Justin where she performs oral sex on him.

The level of sexual autonomy on Mona's part is one element that sets this novel apart from Boehringer's first novel. Mona is the aggressor in her relationship with her male lover. With him, she redefines the boundaries of female sexuality so that she is empowered, no longer a passive victim of masculine desire. There is a reversal of the pattern of male domination that has lead to the female subjugation both Mona and Perdita have faced. Even Perdita seems to move outside of the passive sphere she retreats to after her rape. Following the advice of her therapist, the young girl returns to school in hopes of resuming her routine. Her re-entry into society is disrupted when a group of boys taunt her. Rather than allowing the verbal assault to go unchallenged, Perdita takes matters into her own hands and fights back. Her actions foreshadow those that her mother takes later in the novel when Mona murders Cesar. In light of the young girl's self-assertion in retaliating against the school-yard bullies, it is distressing that she takes her own life. Unable to overcome the psychological wounds she has suffered, Perdita slits her wrists in a shocking act of suicide.

Carol Cooper is perceptive in her observation that *Crossing the Dark* is "a moving allegory about how America fails her children." The place where narrative action occurs lends itself well to a dramatization of this collective failure. It is only fitting, then, that the novel culminates in the Everglades, a no-man's land or interstitial space outside of established geographic and metaphysical bounds. The sub tropical wetlands are, in a symbolic sense, neutral territory—an in-between place that is a locus for exploring the unknown. Mona chooses to exact vengeance upon Cesar in ways that suggests the woman's appropriation of the timeless role of female avenger. The vindictive, guilt-stricken mother decides to work undercover as a prostitute, a masquerade allowing her to assume a proscribed role that undermines the familial identity the dominant male culture would impose. Mona finds Cesar, who is out of jail on bond and prostituting another young woman. Armed with a gun and night stick, symbols of masculine power, Mona brutalizes the man who has terrorized countless women. She shoots him in the head, then dumps his body into a canal:

> It's hard dragging his body over to the canal—he's dead heavy and the double shoes are making me clumsy. Sweat runs from between my breasts. His body stops short of rolling in the water. I climb down the bank and push him in, then scramble up, fearing alligators may be lurking. I wait at the top of the bank, hoping the alligators will come [*Crossing* 238].

Days later, the police find Cesar's dismembered remains. Mona's self-reflective thoughts following her murder of Cesar underscore her liminal state as one who has abandoned all claims to a socially-defined persona: "With the warm weather and access to beach showers, it's a wonder that Florida isn't teeming with homeless people in the winter. Not that I am—a homeless person, that is. I'm just in between things right now. It'll get better. I'll get better" (*Crossing* 240).

In *Crossing the Dark*, Mona's positioning in the Everglades where she announces that she will heal leaves her in a tentative space that summons the one in which Meg finds herself at the end of Boehringer's first novel *Chasing Jordan* when Meg decides to run into the arms of her lover, thereby rejecting the familial identity she once embraced. Perhaps the author is suggesting that, despite its transient nature, the uncharted "wild side," the imaginary space that beckons women in literature and life, continues to exert a pull that is not easy to resist. No matter how hard contemporary women attempt to find a balance between an established role and a non-traditional self, to have it all, it is impossible to ignore the insistent call for a life of unrestrained female autonomy. In any case, Heidi Boehringer makes a bold appearance on the contemporary literary scene with her gripping works of fiction and their portrait of lush, sultry landscape that refuses allegiance to fixed notions of place.

Works Cited

Boehringer, Heidi W. *Chasing Jordan*. London: Serpent's Tail, 2005.
_____. *Crossing the Dark*. London: Serpent's Tail, 2007.
_____. "Q/A." *Heidi W. Boehringer*. 2014. Web. 31 May 2013. http://www.midnite-mysteries.com/QA.aspx.
Cooper, Carol. "Noir Mom." *Village Voice*, 30 Oct. 2007. Web. 31 May 2013.
Morrison, Toni. *Beloved*. New York: Knopf, 1987.
Showalter, Elaine. "Feminist Criticism in the Wilderness." *Writing and Sexual Difference. Critical Inquiry* 8.2 (1981): 179–205.

8

Angela Hunt

Angela Hunt is the epitome of an author who has truly focused on the craft of writing. She is prolific and versatile, with well over a hundred book titles and almost "four million copies of her books [have] sold worldwide" (*Angela Hunt: Expect*). This versatility has enabled her to publish in a variety of genres: children's books, young adult novels, young adult mysteries, Christian romance novels, historical novels, Biblical adaptations, how-to nonfiction books, and contemporary fiction. When asked about how she became an author, her motivations were very practical:

> I became a writer for the most ordinary of reasons: I needed a job, and wanted a job where I could work at home. As a young mother, I wanted to be home with my children, plus I'd been told I had a 'way with words.' I never dreamed of writing a book, never thought I would. I was happy to bring in a paycheck ["Angela Elwell Hunt"].

Although Angela Hunt's long list of awards date back to very early in her career, her more notable awards include receiving eight Angel Award of Excellence in media, most recently for *The Truth Teller* and *The Velvet Shadow* in 2000; *The Island of Heavenly Daze* in 2001; and *The Note* in 2002. She won the 2000 Aspen Gold Award for *The Truth Teller* and the Christy Award in 2000 for *By Dawn's Early Light*. In 2006, she was given the Lifetime Achievement Award from the Romantic Times Book Club. One of her better known novels, *The Note*, a story about a journalist who tries to find out the origins of a note that washed up after an air plane crash, was adapted into a Hallmark movie in 2007 ("Angela Elwell Hunt"). Before becoming a full-time writer, Hunt taught English, and today, she often presents at writing conferences and workshops such as the Southern Christian Writers' Conference (*Angela Hunt: Expect*).

A Florida native, the author was born in Winter Haven, Florida, in 1957, and she continues to reside in the state with her husband, Gary A. Hunt ("Angela Elwell Hunt"), and their beloved mastiffs. In fact, along with professional writing she is also a professional photographer and specializes in taking pet portraits, a calling she discovered while volunteering to take photographs of animals at local animal shelters (*Angela Hunt: Expect*). She is a 1980 graduate of Liberty University and later received a Master of Biblical Studies in Theology in 2006 and a Doctorate of Biblical Studies in 2008 ("Author Bio").

While her readership is strongly based in the Christian book market, her work also often appeals to a general audience, and a good number of her books are set in her home state of Florida. For example, her Fairlawn series is set in a Mt. Dora funeral home and follows the life of protagonist Jennifer Graham. This series is made up of three novels: *Doesn't She Look Natural?* (2008), *She Always Wore Red* (2008), and *She's in a Better Place* (2009). *The Elevator*, published in 2007, is located in a Tampa elevator where three women are trapped during a hurricane. More recent Florida novels include *Five Miles South of Peculiar* (2012) and *The Offering* (2013) (*Angela Hunt: Expect*).

Works Cited

"Angela Elwell Hunt." *Contemporary Authors Online*. Detroit: Gale, 2008. *Biography in Context*. Web. 27 May 2013.

Angela Hunt: Expect the Unexpected. 2012. Web. 28 May 2013. http://www.angelahuntbooks.com/.

"Author Bio: Angela Hunt." *Tyndale Media Center*. 2009. Tyndale House Publishers. Web 29 May 2013. http://mediacenter.tyndale.com/2_authors/author_bio.aspx?authorID=310.

Romance Fiction in Florida
The Crisscross of Jane Austen and Angela Hunt

TAMMY POWLEY

Romance fiction is an eternally popular genre with a large readership. Even early novelists such as Samuel Richardson knew that the search for love was a topic that could be used to hook his readers, and Jane Austen later came along to organize and develop what is now a well-established formula for the perfect romance novel. Austen "wrought novels distinguished from those of her predecessors," such as Richardson, and created "a tight, precise structure" ("Getting Married" 89). Today's contemporary writers are well aware of Austen's romantic formula, and one Florida author who has used it successfully in a few of her books is Angela Hunt. *Gentle Touch, Doesn't She Look Natural?*, and *Five Miles South of Peculiar* are three of Hunt's novels that in some way employ the romance tradition, and all three are set in Florida. In *Gentle Touch*, the female protagonist lives in Winter Haven, Florida. She works as an oncology nurse, and of course, she ends up meeting a doctor who she at first does not like but who eventually changes her life and her heart. Hunt's novel *Doesn't She Look Natural?* follows another female protagonist, this time to the quirky town of Mt. Dora, where she rebuilds her life, both figuratively and literally, after a divorce. Throughout most of the book, she struggles with heartache and hope as she dreams of reuniting with her ex-husband. A more recent novel by Hunt, entitled *Five Miles South of Peculiar*, was published in 2012, and Peculiar is the name of the fictional Florida town the author created where three sisters grow up together in a cracker-style house, part of the Sycamores Estate. The Caldwell sisters, Darlene, Carlene, and Nolie, are still learning about romantic love and one another.

Often contemporary romance fiction is dismissed by literary scholars. Classified as "commercial fiction" by many English teachers, a literature class discussion might turn to comparing commercial to literary fiction in hopes of training students to distinguish between the two and ultimately understand how one (literary) is better than the other (commercial). However, even with these persuasive campaigns to urge future scholars and readers to select the classics over modern day works, today's commercial romance fiction continues to be a robust market, and many romance authors boast very successful writing careers. Angela Hunt is one such author, though her work is not limited to romance novels. This prolific writer, who also happens to be a native Floridian, has a huge following in the Christian book market. One of her best-known works, *The Note*, a narrative that mixes mystery and romance, was made into a television movie. Hunt makes appearances at writing conferences and also runs writing workshops. In short, she is an extremely popular author, yet because her writing is deemed commercial and she has the added stigma of a Christian-based readership, her work does not receive scholarly attention.

Dismissing authors like Hunt is not uncommon, especially when critics try judging their works' significance against traditional literature such as the novels of Jane Austen. However, it might be possible that commercial fiction is not that far removed from the classics and, therefore, worth exploring, at least in the sense of their relationship to one another. In fact, in *Why Jane Austen?*, Rachel M. Brownstein points out that "the eager mass-marketing of Jane Austen–related books and film, from the by-now old movies of the 1990s through the continuing stream of sequels, etc., to the latest mash-ups, have confusingly confounded [Austen's] works with popular genre fiction" (196). This examination of classic romance forged by authors such as Jane Austen and commercial romance written by the contemporary author Angela Hunt starts with basic literary elements such as the plot's structure and characters to determine how three of Hunt's novels fulfill the classically established romance formula. By holding up Austen and Hunt together and questioning the popularity that the romance genre continues to generate, it might be possible to conclude if there is any place for commercial romance in Florida's literary canon.

Jane Austen is not the first woman to pen a novel. The notion of "a woman-centered domestic novel about courtship that ends in marriage" was by the time Austen began to write and publish "a conventional form of fiction for a woman writer to choose" (*Why Jane Austen?* 152). Not coincidentally, one of her heroines, Katherine in *Northanger Abbey*, mentions reading other female authors' works such as *The Mysteries of Udolpho* by Ann Radcliffe. What distinguishes Austen is that she "help[s] to establish the woman's authority over a specific domain of knowledge—that of the emotions" (Armstrong 43) and is the first to polish and shape the romance novel into an organized package that requires specific elements. Austen's world is "regulated by a strict code of behavior" ("Getting Married" 89). First, there is the heroine. She is the central character of the story and must be introduced almost immediately. In *Pride and Prejudice*, undeniably the most popular among the handful of novels Austen completed, Elizabeth Bennet is mentioned in the first bit of dialogue between Mr. and Mrs. Bennet and shown to be the favorite of her father when he describes her as having "something more of quickness than her sisters" (Austen 2). Elizabeth is the heroine prototype: she is beautiful, smart, and witty. Though she is not wealthy, she has a refined quality about her that stands out among other female characters. Brownstein describes the Austen heroine:

> A heroine must stick to the social code and then some. She is governed by constraints.... A heroine must be perfectly well-behaved, well-spoken and well-spoken-of. She must be just like other girls and also she must be better, to be singled out once for all by the best of men ["Getting Married" 83].

Once the heroine is established, the hero must soon follow. He is "exempt from the rules of society" ("Getting Married" 83) yet also has similar qualities to the heroine. At first, though, she misjudges him, and he misjudges her. This causes him to become, at least for part of the novel, an antagonist in the story. However the "restraint" between the hero and heroine "heightens the tension" and "enhances the excitement" (85). Eventually, the misunderstanding between the hero and heroine is resolved, and they realize they are attracted to one another, which in Austen's society, of course, leads to marriage. As a result, the heroine "is rewarded in the end ... by marriage to an admirable, admiring man" because Brownstein argues "what qualifies a girl as our heroine and Austen's is not so much that she is inherently a heroine but that she knows, or very nearly knows, what a real heroine is" (91). Establishing the heroine and hero is the most important element of any romance novel that is based on the

Austen formula. In addition to this requirement, any number of other components may be included as well, most likely as subplots to the primary story of the lovers, such as an untrustworthy friend (male or female); a mystery that is solved by the end of the story; and a family crisis.

This Austen formula may come off as rote, but it worked for Jane Austen and continues to also work for present-day writers of romantic fiction. One of Angela Hunt's novels that fits almost precisely within the boundaries created by Austen is *Gentle Touch*. The heroine is introduced on the first page. Like Elizabeth Bennet, Jacquelyn Wilkes is beautiful, intelligent, and accomplished. She works as an oncology nurse at a clinic located in Winter Haven, Florida, and is very proud that she has been awarded nurse of the year two years in a row. Other than her mastiff, Bailey, Jacquelyn's job is the priority in her life. She refers to her "workplace" as "her home away from home" and "the job she'd been longing for" when she had to go on vacation (*Gentle Touch* 9). After this female protagonist is established as independent and beautiful, it is not too long before the hero and soon to be antagonist is introduced: Jonah Martin is a good-looking and gifted oncology doctor. Though they are attracted to one another from the start, their first few meetings do not go well. Much like Elizabeth and Darcy are "equally proud and prejudiced" (Juhasz 37) so are Jacquelyn and Jonah. She believes he jokes too much with the patients and is rude to the nursing staff while "he couldn't say what drove him to alienate her so ruthlessly. Perhaps it was her calm self-confidence, her always professional demeanor. [...] Then again, maybe it was those green eyes" (*Gentle Touch* 49). This reference to her eyes points directly to Darcy who remarks on "the very great pleasure which a pair of fine eyes in the face of a pretty woman can bestow" (Austen 19). Of course, Darcy is talking about Elizabeth, and this is the first hint in the novel that these two characters will eventually unite.

In both *Pride and Prejudice* and *Gentle Touch*, the plots focus on the two lovers who slowly learn more about each others' qualities, and as a result, they gravitate toward each other until all their misconceptions are resolved and they realize they are desperately in love with each other. Other boilerplate parts of the Austen formula are also woven into Hunt's novel. For example, just as there is the mystery surrounding the relationship between Darcy and Wickham, there is the mystery about why Jonah Martin moves from hospital to hospital. Family tragedies include the elopement of Wickham and Lydia in Austen's novel, and in Hunt's, Jacquelyn is isolated from her family when she discovers she has cancer. As for the untrustworthy friend, Wickham feeds Elizabeth incorrect information about Darcy, and in Hunt's story, Craig Bishop is supposed to be in love with Jacquelyn; however, he leaves her when he finds out that she has cancer, and she will need him to care for her while she recovers from chemotherapy.

The Austen formula is not as directly apparent in Hunt's novel *Doesn't She Look Natural?*, but this story still encompasses many of the same romance tropes. Since now the female protagonist is a divorced mother of two, Jennifer Graham is not the same virginal heroine portrayed by Elizabeth Bennet and Jacquelyn Wilkes. She is bitter and grieving about her divorce, even though she has been divorced a full year when the story begins. Still, she shares many other qualities required of a romance heroine. Before her divorce, she was a dedicated career woman who had a successful job where she worked for a U.S. senator on Capitol Hill. She loses her job and her dignity after her husband, who also works in the same senator's office, runs away with the family's nanny; however, Jennifer Graham is obviously a smart and determined woman. She is tough and compares herself to "crème brulee" [...] [that] begins in a liquid state, endures a period of searing heat, and eventually develops a scablike *[sic]* crust" (*Doesn't She* 1).

The romantic hero in Hunt's tale takes some time to emerge, and unlike *Pride and Prejudice* and *Gentle Touch*, his role is not as prominent in the story. There is a love story here because the heroine is looking for love, but she is also rebuilding her life as she moves her family to Mt. Dora, Florida, to renovate an old Victorian-style funeral home she has inherited and hopes to sell. Daniel Sladen comes forward as the lawyer who opens up the possibility of a new life in Florida to Jennifer. As the executor of the will, he tracks her down in Virginia and notifies her about her inheritance. When she arrives in Mt. Dora, he is there again to help her, this time showing her around her new property. Jennifer, though, is understandably not fond of lawyers since her divorce and immediately categories him with all lawyers: "A black BMW pulls into the parking lot, a cloud of dust rising in its wake. This has to be Mr. Sladen. [She] jerk[s] [her] thumb at the car. 'At least the lawyers do all right in this town'" (*Doesn't She* 42). In Jennifer's mind, she repeatedly and condescendingly refers to Daniel Sladen as "the lawyer" while she also notices that "the man does have nice hair" (42). Romance readers know this is her Darcy; Daniel Sladen will not be "the lawyer" to her forever.

While Daniel Sladen is the right man for the heroine, her ex-husband is not. Similarly to Wickham, Thomas Graham is not a trustworthy character, and in this way, Jennifer shares a great deal with Elizabeth Bennet:

> With Wickham, Austen is testing the patriarchal romance premise of love at first sight. The relationship is based upon superficialities, and Elizabeth, as the novel begins, is all too good at that. She prefers it, in fact. Always trying to protect her private, hidden, true self, she is not particularly interested in coming into contact with anyone else's. She likes to show off with her quick judgments. She's clever, but she isn't wise [Juhasz 36].

Like Elizabeth, Jennifer is quick to judge and is not wise when it comes to her ex-husband. Thomas is Jennifer's first love, and she still thinks of him as her husband and longs for them to be reunited, despite the fact that he has been unfaithful to her. Wickham and Thomas are both described as attractive men who know how to charm women. This includes Elizabeth and Jennifer. Additionally, most of the other characters also know not to trust these men. Darcy knows the truth about Wickham. Joella, Jennifer's mother, "knows about men like Thomas," [a]nd, she doesn't want her daughter to be hurt gain" (*Doesn't She* 284). Yet the heroines are too headstrong to listen until they are forced to concede that these men are not the good and faithful companions that they had hoped them to be.

It could be argued that *Five Miles South of Peculiar* has more than one heroine since the novel portrays the lives of three sisters, all of whom struggle with love as well as other emotional issues. This is a much more layered narrative than the previous two Hunt novels discussed, but among the layers is one of romance, in particular, that of the love triangle. Other than their mother's womb, twins Darlene and Carlene Caldwell share little else as far as personality, talents, and looks. When they become teenagers, though, they finally find a common interest: Griffith Young. Both win his heart in different ways, but Carlene leaves the small southern town to find fame in New York while Darlene stays home and shares her life with Griff. They are distant geographically, but all three still feel ties to one another for many years until Griff dies. The triangle continues to push the sisters away from each other even after his death. Though Carlene comes home for the funeral with the idea that her twin might need her, "Darlene barely sp[eaks] to her during that visit," and Carlene believes this is because "Once claimed, Griff belonged only to Darly. She was still jealously clinging to him, unwilling even to share her grief" with her sister (*Five Miles*).

The element of the love triangle is well-established in romance fiction, and Austen is not the only classic author to incorporate it. Just a few examples that can easily turn into a long list include Heathcliff, Kathy, and Linton from Emily Brontë's *Wuthering Heights*; Tess, Angel, and Alec in *Tess of the d'Urbervilles* by Thomas Hardy; and Paris, Romeo, and Juliet from William Shakespeare's play *Romeo and Juliet*. Crossing back over to Jane Austen, the author commonly uses love triangles, even perceived love triangles that do not actually exist, as a way to create tension and force the eventual lovers apart, at least for a time. In *Emma,* named after the protagonist/heroine, there are a number of confusing love triangles and mixed up relationships because Emma believes herself to be a match-maker. She does not completely understand her misguided actions and their affects on other characters in the novel until she believes she is responsible for creating a very alarming love triangle, one between Mr. Knightly, her friend, Harriet Smith, and herself. At this point, Emma realized her previous "affection which Frank Churchill had once, for a short period, occupied" (*Emma* 300) was nothing in comparison to the feelings she has for Mr. Knightly. The idea that Harriet Smith now also was part of Mr. Knightly's affections brings Emma to a shocking realization:

> She saw that there never had been a time when she did not consider Mr. Knightly as infinitely the superior, or when his regard for her had not been infinitely the most dear. She saw, that in persuading herself, in fancying, in acting to the contrary, she had been entirely under a delusion, totally ignorant of her own heart [*Emma* 301].

Both Caldwell sisters in Hunt's novel know their hearts are with Griffith Young, but Carlene is not ready initially to give up opportunities that New York offers. Darlene uses this as an opportunity to make herself emotionally and sexually available to Griff, and she becomes pregnant. At one point when Carlene becomes fed up with her new life in New York and thinks of coming home to be with her boyfriend, Griff, she discovers that he is now engaged to her sister. The love triangle resumes as she returns to New York. Griff loves Carlene but does not want to live the life she wants to live in New York, and now, his life has been forever changed due to one night of indiscretion, and he manages to build a life with her sister, Darlene. However, even many years after his death when Carlene considers coming home for a fiftieth birthday party celebration the town is throwing for the Caldwell sisters, she becomes melancholy as she thinks about how "[s]he might ... spot familiar faces among the crowd" during the birthday party, but "none of them would be the face she longed to see most" (*Five Miles*).

While the Carlene, Griff, and Darlene love triangle is a conventional part of the novel's plot, there is a second love triangle that also threatens to appear, or at least, the character Darlene fears that it will. Years after losing her husband, Darlene has found another man to make her happy, Henry Hooper, Mayor of Peculiar and the manager of the local Piggly Wiggly. He is the catalyst that brings her twin, Carlene, back to Peculiar because he sends her a birthday party invitation. The timing of this invitation from Henry is right after Carlene learns she is not going to be able to ever sing professionally again. She is not sure what to do with her life, and Henry provides her with an answer, even though it may be a temporary solution to her problem. An innocently sent birthday party invitation results in Carlene's return home and the beginning of Darlene's imagining that her sister is determined to seduce Henry Hooper, her hopefully soon to be fiancé. Darlene constantly pictures scenarios where the two are together or where "Henry" is "beaming at [Carlene's] grand accomplishment" (*Five Miles*).

The multiple triangles in Hunt's novel work in a similar fashion to those in Austen's *Emma* as they create tension and confusion among the lovers. Like Emma, Darlene is misinformed and develops conclusions and ideas based off of her emotional uncertainty. In addition, an accident during a potluck dinner forces Darlene to be bedridden for weeks. Her jealousy of her sister, her guilt about replacing her sister in Griff's life, and finally, her accident, which physically keeps her from being part of the regular events around her, combine to cause Darlene to picture all kinds of unrealistic scenarios:

> A tear slid from the corner of Darlene's eye as she struggled to ignore the sounds of laughter from the kitchen.... Because Carlene decided to stick around, she was now in the kitchen with Darlene's boyfriend, laughing and batting her lashes and no doubt doing her best to charm the small-town man.... How could he not be dazzled by Carlene? Griff certainly had been [*Five Miles*].

Of course, once the heroines, Emma and Darlene, discover the truth, they are able to alleviate their concerns and reunite with their men. They also learn a few lessons about making assumptions and not attempting to control the lives of other. In both cases, this means love, happiness, and marriage.

These three novels of Angela Hunt's, *Gentle Touch, Doesn't She Look Natural?*, and *Five Miles South of Peculiar*, in many ways follow the Austen formula; however, this information alone is not really enough to understand the popularity of both authors' works. Austen's writing is entertaining but also revolutionary. Nancy Armstrong examines the political history of the novel in her book *Desire and Domestic Fiction* and continually points to Austen as an author whose narratives empowered her readership:

> Domestic fiction mapped out a new domain of discourse as it invested common forms of social behavior with the emotional values of women. Consequently, these stories of courtship and marriage offered their readers a way of indulging, with a kind of impunity, in fantasies of political power that were the more acceptable because they were played out within a domestic framework where legitimate monogamy—and the subordination of female to male—would ultimately be affirmed [29].

Indulging fantasies and emotional values—these are all ingredients that attract readers to romance fiction. Escaping for a few hours in a fantasy world is an indulgence, no matter what the genre. With romance fiction, however, there is an assurance of enough conflict and tension to make a novel interesting with the added guarantee that the resolution will emotionally satisfy. Seasoned romance readers, even with new romance fiction, know the storyline already because Austen wrote it first. Suzanne Juhasz explains that Austen "makes us believe in the possibility of love and identity, the chance for true love, because she shows it happening, not in some fairy tale world but in the very midst of the forces that have traditionally worked against it" (30).

Safe and predictable, contemporary romance may be popular when it comes to book sales, but in critical circles it is typically not mentioned, even though it is obviously rooted in classic domestic fiction. Writing and literature professors tend to start their students with the classics and usually do not consider seriously teaching texts deemed commercial fiction. However, there may be room for both, and this might require some time and an open mind to make such a connection where Jane Austen meets Angela Hunt. Fans of Angela Hunt most likely do not try to make this connection either. They may simply indulge and enjoy, which tends to be the opposite position of literary scholars who analyze and synthesize, who might even deem commercial success of a novel as evidence that its literary worth is questionable since it is enjoyed by so many common readers.

Stretching from Austen to Hunt is really not that far of a reach when comparing plot and characters. While there is an obvious relationship between traditional and contemporary romance fiction, it might be surprising to discover how close both types of narratives come down to basic elements of fiction writing. Obviously, Angela Hunt is not Jane Austen. However, by using the Austen formula and weaving in the tropes established by Austen, Hunt keeps with tradition, and she brings this to the state of Florida, a semi-tropical world far from an English drawing room or rolling countryside.

Works Cited

Armstrong, Nancy. *Desire and Domestic Fiction*. New York: Oxford University Press, 1987. Print.
Austen, Jane. *Emma*. Birmingham: Sweetwater Press, 1998. Print.
_____. *Pride and Prejudice*. New York: Bantam Books, 1981. Print.
Brownstein, Rachel M. "Getting Married: Jane Austen." *Becoming a Heroine*. New York: Columbia University Press, 1994. 81–134. Print.
_____. *Why Jane Austen?* New York: New York: Columbia University Press, 2011. Print.
Hunt, Angela. *Doesn't She Look Natural?* Carol Stream: Tyndale House Publishers, Inc. 2007. Print.
_____. *Five Miles South of Peculiar*. New York: Howard Books, 2012. E-book.
_____. *Gentle Touch*. Minneapolis : Bethany House Publishers, 1997. Print.
Juhasz, Suzanne. "Becoming a Romance Reader: Jane Austen's *Pride and Prejudice* and Elswyth Thane's *Tryst*." *Reading from the Heart: Women, Literature, and the Search for True Love*. New York: Penguin Books, 1994. 25–68. Print.

Angela Hunt's Uncanny Florida

Lisa K. Perdigao

In *Land of Sunshine, State of Dreams*, Gary R. Mormino characterizes the development of Florida where progress is measured in "the loss of grove and forest" and "newly minted words coined to explain Florida's growth: megalopolis, exurbs, microburbs, and boomburbs" (415). According to Mormino and critics within the fields of Florida studies and its subset Disney studies, Florida has become a hyperreal landscape, artificially developed like its epicenter Orlando and its tourist center in Walt Disney World. The hyperreality, surreality, and unreality of Florida can be traced not only through social histories but also through representations in film, television, and fiction that create and perpetuate distinct versions of the Florida mythos. After all, "Modern Florida is simply irresistible to writers and cultural critics" (Mormino 29). As Ron Howard's 1985 film *Cocoon* exposes the "Fountain of Youth" to a group of senior citizens and the television series *The Golden Girls* (1985–1992) depicts its characters finding new life with each other, both highlight how Florida is transformative and regenerative. In contrast, television series *Miami Vice* (1984–1990), *Silk Stalkings* (1991–1999), *Nip/Tuck* (2003–2010), and *Dexter* (2006-2013) are darker representations of the Sunshine State, suggesting what lurks beneath and behind its luminous surface. From television and film to the Florida novel, Florida is reinvigorated, transformed with new perspectives.

Florida fiction takes its own shape and form to reflect ideas about the changing nature of the state. Mormino writes, "Florida's excesses and surreal synchronicities have inspired a distinctive reporting and literary genre" (30); that distinctive literary genre can be read in the following terms: "Typically, modern novelists depict Florida as a lost utopia—a dystopian, overdeveloped land overrun by corporate theme parks, rapacious developers, and crazed drug lords" (Mormino 30). In Carl Hiaasen's novel *Native Tongue* (1991), Molly McNamara, Mother of Wilderness, witnesses the destruction of the Amazing Kingdom, a parody of and rival to Disney, and says, "Nature is a wonder.... Such power to renew, or to destroy. It's an awesome paradox" (472). Facing the "loss of grove and forest" and its replacement with the hyperreal, the Florida landscape is one underwritten and overwritten with a sense of loss as well as possibility. For Suzanne Fox, "Hiaasen's Florida is a strange amalgam: part natural and part artificial, at once self-destructive and self-protective, drawn from the real but wholly improbable" (18). Surveying the field of Florida fiction, the peculiarities of the place can be mapped along these lines.

Yet perhaps the sense of loss evoked in both Mormino's and Hiaasen's language is not the result of modernization but what was always already inherent in the Florida landscape and story. Michele Currie Navakas references Amos Doolittle's 1784 *Map of the United States of America* and its representation of Florida. She writes, "[O]ne portion of Doolittle's map suggests that some parts of the continent had the potential to fragment and dissolve.... Thus, Florida persisted as 'fragmented, elusive territory' on some of the same maps through which America asserted its 'continental status'" (Navakas 244, 245). This representation of a fragmented and elusive state persists throughout Florida fiction. Describing Florida novels, Fox notes, "But like the state all of them depict, it is still a place of paradox: at once natural and artificial, frontier and theme park, stubbornly enduring and deeply vulnerable to change" (19). While Florida writers, a list that includes both Mormino and Hiaasen, expose a dystopic Florida, in her 2012 novel *Five Miles South of Peculiar*, Angela Hunt shifts the gaze to offer a return to a pastoral Florida that signifies a renewal of its characters as well as a regenerative site in and of Florida fiction.

Like other works of Florida fiction, Hunt's *Five Miles South of Peculiar* exposes a "weird Florida" but with a difference. Five miles south of Peculiar lies Sycamores, a family homestead that preserves—or attempts to preserve—a historic Florida, what is lost to the story of Florida development. Recalling Hiaasen's sense of Florida as a contradictory place, Mormino's description of Florida history yields dichotomies, as he writes, "From its founding as an imperial outpost to its modern identity as a tourist empire, Florida has evoked contrasting and compelling images of the sacred and profane: a Fountain of Youth and a Garden of Earthly Delights, a miasmic hellhole and scuzzy wasteland" (2). As a result, according to Mormino, Florida is a "powerful symbol of renewal and regeneration" whose "dreamscape constantly shifts" (2). Hunt's Sycamores and its reference point Peculiar, Florida suggest the liminality that Mormino argues is featured in the Florida story. In Hunt's novel, as three sisters try to redefine their relationships with each other after decades of estrangement, they struggle to identify who they have become in a contemporary world. What emerges from the pages of Hunt's novel is an uncanny Florida, one that is both familiar and strange, a fictional place that is tropic for the story of Florida itself.

Five Miles South of Peculiar identifies the novel's setting and suggests more figurative meanings. The three Caldwell sisters are isolated from the rest of the community in Peculiar and, in many ways, remain trapped in the past. Darlene Caldwell performs as her mother and grandmother had before her, as the perfect hostess, homemaker, cook, and baker. Her sister Magnolia ("Nolie") is the odd sister, the one who constantly reads Emily Dickinson's poems, and, like the poet, has worn all white since the "tragedy" that she is unable to move on from. But perhaps Carlene is the most static character of the three. She left Peculiar years ago to attend Julliard and, since then, had pursued a career in New York City on Broadway. Although she returned home for key events over the years—most notably the funerals of family members—the community and her sisters constantly think of her as the child and young woman she was before she left because they are unfamiliar with the woman that she has become. Haunting the novel is the uncanny return of Carlene, made quite literally so since she and Darlene are twins, yet, as Darlene notes, "'We're twins, but we're far from identical…. I guess we're about as different as twins can be'" (47). When Carlene returns home for the twins' fiftieth birthday celebration, struggling with what her life will be now that she has lost her singing voice, Darlene is similarly confronted with an identity crisis, wondering who she is when she again becomes her sister's shadow.

Sigmund Freud's description of the uncanny is a useful one to apply to the novel's framework. Robin Lydenberg writes,

> The ambiguity of the uncanny as both familiar and unfamiliar is reinforced by Freud's examination of the German word *unheimlich*: the root, *heimlich*, carries the primary signification "familiar and agreeable" … but

in its secondary meaning it coincides with its opposite, *unheimlich*, "concealed and kept out of sight" .... What is most intimately known and familiar, then, is always already divided within by something potentially alien and threatening [1073].

The "blurring of boundaries" that Lydenberg highlights in Freud's theory is central to the occurrences of the uncanny in Hunt's novel. Imagination and reality are confused in Hunt's novel, as the past collides with the present and the characters face the return of the repressed. Toward the end of the novel, Carlene struggles with Darlene's confession that she had seduced Carlene's high school boyfriend Griff before Carlene left for New York, on the night of the Buttercup Squash Pageant. Although Carlene thought that her departure brought the couple together, Darlene's story rewrites the past and challenges her perspective on it.

While Darlene's confession threatens what is "most intimately known and familiar" (Lydenberg 1073), Carlene actively attempts to heal their relationship, making things "familiar and agreeable" (Lydenberg 1073) again, by concealing facts of her own. When Carlene reads a letter that Griff sent her before he died, she omits a passage. Facts are re-presented and reconstructed to suit the needs of the different characters. Carlene thinks that "Darlene seemed to believe that confession brought relief, but maybe every truth didn't need to be exposed. In some cases, maybe love won the day when the truth remained cloaked" (336). Reading Griff's lines about Darlene, "She takes such good care of me, the house, the kids, and most of the folks in Peculiar" (338), emphasizes the significance of his wife's roles in the family, house, and community. Yet what goes unspoken is telling, and the readers are given access to Griff's idea of what his life might have been:

> Not a day passes that I don't stand on the driveway, face the northern horizon, and wonder what you're doing up there in the big city. I have a life in Peculiar, a life that fits like a comfortable old coat, but every once in a while I dream of the life you and I might have shared. Last night I dreamed we were together in a taxi, and you were holding some kind of fancy award, a huge statue that nearly took up all the room in the back seat [339].

He ends the note with the lines "I miss you, Carly, and hope you'll set aside a few dozen years for me in eternity" (340). Griff's letter provides a redefinition of space from his perspective on the driveway. That life, a "comfortable old coat" (339), is rooted in the material conditions of

Sycamores, but his dream uproots him, and Carly, from the site. In fact, they are not just in New York but are mobile, in a taxi. The novel's construction of time and space, which extends to the characters' relationships, is countered by these lines. That Carly conceals this part of the letter is significant; always seen as the one who leaves Darlene in the shadows, Carly sustains—or even creates—the solidity of Sycamores, including Darlene's marriage.

Five Miles South of Peculiar highlights the presence of the uncanny in the insistence of the past and the return of the repressed while representing a Florida that is both familiar and strange. Hunt's story is specific to the Caldwell sisters, but it is representative of the larger story of Florida development. The novel begins with a description of Sycamores and its history parallels that of its state. Ironically, the story's beginning marks the sudden death of the founder of the Sycamores estate, Chase Caldwell, as "Residents of Jackson County, Florida, held their breath the morning of July 3, 1968" (1). The residents' attention was directed not on the man but on the property, as his "precious estate" would "officially become county property at 2:03 p.m." (1). The story is undoubtedly one that begins with loss, yet it offers possibilities for Caldwell's descendants.

While the story behind Sycamores suggests auspicious beginnings, particularly with the almost glossed over story of Caldwell's and Sycamores' roles during the Prohibition era, the family homestead is founded on the principle of conservation for future generations. Caldwell protected the land and, by extension, his descendants, guaranteeing their possession of the house and income for the property. Hunt writes, "He not only managed to shelter Sycamores from taxes, but also devised the charitable gift annuity that provided a monthly income for any immediate Caldwell descendant residing on the property" (2). The result of that provision is that it "allowed life at Sycamores to continue as it always had, with a sedate and stately elegance" (2). Conservation and preservation are key and while Hunt's novel is not about the "greening" of Florida in a twenty-first century sense, it does highlight the significance of the survival of the land. Nolie's interests in and dedication to landscaping, performed daily, and new pursuit of breeding dogs indicate how the natural world is thriving at the hands of the Caldwell women.

Hunt's novel and sense of a Peculiar, Florida reenacts the story of Florida development that is intertwined with the characters' personal histories. The story of Florida development is one that stretches over the twentieth century and into the twenty-first century, with "Florida's Big Bang" occurring between 1950 and 2000, with the "state swelling from 2.7 to 15.9 million inhabitants" (Mormino 21). Mormino notes that

> the decades following 1940 changed Florida more than the previous four centuries, altering boundaries, reconfiguring landscapes, and casting new relationships. The march to and across Florida was irresistible and irrepressible, as orange groves became gated communities, small towns were transformed into cities, and big cities sprawled into metropolises and boomburbs [21].

Initially, life in Hunt's Peculiar seems almost untouched by time, as her descriptions of the place and its community members form an idealized tight-knit American town that recalls an earlier decade before the "Big Bang." Darlene keeps herself busy with community meetings and prides herself as playing a prominent role in town. In contrast, Carlene's life takes her away from a more rural life to the city. Yet, at fifty, when her singing career is tragically stopped by a botched vocal surgery, Carlene also takes part, albeit unintentionally, as part of that larger migration south that Mormino refers to as "the graying of Florida" (157). And perhaps like the characters in *Cocoon*, or at least *The Golden Girls*, she quite literally discovers a new lease on life once she crosses that milestone birthday.

While many changes to the state are the results of technological and urban development (for example, air conditioning, automobiles, interstate highways, planned communities), in contrast, Hunt's Peculiar, Florida is one that, like Nolie at the center of the novel, is static. Hunt writes,"'Chase' Caldwell's progeny were more than willing to let the rest of the world rush and worry and gobble meals behind a steering wheel. At Sycamores, and in Peculiar, the nearest town, life was meant to be savored" (2). Carlene, who had resisted coming home for a brief stay much less an extended one, prefers her modern conveniences in New York City and is struck by how much has remained the same back home. When she is faced with the decision whether to stay in New York or return home, she thinks, "Returning to Peculiar meant returning to inertia, and inertia felt far too much like death" (23).

Almost outside of time and with a "peculiar" sense of space, the novel is situated between tradition and modernization that is reflective of Florida development. When Carlene is flying from New York to Florida, she compares the sites: "Ninety minutes ago, she'd watched gray asphalt and soaring buildings recede into the distance; now miles of green woods, blue lakes, and brown farmland filled her window" (72). Mormino writes, "Unrelenting growth (retirees and transplants) and the case of mobility (geographic and economic) have also disrupted small-town Florida," as "Interstate highways and internet technology have closed the distance between small towns and big cities" (65). Hunt describes the novel's dichotomous site, where an interstate highway both divides Sycamores from Peculiar and connects the two sites. As Hunt writes, "A five-mile stretch of Highway 90 lay between the late Chase Caldwell's estate and Peculiar, Florida, current population 493" (24); in a sense, the novel could be read as existing "five miles south of peculiar," along the interstate, or at least passing through. Peculiar, a "way station between Marianna and Chattahoochee by Caldwell and a few of his cronies," "served as a distribution point for home-manufactured medicinal products until the long arm of the law closed down most of the operations" (24), and it becomes the site of the uncanny. It is the familiar Florida story but one made strange by its specific circumstances. Hunt says in her "Author's Note," "While Peculiar, Florida, does not really exist, Peculiar, Missouri, does. I trust that the people who live near Chattahoochee and Tallahassee will forgive me for populating their area with a fictional town." The novel offers an alternative map of Florida that is remarkably like the one Navakas describes, presenting a "fragmented, elusive territory" (244), a liminal state.

The battle between the sisters, their struggle to redefine themselves in the presence of the other, becomes the foreground and background to the story of what will happen with their family land. The novel begins by detailing the history of the property and the Caldwell family, and it also details the provisions of that will, which include its restrictions: in six years, the lease runs out and the three Caldwell sisters need to figure out their futures. Facing and fearing change, all three sisters stake their claims on Sycamores and must figure out how to reconcile their pasts with their present selves and ideas about the future. It is only too fitting that the resolution to the sisters' troubles relocate all three, redefining the center of Sycamores, what it has been and what it can be for future generations.

The tension between the twins is introduced at their fiftieth birthday party that brings the sisters together and reignites old jealousies and rivalries. Carlene is the uncanny reminder of the past that Darlene had attempted to bury or at least rewrite. The pastor Erik, who, after losing his parish after his divorce, relocates to Sycamores to help out the Caldwell women, asks Darlene about the twins' relationship. She tells him,

"Never had time to go to New York. After Carlene left, we got busy livin' our lives. I got married, raised two kids, buried Momma, got my kids married, and then buried Grandma. Not all at once, understand, but over the years. About five years ago I buried Griff, my late husband. So you'll have to excuse me, preacher, but I haven't felt much like going to New York to celebrate my sister's success" [48].

With Carlene's return, Darlene grapples with the person she had wanted to be and the one that she had become. Hunt writes, "Darlene harbored a secret desire to see the world" (49), yet although her children had bought her a plane ticket to France, she fails to use it, at least until the novel's end. Hunt represents Darlene's feelings in relation to the sycamores: "Some days she stood wrist deep in dishwater and stared out the window, feelin' that the sycamores bordering the property were more like malicious guards than benevolent shade trees" (49). When Carly left, she had also left Darly "in the trees' blue shadows," in the shadow of her twin's success, "chained to her responsibilities, and dependent on her routines" (49). Carlene's return signals how things are changing for Darlene as well, as "One by one the others slipped away, leaving Darlene to tend to the family heritage. In a few years, though, the county would ask her to leave, and then where would she go?" (49).

The struggle between the sisters is played out within and over the house. Over the years, on a few visits home, Carlene had preferred to stay with their aunt rather than stay at Sycamores, for reasons we later learn are the result of the situation with Griffin. When she returns home for her fiftieth birthday, Carlene reasserts her place within the house, and her presence forces her sisters to reexamine their relationships with her as well as their own personal histories. The twins' history, as remembered by Darlene, is one marked by the celebration of Carlene's triumphs while Darlene remained unforgotten on the sidelines. In fact, when Carlene appears at the twins' birthday, surprising her sister and the other town residents, Darlene is at first excited and then quickly realizes that she is again cast into the shadows. At the party, when she sees Henry, the mayor and her boyfriend, doting on Carlene, she fears that she is again losing the attention of a man to Carlene: "Once, just once, she'd love to find a man who considered her the most beautiful, talented, and wonderful Caldwell sister" (49). While Darlene sees Carlene—and their relationship—as unchanged over time, Hunt extends that reading into Carlene's sense of Sycamores itself: "Some aspects of home hadn't changed at all" (94). And what Sycamores represents is more than an idea; the physical landscape tells that story, as "Trees still surrounded the property, live oaks and magnolias, tall pines and sycamores" (94), including "[t]he twin trees her grandfather had planted at the right and left sides of the porch" (94); like the twins, they have changed, grown, but they are still rooted, fixed in place.

Darlene constantly tries to resuscitate a Sycamores of old and when Carlene decides to extend her stay indefinitely, the battle between the two is one of tradition versus modernization. According to Darlene, Carlene does not value the tradition behind Sycamores and Darlene's more traditional role there. When Carlene begins to question Nolie's behavior and lifestyle, Darlene quickly admonishes her, telling her that she can't just come into their lives and try to change things. Their argument over their lifestyles translates to one about the house itself. When Carlene suggests updating the house, she offers suggestions in terms of integration, saying, "'I've been thinking about how my furniture will fit in the house'" (266), yet Darlene interprets her words as a critique of her taste, belongings, and way of life. Carlene wants to keep their grandmother's bed, a "massive oak bed" that is symbolic of the idea behind Sycamores, suggesting her appreciation of the past, but Darlene regards her plans as an attack on it, particularly when Carlene says that they should replace the old couch that Darlene loves. Darlene acknowledges that she has "lived a sizable portion of her life on this piece of furniture" (267). For Darlene, the couch is an extension of her way of life, but Carlene fails to recognize its significance (267). Hunt writes, "in a few words, a mere throwaway sentence, Carlene had condemned the sectional and forced Darlene to see it as it was—an ugly, slightly smelly, uncomfortable eyesore" (267).

The couch is depicted as a metaphor for Darlene's life, as she wonders, "But why couldn't Carly see that she was ripping apart the fabric of Darlene's life?" (267), and also serves as a trope for the relationship between the sisters. Carlene is modern; Darlene is the traditionalist. Nolie introduces a middle ground between Darlene's sense of tradition and Carlene's modern aesthetic. When Darlene tells Nolie that Carlene is going to stay on at Sycamores and is moving her things from her New York apartment into the house, Nolie replies, "Wonderful! ... That's so exciting!" (268). For Darlene, it is not wonderful news and she tries to win Nolie over to her cause, saying that Carlene wants to replace their couch with some "hoity-toity sofa I've never heard of" (268), emphasizing the distinction between the two objects, "sagging plaid couch" (267) and "hoity-toity sofa"

(268), their aesthetics and significance. Nolie, surprisingly, given her inability to move on from the past, highlights the ephemeral nature of material possessions and encourages Darlene to embrace Carlene's return (268). Yet even as she rages against Carlene's plans, Darlene acknowledges the necessity and inevitability of change; the losses of her father, mother, grandmother, and husband represent that reality. She concedes the point, recognizing that Sycamores belonged to all three sisters and since Carlene had been so long absent, "she deserved the opportunity to make a few changes now" (267).

For Carlene, change is imperative. She sees the house as one filled with ghosts and painful memories (123). Carlene thinks that putting up "new wallpaper" or getting "some new furniture" (123) would help to keep those ghosts at bay. While Carlene's perspective initially challenges the other two Caldwell sisters' ways of life and thinking, it, like her furniture, is ultimately integrated into Sycamores. And Carlene's perspective isn't entirely modern—it too is rooted in the past. Carlene recalls their mother's insistence on "facing forward" rather than "looking back ... long[ing] for things that could never appear again" (144). Poised between the familiar and unfamiliar, what is known and what is threatening, Sycamores and Peculiar become appropriate settings for the characters' individual and collective stories.

By re-presenting a family history and reconjuring a Sycamores that is representative of all of those entangled relations, Hunt highlights the uncanniness in her Peculiar, Florida. The line "Expect the unexpected" is featured on Hunt's website and while it is representative of the writer's vision for her novels it also bears similarities to the lines advertising Florida. The representations of a "weird Florida" in Florida fiction are extensions of ideas about Florida that were designed to advertise the state as well as those who serve as critical assessments of the peculiarities of its landscape, weather, people, and politics. Mormino recalls a 1980s slogan promoting tourism: "Florida—The rules are different here" (150). Central to the story of Florida is the way that it is identified, represented, and re-presented. Hunt's *Five Miles South of Peculiar* is less Hiaasen and perhaps more Zora Neale Hurston who also takes her female protagonist through Florida development in the quest to redefine or reclaim her identity. The Caldwell women find their voices and reassert their faith in themselves, each other, their community, and the future, one that is not severed from but entirely contingent upon the past.

The world of *Five Miles South of Peculiar* returns us to a pastoral Florida, a pre-developed Florida that is, by the novel's end, a ghost in the imaginations of the Caldwells and inhabitants of Peculiar. The characters are able to move into the future, and the future of Sycamores is re-established and remade. Carlene thinks, once she returns to New York, "All this—all of Peculiar, in fact—would seem like a vague dream" (157). But the idea of Sycamores is persistent. After realizing that she cannot return to New York and contemplating a relocation within Florida— to Tallahassee to tutor voice students—"At the thought of losing this place, loneliness crept into her mood like a fog" (334). Her sense of loss leads to the realization that her identity is an extension of Sycamores, which is connected to her family. Carlene concludes that "[t]hey were her sisters and, like it or not, they held her past, her present, and, undoubtedly, her future" (334). The tragic turn that leads to the loss of Carlene's singing voice allows her the financial resources to start life anew at Sycamores. Although their stay is restricted by the initial grant, Carlene has the ability to transform the site. The halls were once filled with her voice and now voices will again sound throughout the house as it is reborn as a musical academy. That success, Carlene thinks, will lead to financial gain and prosperity for Peculiar, new possibilities.

Navakas' survey of the Florida story yields a new assessment as she writes, "Florida's fragmented, dissolving ground would produce forms of belonging, community, and economy that could never sustain the version of nationhood we find in the discourses of Federalism and expansion ... the tale proposes that American identity must also be based on mobility and dispersal" (247). Similarly, Hunt's novel rewrites the Florida story to highlight how the community defines—or redefines— the site. Space and the idea of home become relative, as Erik tells Nolie in lines that resonate with Hurston's novel, "'I know you're tied to this place, but I know you can break free. It's time for you to cut the apron strings and step in the wide world.... You can't make a place for yourself under the sun if you keep nesting in the shade of the family tree'" (353–354). After Darlene and Nolie leave Sycamores, the borders of Peculiar change; it becomes more expansive and inclusive. Navakas concludes her argument by saying that "the occupations and associations unique to Floridian geography would create Floridians, Americans whose mobility and dispersal—in direct contrast to fixity and integration—would grant them mastery of themselves and a place within the new borders of the republic" (271). Hunt's sense of a Peculiar, Florida can be cast in this light, as the story of the mobility and dispersal of the Caldwell women is set alongside Carlene's return to the site.

By the end of the novel, all three women actively redefine their conceptions of home and self. Carlene, the once estranged sister, is not only welcomed back into the community, but she also becomes part of its revitalization and progress. As Carlene notes, "County officials could do a lot more with money than with an aging homestead" (360). What Carlene is able to do is create a future out of the past. Although Darlene leaves Sycamores, she remains intrinsically connected to Peculiar. In the novel's last act, she becomes the wife to its mayor. Nolie literally moves on, to join her new husband to serve as minister in a penitentiary up north, well, in northern Florida. But Nolie, like Carlene before her, returns to Sycamores in the novel's conclusion, this time for a wedding and not a funeral, reversing the novel's course. Fluidly moving between past, present, and future, the Caldwell sisters offer an alternative way of mapping both personal and communal histories. Carlene's lines are suggestive for all three characters: "She was born in Peculiar and of Peculiar. She would always be, as the townsfolk liked to say, *a Peculiar person*" (334). Hunt's novel ultimately acts as the liminal and peculiar site that it depicts. By sustaining competing and contradictory versions of the Florida mythos, *Five Miles South of Peculiar* becomes a "strange amalgam" (Fox 18), a "powerful symbol of renewal and regeneration" (Mormino 2).

Works Cited

Fox, Suzanne. "Florida Mysteries: Perils, Paradise, Paradox." *Publishers Weekly* 7 May 2012: 18–19. Web. August 2013.

Hiaasen, Carl. *Native Tongue*. New York: Vision, 1991. Print.

Hunt, Angela. *Five Miles South of Peculiar*. New York: Howard, 2012. Print.

Lydenberg, Robin. "Freud's Uncanny Narratives." *PMLA* 112: 5 (1997): 1072–1086. Web. July 2013.

Mormino, Gary R. *Land of Sunshine, State of Dreams: A Social History of Modern Florida*. 2005. Gainesville: University of Florida Press, 2008. Nook file.

Navakas, Michele Currie. "Island Nation: Mapping Florida, Revising America." *Early American Studies: An Interdisciplinary Journal* 11.2 (2013): 243–271. Web. August 2013.

9

Edna Buchanan

Edna Rydzik Buchanan was born March 16, 1939, in Patterson, New Jersey, and attended Montclair State Teachers College, which is now Montclair State College. She moved to Miami, Florida, in the 1960s, where she began an illustrious career as a journalist, first for the *Miami Beach Daily Sun* and then later as a "police beat reporter" for the *Miami Herald*. Buchanan worked relentlessly, researching and reporting on some of the most heinous crimes of the decade until her tenacity, talent, and grit earned her a Pulitzer Prize. In 2012, Buchanan was presented the Literary Legend Award by the Florida Heritage Book Festival in Saint Augustine, Florida (*Edna Buchanan*). Her first book, and arguably her most disturbing, is *Carr: Five Years of Rape and Murder,* a book that chronicles pedophile and murderer Robert Frederick Carr's detailed confession as told to Buchanan herself. The June 8, 2000, edition of the *Miami Herald* calls Carr's crimes so wicked that his death in 1997 meant only that he would "meet his maker 1,400 years before Florida [would let] him out of prison" (Blanco). Her two books—*The Corpse Had a Familiar Face* (1991) and *Never Let Them See You Cry* (1993)—each offer accounts of real stories that Buchanan covered during her career with the *Miami Herald*.

Miami's penchant for blatant drama, brazen decadence, and baneful drugs offered Buchanan an eyewitness account of kidnapping, rape, murder, and natural disasters from the victims' and the villains' point of view; consequently, her move from journalism to fiction was a natural migration, and although Buchanan retired from her reporting career long ago to pursue novel writing, she feels lucky to have been a journalist because "[t]here is something noble and exciting about venturing out every day to seek the truth" (*Edna Buchanan*). In pursuit of such truth, Britt Montero, Buchanan's sassy, doggedly determined protagonist, lands squarely in the thralls of Miami's ugliest national and international crime and corruption. Nine Britt Montero novels later and a new book, *Dead Man's Daughter*, on the horizon are an indication that Buchanan really knows her stuff!

Although Buchanan began writing professionally after college, she knew "she wanted to be a writer since she was 4 years old" (Goodreads). She offers a pragmatic, albeit cheeky, list of her life's philosophy on her personal website, which speak to the journalistic influence in her career and her own humorous view of the world. Here are two of Buchanan's especially interesting suggestions for living the good, safe, and practicable life:

> The person most likely to murder you sits across the breakfast table, your nearest and dearest, the one who sleeps on the pillow next to yours and shares your checking account, can be far more lethal than any sinister stranger lurking in the shadow. Love kills.... If kidnapped, ask for fried chicken when your captors offer food. The FBI will find your fingerprints in their hideout even if they never find you [*Edna Buchanan*].

Buchanan is funny and serious, witty and tender, raw and genteel. She knows her way around a crime novel because she knows her way around crime and criminals. Her work is alive and breathing because she has spent time with the dead and their killers. She is one of Florida's finest women writers.

Works Cited

Blanco, Juan Ignacio. "Robert Frederick Carr." *Murderpedia*. 2014. Web. 11 Mar. 2014. http://murderpedia.org/male.C/c/carr-robert-frederick.htm.

Edna Buchanan: The Queen of Crime. Edna Buchanan. 2012. Web. 7 Mar. 2014. http://www.ednabuchanan.com/.

Goodreads. "Edna Buchanan." 2014. *Goodreads, Inc.* 2014. Web. 7 Mar. 2014. http://www.goodreads.com/author/show/29245.Edna_Buchanan.

Florida's Femme Fatale

Wendy Dwyer

In a city known for departures, Miami would much prefer its reputation limited simply to farewells from hordes of happy passengers waving and cheering from luxurious cruise ship decks, en route to glamorous ports of call, white sandy beaches, and evenings spent gambling in a ship's casino. Some Miami departures, though, are final and fatal, and it is to those that Pulitzer prize-winning journalist Edna Buchanan has been drawn for decades.

Likewise, it is Florida's exquisite beauty, exceptional weather, and extreme contrast between good and evil, beauty and revulsion, and light and darkness that make the sunshine state a major character in Buchanan's writing, both fictional and memoir. Unimaginable horror and destruction dwell equally in Buchanan's beautiful Florida settings, a reminder that life includes angst, ennui, abhorrence, pleasure, grief, redemption, give and take: The binaries that draw and repulse Buchanan and her characters.

Reverently hailed by the *Los Angeles Times* as the queen of crime, Buchanan is truly the original goodbye girl, Florida's femme fatale of fiction. She spent two decades uncovering and sharing the stories of the deceased, first as a journalist for the *Miami Herald* and then after as a novelist featuring Cuban-American crime reporter Britt Montero. While Buchanan may not have been born in Miami or raised on the sweet tea and heady scent of citrus blossoms, Miami warmed her blood and sparked desire to punctuate a murder victim's life.

In her memoir, *The Corpse Had a Familiar Face*, Buchanan confesses her purpose for writing, and hints why Florida is as essential a character in her writing as is crime reporter, Montero. According to Buchanan, "The face of Miami changes so quickly, but the dead stay that way. I feel haunted by the restless souls of those whose killers walk free" (*Familiar Face* 24). Whether writing in a memoir or in the voice of her hard-as-nails alter-ego, Montero, the Florida setting is as much a living, breathing, changing character as any protagonist.

Florida's legendary natural beauty, from the muck to the ghetto, is the backdrop for all of Buchanan's crime novels—but not a static backdrop. Buchanan uses this tropical and terrible paradise's constantly evolving nature to reveal her novels' many and varied characters. Florida landscape is both a cause and justification for their behavior—bad and good. Whether it is the steaming heat rising from sultry Miami pavements, Mother Nature's fury letting loose in a hurricane or sudden storm, or the breathtaking azure sky and mismatched architectural soup of Miami landscape, Florida is a central theme and participatory character.

Whether Buchanan is writing as herself about Edward Becher, a senior citizen from New Jersey whose death occurred while walking back to the hotel after parking his car, or whether she is chronicling the story of the still-missing Amy Billig, who disappeared at seventeen and whose unfinished story nearly forty years later is as haunting and heartbreaking as it was that winter afternoon when she disappeared, Florida's setting is both predator and prey. The same is true in her historical fiction. Legendary John and Laura Ashley, members of Florida's famed, but doomed Ashley Gang are brought back to life in Buchanan's novel, *A Dark and Lonely Place,* where Florida, with all of its extremes, is a major character in every chapter and between every line. Like the state that boasts delicate, rare orchids and a shoreline strong enough to withstand multiple beatings and Mother Nature's whims, Buchanan's writing is hard-shelled, fact-filled, and sensitive enough to remind the most jaded that every face, and indeed every corpse, is someone's daughter, son, wife, father, cousin, friend, lover, or ex. In her *Miami Herald* articles and in her many novels, Buchanan shares the gift of humanity with the deceased, providing a reason to care for the life lost and a shadow of guilt for human memory reduced to column inches. Buchanan provides hard news with a human touch.

Florida's extremes suit Buchanan's personality and enhance her ability to tell a story. Rich, lush descriptions of long, hot days when the mercury soars past the triple-digit mark and the humidity is not far behind are juxtaposed with curt, matter-of-fact headlines for which Buchanan and her alter-ego Montero are known for in reality and fiction respectively. Midst gritty snapshots of death, crimes of passion diffused and dissected to reveal the victim and the villain, and suspense-filled mysteries which need to be resolved comes a veritable photo album of Florida as active participant in vacations and crimes, beginnings and endings, or love and hate. Florida's beauty is both the muse and tormentor of humanity's inner beast.

Buchanan has earned her place as a resident of the transient state through a love affair with Miami that has lasted more than fifty years. She speaks reverently of the moment she fell in love with Miami: "Some people avoid Florida in July because of its scorching heat. But July was when I first saw Miami, and I knew at once it was for me. That first deep breath of steamy summer air, heat waves shimmying off the sizzling pavement, palm fronds feathered against a sharp and brilliant blue sky—it was like coming home at last" (*Familiar Face* 41).

For her part, Buchanan not only appreciates the steamy atmosphere, but embraces it and uses it to enhance her writing and her life. She admits that the heat is exhilarating and inspiring for her personally, but she is constantly aware that the high temperatures and the humidity which can sometimes seem suffocating are equal parts alluring and revolting for a journalist working the dead beat. Buchanan makes the contrast vividly clear in her autobiography: "The summer sun and the salty sea breeze feel good on my skin.... The same oven-like heat will, in a matter of minutes, kill pets and small children left in a closed car. What it will do to a dead body in the trunk for twenty-four hours is unspeakable" (*Familiar Face* 41).

The same can be said for the effect of the heat on ordinary individuals. Like the manic nature of many whom Brit Montero must address in Buchanan's suspenseful novels, the idyllic weather in Florida can turn without a moment's notice, unleashing a fury on those who call Florida home and on those who rejuvenate in Florida's sunshine. The schizophrenic changes in the state's personality only add to the intensity of an individual's behavior, so the hotter it gets in Florida, the hotter the tempers and the higher the crime rate. The hotter the temperatures and the more passionate the crime, the shorter the headline in Buchanan's stories on the crime beat and often, the more condensed and powerful the sentences in her novels.

In an article for *The New Yorker*, Calvin Trillin quips that there was a conversation in the *Miami Herald* newsroom about Buchanan's attention to detail and her penchant for succinct and gripping leads. Four simple words likely to cause a craving in readers to hear the rest of the story serve as an example for why Edna Buchanan's writing is unequivocally intriguing and hard to put down: "Gary Robinson died hungry" was the lead for a story about the unfortunate timing of a fried chicken shortage and the final moments of a man's life cut short by a desire to eat and a temper, both equal ingredients in his death. According to Trillin, the other contender for a classic Buchanan lead is nearly as simple and succinct: "Bad things happen to the husbands of Widow Elkin." Buchanan's matter-of-fact leads not only grab attention, but they also testify to Miami's influence, its residents, and its law-keepers' *here and now, it-is-what-it-is* attitude. In *A Dark and Lonely Place*, a high-profile lawyer with a notoriously sketchy moral compass crashes his speedboat spectacularly into a beachside resort hotel. The detective checking the body notes flatly, "The flattened face looked familiar. So did the gold Presidential Rolex on the dead man's left wrist. It still worked perfectly, but time had run out for the man who wore it" (*Dark and Lonely* 9). The brevity of the description of the dead man sharpens the bitter irony of a life that has, quite literally, run out of time.

The glitz and art deco of Miami that entice so many tourists and transients are Buchanan's addiction and Montero's gods. Both the author's and character's lives are illustrated with intensity of colors and lit by Miami's extreme brightness of day and shadows of darkness. The disparity between wealth and poverty, good and evil, and celebrity and anonymity are all leveled in death, and Buchanan describes the two with a level and even-handed abruptness that it both dismissive and alluring. Even on the darkest of Florida nights, deep in the thick wilds of the Everglades, Buchanan finds a way to add more than moonlight to illuminate and dissipate the shadows: "The young woman in white stumbled as she ran, her blond hair pale in the moonlight. The endless woods looked so different, so forbidding at night. The only light was the quarter moon, and the path, when she could see it, lay in shadow. But, on a mission, she felt no fear" (*Dark and Lonely* 227).

Buchanan, whose figure, glamor, and elegance defy the abruptness of her sentence structure explains with customary succinctness that Florida inspires her writing since "[i]t's sort of like we're down here alone, and we're on our own. It's flat; we're at sea level. The full moon rises. The temperature soars. The barometric pressure drops, and all hell breaks loose" ("Edna Buchanan: Florida Inspires"). Florida's prominence in Buchanan's novels and her references to Miami heat lend some credence and supporting evidence to the possibility that extreme heat and humidity cause people on the edge to snap and commit heinous crimes. When the temperature gets too hot, it is the "little things in life [that] sometimes trigger the urge to kill: a stereo too loud, a game of checkers. One man killed his neighbor over the clippings from a Florida cherry hedge. Temperatures in the nineties sparked a fatal family fight over a fan" (Buchanan, *Familiar Face* 30).

When the Florida sunshine and heat do not create an atmosphere conducive to murder, the pair often works hand-in-hand to make a Florida murder worse because of the incongruity between storminess and endless teardrops shed over lives lost or forever changed despite Florida's near paradise setting with swaying palms and shimmering waters—often a pathetic fallacy in reverse. Buchanan describes a trip to interview the family of a Haitian-born cabbie who was shot four times for not giving his fare money to robbers. She recalls, "The temperature suddenly dropped ten degrees, and a chilly rain began to fall.... The day took on an eerie, other-worldly quality. I moved toward my car in the pelting rain, and the cluster of sad-faced Haitians moved with me, disregarding the downpour, wanting to tell me more of whatever it was I needed to know (Buchanan, *Familiar Face* 32).

These extreme contrasts appeal to Buchanan because they are also the reason people come to Florida and Miami in particular. Miami is so large that it is easy to feel or to become anonymous in the sea of humanity and heat. As is true with much of Florida, Miami is an escape or final destination for tourists and retirees who come to visit, fall in love with the weather and the beauty, and choose to stay in Florida until death —most experience a natural, expected death unlike Buchanan's folks. Florida is a study in contrasts, and there often seems to be very little gray area in the land of sunshine and citrus. This kind of contradiction and polarization of life makes people who are already inclined toward the sinister lose track of their center and blur the lines between right and wrong and good and evil. Its transient population and warm, moist climate make Florida a veritable petri dish for questionable and strange occurrences.

Florida figures so prominently and equally in drug and human trafficking and such bizarre crimes that entire websites are dedicated to the strange behavior that seems to happen solely in Florida, including homeless men whose faces are chewed off by strangers, a first-date turned carjacking, and a trio of criminals who return to the scene of a break-in with a U-Haul because there is simply too much great stuff to leave behind (Lammle). Is it the extreme heat that causes those struggling with making the right decision to forego common sense completely, throw caution to the wind, and make that life-altering, albeit poor choice that will change or end life forever? Buchanan would suggest this is so.

For Buchanan, the contrasts are often a poignant reminder of the fleeting nature of life and the reckless disregard for it shown by those who take it away from others. Florida's majesty and vast expanses of mystery and awe sometimes set the scene for stories that have no end, like that of Amy Billig, the seventeen year-old woman who disappeared in 1974 en route to borrow a couple of dollars before meeting a friend for lunch. Although forty years have passed, Buchanan does not need to look at the files on her desk to know "Amy has three silver fillings in three premolars and porcelain fillings in two upper front teeth. Amy walked her happy walk into a sunny day at noon and disappeared" (Buchanan, *Familiar Face* 191). Buchanan's facts, as simple as a weather report, evoke the interruptions and hesitations that Amy Billig's family must endure every time the telephone rings, even so many years later, hoping against hope that this one phone call will not be a prank or an extortion attempt but a real answer to provide closure and, alive or dead, bring Amy home.

As a character in her novels, Florida is central, moving a plot forward and defining the location of an event or a scene; the state becomes a character. Moody, brooding, or lighthearted and celebratory, the landscape is breathing, ever-evolving, and highly emotional. When writing the background to the infamous Ashley Gang, a Florida-based crime family killed in 1929, Buchanan seasons the entire story with heavy doses of Florida history, including lush descriptions of the swamps, snakes, mosquitos, and unbearable humidity as well as the breathtaking beauty of the state's moon risings, Mediterranean-style architecture, sky lights, and ever-present water.

In the preface of *A Dark and Lonely Place*, Buchanan claims that the novel is the one she has yearned to write for half her life. Based loosely on Florida's own storied outlaw, John Ashley of the Ashley Gang, it is clear that Buchanan considers Florida to be not only her true home, but also her final frontier. In an interview in 2012 about the book, Buchanan laments history's neglect of Florida's most notorious couple, John and Laura Ashley, the peninsula's Bonnie and Clyde, "whose story is far more riveting, breathtaking, and poignant. They spent more on the run, escaping from city, state, and federal lawmen.... What a story" (Butki).

As evidence that even an ice cold case is not intimidating for Buchanan as a crime reporter or crime novelist, December, 2011, marked the centennial of the killing of John Ashley, whose crime spree with his nephew and friends ended when the entire gang was shot execution-style without the benefit of a trial, sparking the suicide of his sweetheart, Laura, at the gang's Everglades hideout and reminding, yet again, that every murder is major to the victim.

In *A Dark and Lonely Place*, the brutality and senseless awe of crime is seamlessly shared with a powerful sense of empathy for the victims affected. In a novel that stretches across two centuries and flirts with mysticism and reincarnation, *A Dark and Lonely Place* effectively marries historical fiction and the crime novel with more than a passing nod of adoration to the beauty and rugged landscape of Florida. John and Laura are star-crossed lovers in both centuries, and both sets of lovers have a deep and intrinsic connection to the land, the water, and the rich history of Florida. Buchanan was compelled to write the Ashley Gang story, and particularly John and Laura's love story, and she alludes to the rugged Florida terrain and the passion of love and family loyalty that " haunted [her] dreams and stirred [her] soul from the moment [she] first heard their names decades ago. To tough, hardworking, self-reliant Florida frontiersmen, John Ashley was a folk hero, a symbol of resistance to Yankee government, greedy bankers, and the law. To vindictive lawmen, he became a deadly obsession" (Butki).

Buchanan describes seeing a photo of John Ashley as she was searching the newspaper morgue. There "[h]e stood at the threshold of manhood, ... his life stretched out before him like a promise. Never in his wildest dreams could he have imagined then how broken that promise would be, or that he would soon become the most controversial and notorious character in Florida's colorful and violent history" (Butki). Yet even in recounting John Ashley's final, horrifying moments, the everlasting beauty of Florida is not lost on either Ashley or Buchanan.

As Ashley's imminent death approaches, a "cold wind in the trees raised the hair on the back of his neck. This time, he knew, was different. A bright quarter moon reigned over a star-studded night made for love, fresh starts, and new beginnings, not bad endings. How did this go so wrong?" (Buchanan, *Dark and Lonely* 376).

9. Edna Buchanan

The string of wrongs that never ended with any rights in the case of John Ashley and the notorious Ashley Gang is succinct and gripping, the perfect post script and punctuation point for a piece on Florida's influence on arguably its finest homespun, if not homegrown writer. *The Corpse Had a Familiar Face: Covering Miami, America's Hottest Beat* and *A Dark and Lonely Place* are testaments to the extremes at play in both Florida's lush landscape and Buchanan's terse, matter-of-fact storytelling style. Buchanan herself says that Florida is about "[l]ost lives and broken hearts. The more things change, the more they remain the same. Florida has always been the last stop for sun-seeking drifters and people on the run from trouble" (Butki). As long as this is true, there will always be room for another Buchanan novel.

Works Cited

Buchanan, Edna. *The Corpse Had a Familiar Face: Covering Miami, America's Hottest Beat.* New York: Pocket Books—Simon & Schuster, Inc., 1987. Print.

———. *A Dark and Lonely Place.* New York: Simon and Schuster, 2011. E-book.

Butki, Scott. "An Interview with Author Edna Buchanan About Her New Novel, *A Dark and Lonely Place.*" *BlogCritics.org.* N.p., 23 February 2012. Web. 11 January 2014. http://www.seattlepi.com/lifestyle/blogcritics/article/An-Interview-With-Author-Edna-Buchanan-About-Her–3360284.php.

"Edna Buchanan: Florida Inspires." Interview. *Florida Inspires.* History Channel, 2013. Video.

Lammle, Rob. "Ten Weird Crimes that Could Only Happen in Florida." *Mental Floss* 27 Sept 2013: N. pag. *Mental Floss.com.* Web. 11 January 2014. http://mentalfloss.com/article/52914/10-weird-crimes-could-only-happen-florida.

Trillin, Calvin. "Profiles: Covering the Cops." *New Yorker* 17 February 1986: N. pag. *NewYorker.* Web. 09 March 2014. http://niemanstoryboard.org/stories/whys-this-so-good-number–47-calvin-trillin-and-classic-edna-buchanan/.

10

Ana Menéndez

Miami, Florida, is known for its mix of Cuban and American cultures, and fiction writer Ana Menéndez, a product of both cultures, uses this mix in many of her stories and novels. Her parents were part of the exodus that occurred when Cubans fled to America during the early 1960s. The Menendez family settled in Los Angeles, California, where Ana Menéndez was later born in 1970. Eventually, her family relocated to Florida and settled in Miami ("Ana Menéndez." *Contemporary*).

In 1992, Ana Menéndez earned her bachelor's in English at Florida International University and then received her master's of fine art at New York University in 2001 (*Ana Menéndez*). During the early part of her writing career, she worked as a newspaper journalist for the *Miami Herald*, then moved on to work at Southern California's *Orange County Register*, and then went back to work in 2005 for the *Miami Herald*. Finally, in 2008 she left the *Miami Herald* after becoming a Fulbright scholar at American University in Cairo, Egypt ("Ana Menéndez." *Contemporary*).

Ana Menéndez is the author of two short story collections and two novels. Her first collection of stories, *In Cuba I Was a German Shepherd*, was published in 2001, and it includes eleven stories "about Cuban immigrants who fled to the United States and tried to create new lives and adjust to mainstream American culture" ("Ana Menéndez." *Contemporary*). This collection earned her the Pushcart Prize and also became a New York Times Notable book of the year in 2001. *Loving Che*, a novel, was published by Atlantic Monthly Press in 2003. It follows the journey of a young Cuban-American from Miami who searches for answers to her parentage, which "she gleans from [making] several trips back to Havana, [and as she does so] the daughter reconstructs the life of her mother, her youthful affair with the enigmatic Che, and the child she bore by the handsome rebel" (*Ana Menéndez*). Her second novel was selected by *Publishers Weekly* to add to its top 100 books of the year and is entitled *The Last War*. Harper Collins published it in 2009, and events in the story are loosely based on her life ("Ana Menéndez." *Contemporary*). In this novel, Flash, a journalist traveling to the Middle East, is confronted with the possibility that her husband has been unfaithful, and this leads her to an examination of her life as well as their relationship. Finally, her second collection of short stories, *Adios, Happy Homeland!*, was published in 2011. This collection provides a "modern take on the idea of migration and flight" (*Ana Menéndez*).

Works Cited

"Ana Menéndez." *Contemporary Authors Online.* Detroit: Gale, 2010. *Biography In Context.* Web. 27 May 2013.
Ana Menéndez. Web. 28 May 2013. http://www.anamenendezonline.com/index.htm.

Entrapment and Escape

Jane Anderson Jones

Although Ana Menéndez was born in Los Angeles, grew up in Tampa and Miami, and worked for many years as a reporter for *The Miami Herald*, she is primarily identified and identifies herself as "the daughter of Cuban exiles" (*Ana*, Birnbaum). Three of her four published books—*In Cuba I Was a German Shepherd* (2001), *Loving Che* (2003), *The Last War* (2009), *Adios, Happy Homeland!* (2011)—are concerned with the question of Cuban identity, and all four contain the theme of displacement. In an interview with Janelle Garcia, Menéndez acknowledged, "For me, the theme of displacement is a natural one. It's the context in which I grew up and it's the context in which I try to make sense of the things I see. It's my obsession, and you can't write without an obsession. The work is too dull and tedious otherwise" (Garcia). How the theme of displacement plays out in her works has evolved from her first collection of stories, *In Cuba I Was a German Shepherd*, to the recent collection, *Adios, Happy Homeland!*

The stories from *In Cuba* are concerned with the exiled Cuban community in Miami, almost all from the wealthy first-wave of exiles, who suffer from a variety of displacement disorders. As the years go by and their hopes of returning to Cuba fade, their children grow up; some marry outside the Cuban community, and they regain prosperity in a variety of commercial ventures, but there is little sense of assimilation into a broader American society. Many remain entrapped in elusive memories of their lost lives in Cuba. In contrast, the tales in *Adios, Happy Homeland!* are stories of escape artists, starting with the author herself. Each tale is attributed to a concocted author, for whom Menéndez has supplied an appropriately imaginative biographical note, including one for herself: "*Ana Menéndez* is the pseudonym of an imaginary writer and translator, invented, if not to lend coherence to this collection, at least to offer it the pretense of contemporary relevance" (*Adios* 264).

For the first generation exiles of *In Cuba I Was a German Shepherd*, Miami is, in the words of Maya Socolovsky, "a placeholder for Cuban memory" (246). Jose Quiroga goes a step further – "In the symbolic grammar of Cuban discourse, Miami is a necropolis to life that was always lived elsewhere" (198). These exiles have always expected to go back home to Cuba and to resume a life that no longer exists.

The realistic stories with a cast of named characters of *In Cuba* are interspersed with stories narrated by unnamed young women and parable-like tales evoking, if not naming, Fidel Castro. In an interview with Melissa Scholes Young, Menéndez explains that the collection began with the invention of Máximo: "And almost every story grew out of his relationships. It was a fictional treatment of what I had seen in my own community." The protagonist of the opening title story, "In Cuba I Was a German Shepherd," Máximo had been a professor in Havana before the revolution. When he fled to Miami, he and his wife, Rosa, started a food wagon to feed Cuban laborers, and it eventually grew into a small restaurant in Little Havana. Máximo, now retired, and his friend and former employee, Raúl, spend their afternoons in a small park off Eighth Street (Calle Ocho), playing dominoes with Antonio and Carlos, Dominican immigrants. Quiroga, in discussing the political and cultural situation of Cuba in the 20th Century, uses the domino game as a representation of the forces in play with the Cuban psyche: "The Cuban domino game has four players: History, Memory, Representation and Chance. They have all played their game on the streets of Havana and in a little park off Miami's Calle Ocho, and they have paired off in different teams or played on their own" (25). Máximo is the storyteller, the memory-keeper of this quartet, but his stories of Cuba and Fidel have become stale and repetitive, a reflection of his own life now that Rosa has died, his daughters have moved far from Miami, he has sold the restaurant, and lost the convivial group that would gather at the restaurant after closing hours to eat and talk and tell stories that always began with "In Cuba I remember" (*In Cuba* 7). His audience is now reduced to Raúl and the two Dominicans, who while polite, tire of the continual aggrandizement of all things Cuban. Dalia Kandiyoti theorizes, "The consistent devaluation of the present in praise of the past, characteristic of nostalgia and the Cuban community, which define one another ... is a mark of the exiles' self-differentiation as superior" (92). Tourists, brought by tour buses or led by maps that mark interesting sites of ethnic tourism, regularly intrude upon the haven of Domino Park. Máximo is equally infuriated by the gawkers and those players who exaggerate their Cubanness to play up to the tourists. But Máximo's inability to truly connect to anyone outside his Cuban-centric memory world is most painfully illustrated when Antonio comes to the park one day and proudly displays an antique set of dominos made of ebony and ivory. When asked his opinion, Máximo can only reply, "Very nice." Antonio is offended: "My daughter walked all over New Orleans to find this and the Cuban thinks it's 'very nice'?" (*In Cuba* 19). Yet it is Antonio who calms and defends Máximo when he is about to attack a picture-taking tourist. Máximo's last joke about Juanito, a mangy dog from Cuba who lands in Miami, brings the story back to the title and to the loss of identity experienced by the exiles. When Juanito's advances are spurned by an impeccably groomed French poodle, he protests: "Pardon me, your highness, here in America, I may be a short, insignificant mutt, but in Cuba I was a German shepherd" (*In Cuba* 28).

Intrusions from Florida's natural world that are reminders of life in Cuba also serve to disrupt and disturb the equilibrium of idealization and emphasize the inability of the characters to psychically adapt to a new environment. Richard Eder in his *New York Times* review of *In Cuba*, noted that "Menéndez suggests the quality of what is neither entirely migration nor entirely exile. Part of exile's peculiar pain is the absence of the old geography, the smells, the weather. For the Cubans, the pain is their continuing presence." In "The Perfect Fruit" and "Story of a Parrot," a banana tree and the entrance of a wild parrot provoke disturbing memories in two women. Anselmo, the son of Raúl and Matilde, asks to bring his girlfriend, Meegan, to dinner to make an important announcement in "The Perfect Fruit." As Matilde is planning the menu, she reminisces about Anselmo's birth and childhood until she catches sight of a patch of yellow in the far corner of her otherwise perfectly green lawn. The banana trees that Raúl had planted eight years ago have suddenly fruited. Raúl's planting of the trees had initially angered Matilde, but as they grew dormant and green, she thought less and less about the trees until they passed into a deep part of her memory that was almost like forgetting" (*In Cuba* 51). On one level, the sudden intrusion of the bananas is parallel to the intrusion of Meegan, the Anglo girlfriend, into the relationship of Matilde and her son—she is garishly unwelcome. But on another, almost subconscious, level, they represent the buried memories of the past: her husband's philandering, her life in Cuba, perhaps even the disruption of Castro's revolution. Matilde becomes obsessed with getting rid of the bananas that are spoiling the perfection of greenness. She can't put them in the trash because the smell of their rot would permeate the property during the dinner. So she decides to bake—for two days she furiously bakes banana bread, banana pie, banana brownies, banana flan—until an hour before Anselmo and Meegan are due to arrive. Throughout her baking, flashes of Raúl's past infidelities surface—secrets she had kept throughout her marriage. When Raúl confronts her with the banana array as their guests are about to arrive, she counters with a memory of their wedding in Cuba and a photograph of Raúl's being kissed on the cheek by a beautiful young woman: "the camera caught the stars in your eyes. I've never seen you as happy since. That smile!" (*In Cuba* 72). As the young couple approach the front door, Matilde places a perfect banana cream pie in front of Raúl and urges him, "'Please eat,' she said. 'I made it just for you'" (*In Cuba* 74). But the illusions have been broken.

Illusions and delusions also haunt the "Story of a Parrot." Sixty-year old Hortencia de la Cruz lives in a small Sweetwater house in circumstances much reduced from her childhood wealth in Cuba. Her husband Felipe, an aspiring novelist, continuously types away after his shift at Máximo's restaurant as she lounges away her life. One day a wild parrot flies into the house. Hortencia is frantic to have Felipe get it out of the house. "'It's a ball of microbes and worms under all that fancy plumage'" (*In Cuba* 91). It eventually flies out the open back door. Four days later Hortencia accuses Felipe of chasing away the beautiful parrot, its green feathers now transformed into a more exotic blue, and she leaves the back door open for a month to lure it back. Memories of her Cuban youth and imagined theatrical career flood over her and bring back a song she had not heard for thirty-five years. The song invokes *las ilusiones del ayer* (the illusions of yesterday) with its *promesas cruelas* (cruel promises). Finally she agrees with Felipe that the parrot will not return—anymore than her dreams or their passion will return. She muses that when she came to Miami, she could have joined a choir or become involved with the theater on Eighth Street, but she admits to herself, "You were waiting for bigger things. You deserved bigger things" (*In Cuba* 102).

The first-generation exiles are featured once more in "The Party" at Máximo's restaurant. They have gathered to welcome Joaquin Rivera to Miami. A friend of their youth, he had been a revolutionary and supporter of Castro. As they reminisce, they each project their own image on the figure of Joaquin—to Ernesto he was the clever comrade who rescued his friends from a potentially dangerous situation, to Hortencia he was a great singer, Matilde remembered his liking to bake, and Raúl had stories about his legendary womanizing. It is only an old woman, who continually asks Ernesto why they have gathered, who utters the truth when he tells her that "'Joaquin has finally come out of Cuba.' Ernesto steps away and the old woman nods. 'El Alemán,' she says. And then quietly, 'El asesino'" (the assassin) (*In Cuba* 189). At the end of the story when Joaquin's plane has been delayed, she again asks Ernesto why she is there. This time he replies, "'You see Señora,' he says, 'We have been in this country for almost forty years'" (*In Cuba* 202).

"Baseball Dreams" and "Miami Relatives" are both narrated by daughters—one speculating about her father's past and the other trying to come to terms with her crazy family. The daughter in "Baseball Dreams" looks at a photograph of her father, then three years old, holding a baseball bat, and she tells the story of his disastrous first baseball game:

> If only…. That's how I always start the story. If only baseball had held him like a tender parent. How different it all would be. He would have come to see me on the beach that day. He would have married my mother. I am the little girl who wants a life of baseball rules: nine innings, pads on the catcher, may the best team win [*In Cuba* 133].

There is also a photo hidden in the closet of the "Miami Relatives," a photo of the old uncle in Cuba. The narrator worries about her family—the Aunt Julia who bites people, the grandmother who perches on a tree branch, the grandfather who has a radio growing out of his ear, and her mother who regularly emerges from the closet with bleeding fingernails. Everyone in the family claims to hate the old uncle, but the narrator comes to believe that the situation is far more complicated. Stories about Castro's love of baseball and possible early baseball career and rumors about his convoluted family life have swirled throughout the Cuban community in Miami for decades. In these two parable-like stories, Menéndez subtly reveals a generational shift in Cuban-American attitudes. The girl in "Baseball Dreams," a first-generation exile from Cuba, is soaked in "what if" nostalgia, while the daughter of "Miami Relatives" questions with her outsider boyfriend if the stories the family tells are completely truthful. She finally concludes, "He is crazy because of us and we are crazy because of him" (*In Cuba* 177).

Although an attitudinal shift is occurring across the generations, there remains a displacement anxiety in the younger generation. As a member of the second generation, Menéndez described her own experience to an interviewer:

> The children of exiles grow up with a kind of void at their back. In time, at least in me, (this unknowable world) transformed itself from a physical displacement to a metaphorical, or spiritual displacement—a disconnection from clan and tribe that perhaps inspired me to wander the world (the exile and the nomad are cousins, after all). (In Letter, "The Exile" 9–10)

The disconnection mentioned by Menéndez plays out in a variety of ways from the inability to sustain relationships to being overwhelmed with anxiety or grief. The anonymous narrator of "Hurricane Stories" fears for her relationship as she fails to fully engage her lover with her own story and her father's story of preparing for hurricanes and riding out storms in boarded-up houses: "But he grew up with snow in the winter and fir trees against gray skies. I had Florida…. Was it always this way between us?" (*In Cuba* 34). He asks if her father were telling the truth? "I wonder what he knows about me. I sit and watch and suddenly there is so much more I want to tell him" (*In Cuba* 48), but she realizes that he is drifting away. In "Why We Left," the narrator and her husband have moved North from Miami to escape the pain of losing a baby to a miscarriage. As winter intrudes, her longing for her lost child and for Miami leads to delusions of a frozen forest transformed into palm trees and hibiscus, humming with a chorus of insects. There is an inability to separate the real and the illusion. Sorrow and loss permeate "Confusing the Saints." Clarita, a waitress at Máximo's restaurant, has married Orlandito while visiting her grandmother in Cuba, but the marriage has not been officialized, so when Clarita returns to Miami, Orlandito is left behind. Desperate to leave, Orlandito boards a raft. Waiting frantically for Olandito's arrival, Clarita seeks advice from an old herbalist who tells her the story of Oshun, the orisha who sacrificed herself to bring rain back to the earth: "'Suffering is very old,' the herb woman says when I stand to go. 'Older than man'" (*In Cuba* 120). In "the Last Rescue," Anselmo, wracked with doubts about his marriage and his wife, cannot sleep although he must fly in the morning to search for rafters. The previous evening at a party for the pilots, he had heard his American wife Meegan express her doubts about the Cuban embargo with the only Anglo pilot in the crew. The sense of uneasiness in their own skins and a questioning of their place in community around them mark each of these second generation characters.

It is only in the final story of the collection, "Her Mother's House," that a kind of resolution is effected. Lisette, now an editor, reflects upon an earlier assignment to Cuba, when she sought out her mother's childhood home. Growing up she had heard from her mother countless descriptions of the fabulous mansion abandoned in Aruna when the family fled Cuba. Her mother reluctantly gives her the location. The house is ordinary, now inhabited by an old couple, Matún and Alicia, who had worked for Lisette's grandparents. With the reminiscences about her grandparents and mother, Lisette gains new perspectives on her family, yet on her return home at a family gathering, she validates her mother's grand illusions about the abandoned home. Neither puncturing the stories of the past nor any longer deluded by them, Lisette seems able to recreate a new identity for herself.

Between the publications of *In Cuba I Was a German Shepherd* (2001) and *Adios, Happy Homeland* (2011), Menéndez published two novels, lived in Istanbul, ended her marriage, lived in Egypt as a Fulbright Scholar, and worked as a journalist. *Loving Che* (2003) and *The Last War* (2009), the former set in Florida and Cuba, the latter in Istanbul during the Iraq War, continue to explore the themes of the play between illusion and reality mediated by imagination and storytelling and the need to find one's true self. But it is in *Adios, Happy Homeland!* that Menéndez celebrates the act of departure as an act of self-creation. "For me, leaving is the way we learn about identity and place. Travel far and long enough and you realize there is no such thing as a fixed 'identity' – though this is often so difficult a realization that we cling to the outlines of who we thought we were" (Menéndez in Young).

Adios, Happy Homeland! is a flight of fancy through the Cuban/Caribbean/Floridian world, or rather, a collection of flights of fancy. Some are uplifting; some lead to nowhere; some are thoroughly grounded in reality; some leap off into magical realism, but all play within the high metafiction of masquerade. As Amy Letter has pointed out: "It is part of this book's marvelous metafictional bravado that its characters are its 'authors,' and its 'editor' is a borrowed (and liberally re-written) character, while its author's name is described as a character's pseudonym" ("Escaping" 1).

Each of the protagonists is highly distinctive in motive and means of escape. A maker of parachutes realizes that the village's plutocrat, who has rented sewing machines to the villagers, is about to ruin the town's industry. He sews up a masterpiece and floats away. An old woman, confused by dementia, begins to rewind her past until she reenters the space from which she was born. A grandfather, nearing death, tells his granddaughter of his participation in the development of the Redstone rocket and the scheme to display it at the Grand Central Terminal in New York. A young woman defends the practice of flying: "How often have I been at a party and people will start to talk about their dreams of swimming and how they wish to move through the water like fish. And I want to say to them, 'But you can fly, and so few of you do!' People dream of swimming only because they can't do it" (*Adios* 60).

In *Adios, Happy Homeland!* Menéndez lovingly pays homage to Cuban and Caribbean literary and cultural traditions. There are some wonderfully brief, quirky chapters that provide valuable insights such as: "Glossary of Caribbean Winds" describing blows like the "**Bayamo:** A very violent wind born, like many poets, in the Bight of Bayamo. It often vanishes as quickly as it came, but sometimes can persist for years, impeding those who wish to return quickly home" (*Adios* 65). One chapter includes quotes from poets translated by Google, some astoundingly apt:

> ***A Found Poem*** *by Alejo Carpentier*
> *I wondered sometimes*
> *if the highest forms of aesthetic*
> *emotion does not consist simply*
> *of a supreme understanding of creation.*
> *One day, the men find an alphabet*
> *in the eyes of the chalcedony,*
> *the brown velvet of the moth,*
> *and then astonished to know*
> *each snail was spotted, always,*
> *a poem* [*Adios* 192–93].

Most of the stories set in Florida occur in the 1990s during the time known as the Special Period (*Periodo Especial*) in Cuba when Cuba lost the support of the Soviet Union, and harsh economic conditions ensued. Facing what they believed a hopeless future, thousands of Cubans tried to make their way to Florida using any means available, most notably handmade rafts. Many of these rafters, like Orlandito of *In Cuba's* "Confusing the Saints," lost their lives. Certainly the best known of the survivors is Elián González, the six-year old boy who, in 1999, was found floating in an inner tube and rescued by fishermen. In a trio of stories, "Cojimar," "The Boy Who Was Rescued by Fish," and "The Boy's Triumphant Return," Menéndez revisions Elián's tale from different perspectives without explicitly naming the boy. The little boy in the poignant tale, "Cojimar," is awakened one November morning by his mother and told they are travelling to Miami by ship. He believes Miami "was someplace in the sky behind the clouds" (*Adios* 24) and worries that the ship will not be able to fly. When he and his mother arrive at the beach, he is terrified when he sees the raft and tries to jump out. Later in the day a body is spotted in the surf, and all are sure it is the boy until an old man discovers it is not a body, but "a giant jellyfish ... almost the exact size of a small boy caught inside a balloon" (*Adios* 28). Quickly the man pierces it, and it is washed out to sea. "The Boy Who Was Rescued by Fish" humorously and satirically counterpoints "Cojimar" by skewering both the Miami-Cuban social-political machine as well as the American penchant for New Age positive thinking. Beatrice, founder and leader of the Cuban American National Treasury (CANT), dedicated to promoting a "Free and Democratic Cuba," comes under the spell of a self-help manual titled *The Undisclosed* (an obvious reference to Rhonda Byrne's *The Secret*). The connotations of the word "freedom" to the Cuban American community in Miami is highly fraught as Jose Quiroga has illuminated: "Freedom was something that had to be attained, that had to be gained. It involved a journey from poverty to influence, and it also meant the freedom to pursue that influence and use it for political purposes" (199). Beatrice spearheads the effort to prevent the young boy, dubbed "the Little Pisces" because dolphins buoyed him in the sea, from being returned to his father's custody in Cuba. When her efforts inevitably fail, her faith in positive thinking deserts her. But the narrator of the story, one of Beatrice's employees confesses,

> For my part (though I would never admit this publicly and have kept it to myself these many years) the return of the Little Pisces was one of my life's most joyous moments, like a fever breaking, a great unburdening, a reprieve from the land of yes. I have seen tiny spiders crawl to the edge of a twig, spin out their delicate silk threads, and launch themselves into the wind. That's how I felt [*Adios* 49].

"The Boy's Triumphant Return" immediately follows with a propagandistic account of his repatriation. "Today a miraculous and heroic sight: a kidnapped Cuban boy returned triumphantly to the fatherland on a jet that soared over the clear skies of the capital, passing once, twice like a bird before nimbly landing on native soil" (*Adios* 53). The counterpointing of the motifs of freedom and flight in the three stories provides ironic contrasts as well as Menéndez's characteristic quest for a highly elusive truth.

Two more escape artists pursue diverse methods to bring about their departures. Laika, "The Boy Who Fell from Heaven," escapes from Cuba in the wheel well of an airplane, parachuting into the sea near Miami. Laika can't explain his reasons for leaving Cuba:

> Why had he left? There were no reasons and an infinite number of them, but he could not list them for the men ... what would they understand anyway of flight? Their notions of escape were of the crudest kind. Laika's were as tiny and joyful as Lucretius's clinamen. He was happy to leave them inexpressible and ungraspable [*Adios* 166–67].

In Miami, he works in landscape maintenance until he discovers windsurfing. He buys a kite board with a large golden sail and one day turns his kite into the wind and disappears "into the mists of distance" (170).

In a very different vein in "Three Betrayals," Gertrudis Gómez has decided to divorce her husband, whom she had good reasons to suspect of cheating. She reveals to her lawyer, the narrator of the story, that she herself has been carrying on a long-standing affair with a Cuban-Venezuelan poet, but her husband had grown distant, spending longer and longer stays on business trips. When she found a pair of first-class tickets in the names of her husband and his suspected lover, Gertrudis hid them and switched tactics—she began to kill him with kindness. "Gertrudis continued her torture: cooking for him every night, flagellating herself for her failings, watching the guilt work on him like an acid" (232). He changed his behavior, reaffirmed his love for her and apologized for everything. When he left for a short business trip to London with his boss, Gertrudis followed him to the airport and found that only his boss accompanied him. She watched as before his departure, he made a phone call. Gertrudis's phone rang. She didn't answer. "It was her tears she was most ashamed of. She made me promise to never tell anyone that she had wept" (233). Escape can be as painful as it is liberating.

Adios, Happy Homeland! plumbs into the universal curiosity about what else is out there—and what happens if we dare to fly into unknown realms. However, Ana Menéndez offers no easy answers or panaceas. The stories in *Adios, Happy Homeland!* reveal a writer whose view of the world has broadened since the publication of *In Cuba I Was a German Shepherd*, undoubtedly enriched by her experience of travelling and living abroad. Menendez's examination of an individual's place or displacement, whether it be in Florida or in the wider world, continues to grow more sophisticated and experimental.

Works Cited

Ana Menéndez. Official Website. Web. 24 June 2013. http://www.anamenendezonline.com/index.htm.

Birnbaum, Robert. "Ana Menéndez: A Conversation." *The Morning News*. 18 Feb 2004. Web. 18 June 2013. http://www.themorningnews.org/article/birnbaum-v.-ana-menendez.

Eder, Richard. "Baying at a Havana Moon." Rev. *In Cuba I Was a German Shepherd* by Ana Menéndez. *The New York Times*. 24 June 2001. Web. 29 May 2013. http://www.nytimes.com/books/01/06/24/reviews/010624.24ederlt.html.

Garcia, Janelle. "An Interview with Ana Menéndez." *Coastline Literary Magazine*. Web. 11 June 2013. www.fau.edu/coastlines/pdf/menendez.pdf.

Kandiyoti, Dalia. "Consuming Nostalgia: Nostalgia and the Marketplace in Cristina Garcia and Ana Menéndez." *MELUS* 31.1 (Spring, 2006: 81–97. JStor. Web. 29 May 2013.

Letter, Amy. "Escaping isn't what it used to be: Review of Ana Menéndez's *Adios, Happy Homeland!*" Anthurium: A Caribbean Studies Journal 10. 1 (2013): Article 8. Web. 16 June 2013. http://scholarlyrepository.miami.edu/anthurium/vol10/iss1/8

_____. "The Exile and the Nomad Are Cousins: An Interview with Ana Menéndez" P.S. About the book. *The Last War: A Novel* by Ana Menéndez. New York: Harper Perennial, 2009. 5–10.

Menéndez, Ana. *Adios, Happy Homeland!* New York: Black Cat-Grove/Atlantic, 2011.

_____. "The Bilingual Imagination: Searching for the Real and the True." *Poets and Writers Magazine* 39.1 (January/February 2011): 23–26. Web. 16 June 2013.

_____. *In Cuba I Was a German Shepherd*. New York: Grove Press, 2001.

_____. *The Last War*. New York: Harper Perennial, 2009.

_____. *Loving Che*. New York: Grove Press, 2003.

Quiroga, José. *Cuban Palimpsests*. Cultural Studies of the Americas, Vol. 19. Minneapolis: University of Minnesota Press, 2005.

Socolovsky, Maya. "Cuba Interrupted: The Loss of Center and Story in Ana Menéndez's Collection *In Cuba I Was a German Shepherd*." *Critique: Studies in Contemporary* Fiction. 46.3 (Spring 2005): 235–51. Web. 11 June 2013.

Young, Melissa Scholes. "The Mystery of Fiction: An Interview with Ana Menéndez." *Fiction Writers Review (21 Feb 2012)*. Web. 16 June 2013. http://fictionwritersreview.com/?s=ana+menendez

11

Vicki Hendricks

Vicki Hendricks was born in Covington, Kentucky, and raised in neighboring Cincinnati, Ohio; however, she has lived in Florida for over thirty years and considers herself a native Floridian. She has a B.S. degree from Ohio State University, an M.A. degree from Florida Atlantic University, and an M.F.A. degree from Florida International University. She is an English professor at Broward College and has taught there since 1981. She has written six novels, the last of which is *Fur People*, published in December 2013. Her fifth book, *Cruel Poetry*, was a finalist for an Edgar award in 2008. She has two sets of short stories, *Florida Gothic Stories* and *Dangerous Sex: Three Stories*. Hendricks has been called the Queen of Noir, having written some of Florida's darkest, most disturbing crime and erotic fiction.

Hendricks admits her characters are unsympathetic and her sex scenes are lengthy, but her interest in "the obsessive and sexually passionate unraveling of a psychologically twisted individual" overrides her desire to comply with content that Hendricks believes sells books (Smith 66). Consequently, Hendricks's work is read largely by writers, budding writers, literature teachers, and folks outside the United States. In fact, British writers Laura Henderson and Stella Duffy include Hendricks's "Stormy, Mon Amour" in their anthology titled *Tart Noir* (2002). *Booklist* review magazine states, "Hendricks may be the least commercial but most literary of Florida crime writers.... Her stories evoke Flannery O'Connor and Erskine Caldwell" (qtd. in "Vicki Hendricks").

Hendricks appeal to a literary audience likely stems not only from her edgy subject matter, but also from her mentors. She studied under authors Lynne Barrett, James W. Hall, Les Standiford, and John Dufresne, while attending Florida International University. As a professor herself, she has analyzed, practiced, and taught writing methods. She is challenged with teaching writing to students who are required to take composition as well as to students who are aspiring authors. This daily classroom rigor affects Hendricks's writing, evident in her precision and detail.

An avid sports person and animal lover herself, Hendricks's characters often engage in adventure sports, and her characters are often animals and/or humans engaged with animals—really engaged. Hendricks is "not interested in creating normal people who solve crimes or normal people who commit crimes for money." She is interested in "strange combinations and aberrant personalities" (Smith 67). As a result, Hendricks's personalities participate in activities that frequently blur the lines between magic and reality, the legal and illegal, the holy and the profane.

Hendricks's work is lurid and lovely, odd and ordinary, desirous and distasteful. Regardless of her readers' comments, one truth is certain: Hendricks's work is never, ever boring. She thinks, and rightfully so, that Florida settings appeal to people from everywhere who are longing for beautiful weather and tropical scenery. Hendricks also admits, "No amount of sunshine can blind the world to the fact that I write dark stuff in a limited scope, and it's difficult to reach the low numbers of people of weird taste" (Smith 67). Perhaps this is so; however, after one short story, a reader is likely as trapped in Hendricks's clutches as Darlene is in Big Man's from the story "Must Bite!" If so, then Hendricks's penchant for the peculiar may not be so bizarre after all.

Works Cited

Smith, Ellen. "Vicki Hendricks, South Florida Noir Specialist." *Florida Crime Writers: 24 Interviews*. Ed. Steve Glassman. Jefferson, N.C.: McFarland, 2008. 64–73.

"Vicki Hendricks." *Vicki Hendricks*. 2014. Web. 4 Mar. 2014. http://www.vickihendricks.com/

The Spectacle of the Body in *Florida Gothic Stories*

Angela Tenga

One of the hallmarks of the fiction of Vicki Hendricks is its explicit presentation of human bodies, and particularly sexualized bodies, which she often associates with criminality and other forms of transgression. In *Florida Gothic Stories,* Hendricks showcases transgressive characters who problematize the boundary between normalcy and deviance in a drama that is performed on the stage of the body, which is Gothicized through its depiction as a site of excess, ambiguity, danger, and instability. By placing her characters on display in grotesque and often violent situations in which their embodiment is prominent and instrumental, Hendricks produces a voyeuristic spectacle that resonates strongly with Michelle Massé's description of the Gothic novel as "a peep show of terror" (40). In this spectacle, meaning emerges in the imaginative space created through the exchange of materiality between bodies. The result is an "intercorporeal narrative" that operates on principles similar to those described in Laura Doyle's reading of Toni Morrison's *Beloved*, whose narrator "lingers in bodies, at the horizons of the flesh" (206); in *Florida Gothic Stories,* too, narrators inhabit "the physical world of rotten teeth and misguided lovemaking" (208), a world that is known and articulated in terms of the sensations and interrelations of bodies. Moreover, like the bodies that Hendricks describes, her tales themselves cross borders, resisting generic enclosure just as her characters challenge the limits of enfleshment.

11. Vicki Hendricks

Noir Visions, Gothic Gratifications

No single generic category provides a fully satisfactory label for the stories in this collection. Instead, they are better understood in terms of various generic and stylistic influences, ranging from Gothic and horror to crime fiction and noir. Collectively, these influences provide a useful framework for discussing *Florida Gothic Stories*.

The tales in this volume offer gratifications that are commonly associated with horror fiction. According to dispositional alignment theory—which proposes that an individual's reaction to scenes of horror is based on "dispositional feelings ... for the person involved" (Walters)—some viewers derive satisfaction from witnessing the punishment of those whom they see as transgressive. However, horror's appeal also may be rooted in our own desire to commit transgressive acts; because of our "dual identification with both the threatening antagonists" and the characters whom they menace, "we are exhilarated and alarmed by our enjoyment of the forbidden" (Shaw 11). Hendricks offers opportunities for both types of enjoyment, mediated via the interpersonal bodily dynamics of sex and violence. Several stories in this collection involve murder or attempted murder, and the protagonists of about half of these are abused or oppressed women. The abusive men who populate these tales are generally straightforward stereotypes that provide conveniently unsympathetic targets, so readers might easily align dispositionally with the battered female. However, Hendricks complicates this response through ambivalence; the women who seek revenge against their oppressors are seldom purely sympathetic victims, and they often resort to violence themselves. These tales thus invite a full range of responses; readers may feel gratified or horrified, and quite possibly both.

Dispositional alignment is also useful for describing audience responses to crime fiction, which invites both identification with and judgment of characters. It is a notoriously liminal genre that "explores (and thrives on) the border between good and evil, madness and sanity ... and guilt and innocence" (Schwartz 13). Hendricks highlights the fragile balance between these states by depicting the struggles, schemes, and delusions of characters who cross boundaries. With their focus on dark, troubled individuals (and often a femme fatale), these stories have been described as "near-perfect gems of noir" (Lipkin). In particular, these tales appreciate what crime writer George Pelecanos has called the "core psychological aspects ... of claustrophobia and anxiety which drive noir" (Haut

284); they depict people who are trapped, on the edge, and searching for an exit. Hendricks has labeled herself "the original tart noir writer in the states," citing her trademark combination of "sex, violence, and tough female" characters (Smith 66). Persistently addressing the question of "why an individual might commit murder" (Smith 67), Hendricks creates protagonists who are typically damaged, deluded, or fatally vulnerable; yet for all their aberrance, many of her criminals are pathetically, bleakly commonplace. There are no Dexter Morgans or Hannibal Lecters here; instead, transgression is portrayed as a remarkable state into which many essentially unremarkable individuals fall. Transgression becomes intelligible and even familiar through the presentation of characters whose motivations—envy, greed, lust, rage, gluttony—read like a catalogue of the seven deadly sins; yet these characters transcend the ordinary in their extraordinary vulnerability to temptation. As Megan Abbott remarks in her introduction to the collection, these characters share one key feature: they are desperate (12).

The tales that Hendricks labels "Gothic" share much with that tradition, from its characteristic excess and transgression to its concern with power relations and boundaries. "Gothic writing," notes Fred Botting, is "fascinated by objects and practices that are constructed as negative, irrational, immoral and fantastic" (2) as it explores "power, law, society, family and sexuality" (5). These themes are at the core of this collection of tales that depict spousal dominance/subjugation and domestic violence, tales that interrogate notions of family, tales that are splattered with blood, feces, semen, and mother's milk, and tales that are replete with sexual acts ranging from those that some readers might find adventurous to those that are illegal in most of the United States. Like crime fiction, the Gothic also has a distinct "preoccupation with boundaries and their collapse" (Halberstam 23). While Gothic fiction of the early modern era expressed anxiety about the disintegration of political, social, and geographic boundaries, Hendricks locates her anxiety within the enfleshed individual, where boundaries are depicted as indefinite, unstable, and permeable. Sexual boundaries in particular are integral to her vision, which resonates with a Gothic tendency that "both concretizes and interrogates the borders that demarcate sexuality, through representations of the horrifying Other who lurks on the other side of the sexual border" (Anolik 6). In this collection, Hendricks addresses sexual alterity by presenting unusual and transgressive pairings, including acts of bestiality; some of these unions do indeed serve to strengthen and preserve the very boundaries that they transgress, though others do not as clearly conserve or restore boundaries. Moreover, the vast majority of tales in this collection feature first-person narrators, giving their experiences an added immediacy. That many of these narrators are desperate women who use their bodies for power, profit, or violent revenge highlights Hendricks's concern with sexuality's relation to dominance; such narratives tend to continue the traditional Gothic refusal to offer an alternative to its women's fundamental dilemma: "the either/or decision of being beater or beaten" (Massé 8).

Hendricks is often compared with writers of the Southern Gothic tradition, such as Flannery O'Connor; despite the many shared features of their writings, though—including their emphasis on violence, decadence, and the grotesque—simply placing Hendricks's work within this category does not suffice. Nor does comparison with other Florida crime writers who influenced her, such as James M. Cain and Harry Crews.[1] On one hand, her tales clearly demonstrate that the themes of Gothic fiction and their traditional association with wild, decaying, or fantastic landscapes translate well into Floridian settings; the drunken decadence of Key West tourists, a diverse animal population that includes dolphins and hungry alligators, the problematic introduction and proliferation of exotic species, the trailer parks of Lake Okeechobee, the Sunshine State's elderly population struggling to make ends meet, and a category-two hurricane all set the stage for *Florida Gothic Stories*. On the other hand, despite their Floridian flavor, many of the stories in this collection would be right at home in other landscapes of twenty-first-century America. Judith Wilt argues that "[n]o single aspect of plot, image or mood says 'Gothic' to us so clearly as the aspect of place" (276), but for Hendricks, the body has its own Gothic geography. As Doyle writes of Morrison, "[h]er narrators ... make bodies and objects the favored level of the real, a narrative medium and a narrative locale" (206).

Hendricks also pays homage, often playfully, to her predecessors through embedded intertextual references, inviting readers to explore connections between her fiction and its artistic heritage. While these stories are usefully described in terms of their connections to individual works and various generic conventions, Hendricks adapts, interprets, and refashions them to express her own vision—one that can be described as the spectacle of the body, and in particular of a body that serves as stage, landscape, and primary locus of excess and transgression.

Ambivalent, Ambiguous and Alienated Bodies

"Edith would never hurt a fly..."

One of the strategies that Hendricks uses to portray Gothic excess is exaggerated attention to the corporeality of her characters. Her work features frank, detailed descriptions of bodies, and especially of bodies engaged in sexual activity. Taboos are unceremoniously broken as what polite society prefers to keep hidden is luridly displayed; any body part that can glisten, moisten, or harden will most assuredly do so in these tales. They are dramas of embodiment, of the body as sexual instrument, and of the negotiation of identity through embodiment. For example, in "The Big O" and "Sinny and the Prince," two female protagonists pursue courses of action that lead them to experience the paradox of embodiment.

In "The Big O," narrator Candy's world of competing identities is defined via bodily contrasts and juxtapositions and by her relationships to other bodies. Her fond maternal attention to her baby son Chance's "soft little foot" (147) and "sweet skin" (151) sharply contrasts with the degeneracy suggested by the foul, nearly toothless mouth and extensively tattooed skin of Jimmy, the abusive boyfriend whose murder she arranges. Candy is fleeing from abusive Merle when she meets Jimmy, proprietor of The Big O trailer park at Lake Okeechobee. In that meeting, she reveals cleavage generously to manipulate Jimmy into coming to terms with her on a unit that she wants to rent for less than his asking price: "Nursing was handy in more ways than one. I pulled off the road beside a huge pile of trash, and unbuttoned my shirt…. I put Chance's little hand inside my shirt, and he started to knead like a kitten" (149). Candy (nicely positioned next to the trash) takes measures to draw Jimmy's attention to her lactating breast; as it nourishes her baby, it also becomes fetishized as an object of enticement, conflating her female identities as mother and object of sexual desire. Candy's persuasion has the desired effect; she rents the trailer for a short time before moving in with Jimmy, but he soon begins to abuse her. She is already bruised on the morning when her breast becomes a site of further transgression as Jimmy greedily consumes her mother's milk against her will, violating her body and stealing her baby's nourishment. Forcibly holding her down, he is surprised to find that her nipple is equipped not with "only one hole," as he had thought, but with a whole "sprinkler head" (152). Although Candy protests, she is "wet despite [her]self" and reaches a climax even before Jimmy does (152). Candy freely uses her body as a commodity, as the sweet treat that her name implies, until Jimmy crosses a boundary that brings her body's roles—her roles—as sexual instrument and mother into conflict. However, even in her moment of maternal outrage, she experiences arousal; her body performs as something Other, something over which she has no control and from which she is alienated, something paradoxically of her but separate from her. Kelly Hurley notes that in some Gothic tales, "[f]emale sexuality in particular and the female body in general are ... sites of abjection and danger" (118), and this tale inherits that legacy. The female body is mapped as a Gothic landscape; it is an ambiguous space, a site of contradiction and misrepresentation. The implied "sale" of Candy's body—negotiated between the open buttons of her shirt—does not account for her totality of self; the marketplace of her body thus becomes a site of contested ownership and the marker of an unstable border between her competing identities. Like Florida in summer, the female body is lush, sultry, and dewy, but also changeable; to Candy, Jimmy's transgression justifies her own—shedding his blood is retributive justice based on fluid-for-fluid exchange. In the end, she rids herself of both Jimmy and Merle but is also tricked out of her expected profit, and the story closes at a hurricane shelter where she has already spotted a "looker" in a cowboy hat who appears "free and open to suggestions" (167–68); she winks at him while nursing Chance, suggesting renewal of the process of bodily exchange.

A different type of bodily exchange occurs in "Sinny and the Prince," a tale of classic Gothic doubling that dismantles the boundary of embodied identity when Cindy ("Sinny") murders and then takes over the life of her identical twin, Lydia. Cindy's upbringing is a standard nightmare scenario— after her mother, a heroin addict, gives her over to a foster family, Cindy is raped at age ten and routinely subjected to sexual abuse. Her luckier sister, who was adopted by a wealthy family, now lives a life of comfort, which Cindy schemes to steal. In many ways, the plot revisits *Dead Ringer* (1964), which tells the story of Edith, a jealous, financially distressed twin who kills her affluent sister, Margaret, making it look like her own (Edith's) suicide, then assumes her twin's identity (though of course, Bette Davis, in a dual role as both twins, never "slip[s] [her] hand down the front of her [dead twin's bikini] bottoms" to "find the last of her warmth inside" [190]). Cindy plans to divorce Lydia's low-life husband, Hudson, and enjoy her newfound luxury, until Hudson reveals knowledge of the murder and threatens to tell the authorities if she doesn't cooperate with him. Here, Hendricks emphasizes how thoroughly identity is enfleshed and transacted; Cindy is effectively enslaved by the body that she hoped would free her because that body is the one thing through which Hudson can control her—her true identity can be proven through dental records, he points out, which would reveal her one physical difference from Lydia. Like other protagonists in this collection, Cindy is essentially pathetic and ordinary until she undertakes an extraordinary enterprise. Readers may feel sorry for her because of her background of abuse, yet her willingness to kill her sister marks her as transgressive in a way that would appall many. Her punishment—not only that she can't divorce Hudson, but that she will be forced to participate in the pornographic film business that he and Lydia had been running secretly for years—is one that readers can enjoy without much guilt. It also highlights the sinister boundary between public and private selves, a border that is carefully maintained to protect dirty little secrets; Cindy discovers too late that in appropriating the open glamour of Lydia's life, she also becomes ensnared in her sordid hidden life.

As Elizabeth Grosz has shown, philosophical divisions of mind and body belong to a problematic tradition of "[d]ichotomous thinking ... [that] ranks the two polarized terms so that one becomes the privileged term and the other its suppressed, subordinated, negative counterpart" (*Volatile Bodies* 3). This problem permeates these two tales of characters whose attempts to exploit their bodies for personal gain lead to unwanted outcomes; their fates are consistent with Grosz's description of the Platonic view of the body as "a betrayal of and a prison for the soul, reason, or mind" (*Volatile Bodies* 5). Seeking to renegotiate identities that have been associated with their embodied selves, they find that self and body cannot be easily separated. Their dilemma is dramatized through their betrayal by bodies that misrepresent them—or that accurately represent them in unwelcome ways. The body thus becomes an ambiguous, Gothicized landscape that can misdirect the self and undermine its borders.

Anomalous Bodies

"I've Written a Letter to Daddy"

Florida Gothic Stories also explores the connection between transgression and physical alterity. Anomalous bodies may lead individuals into temptation, or they may provide opportunities for individuals to transcend the physical difference that seems to define them. In "Boozanne, Lemme Be" and "ReBecca," Hendricks explores how protagonists with atypical, though not fantastic, anatomical features respond to their embodiment.

In "Boozanne, Lemme Be," Junior is an undersized ex-con who has violated his parole restrictions by leaving Kentucky to come to Florida. Counseled by a man called Weasel (whose name does not augur well), he gains access to the Miami home of "upper-middle-class workaholics" Bob and Melodie Lambert (37) by cutting a hole under their bed. Each day, he enters through a crawlspace beneath the house to enjoy the Lamberts' comfortable living space while they work, then exits before they return. Although he lives transgressively, Junior exhibits compassion and a sort of decency. To offset the parasitism of his lifestyle, he performs small acts of kindness for Melodie, hoping that they will subtly help while remaining safely unnoticed. However, he goes astray when he meets Boozanne, a generously proportioned woman whose carnal temptation he can't resist, from "her soft gut and jelly thighs" to "that sweet spot you don't never forget" (41). Demanding Boozanne induces him to take greater and greater risks with his living situation, eventually persuading him to burgle the Lamberts' house and use their personal documents to steal their identities, then leaves him to take the fall when the plan goes awry. Although the story closes before the authorities arrive, Junior's future is clear: he is "headed back to the slammer for a long, long time" (53). The contrasting sizes of Junior and Boozanne create an image of bodily incongruity while drawing attention to their sexual and power dynamics; Boozanne is immediately empowered because she is "the only woman ever come on to [Junior] that didn't ask for money up front" (43). Because Junior's height (or his response to it) has been an obstacle to sexual fulfillment and companionship, he is particularly vulnerable to Boozanne's advances and, later, to sexual coercion when she demands that he "make arrangements if [he] want[s] to 'continue enjoying her womanhood'" (42). The tale suggests that embodiment alone does not create masters and slaves. Junior feels inferior due to his size; because he believes that Boozanne is "out of [his] league" (42), he readily accepts a subordinate role. Boozanne, however, is confident even though her embodiment is inconsistent with the aesthetic ideals of a culture that commonly represents oversized individuals as "agents of abhorrence and disgust" (LeBesco 1). Written in the space where Junior's corporeality meets Boozanne's, this tale studies the impact of embodiment on identity formation and interpersonal relations while participating in cultural discourse about the politics of difference.

In "ReBecca," a tale of conjoined twins, Hendricks explores the notion of shared identity, with perhaps a polite nod to Daphne du Maurier's Gothic classic of (virtually) the same title. Both tales use a form of doubling as a thematic device, but while du Maurier's *Rebecca* is a psychological study of a woman's obsessive jealousy of her husband's first wife, "ReBecca" is more a fairy tale about narrator Rebelle and her sister Becca, who are connected at the skull and share a brain. The story reveals an extraordinary bond of sororal love even as it imagines the physical experience of conjoined sexuality ("I know where she's got her fingers. There's a tingle and that certain haziness in our head" [55]). Becca has a crush on Remus, and despite her misgivings, Rebelle generously helps Becca get a date with him—even though doing so means that she will witness, of necessity, their passionate union, that her world and Becca's will no longer be a world of two, that she will have to adjust to "the idea of three" (57). For the night of Remus's visit, the sisters rent a video—*What Ever Happened to Baby Jane?* According to Rebelle, it is her favorite, though Becca hates it (59). That Rebelle's favorite film is a horror classic about a jealous washed-up child star's reign of terror over her wheelchair-bound, totally dependent sister seems to forecast sinister developments, but Rebelle is nothing like Jane Hudson; she supports Becca all the way to the bedroom, and, on some level, loses her virginity with her ("We get impulses from the brain, even when our own physical parts aren't directly stimulated" [61]). Though Becca's new romance makes Rebelle feel like "an invisible attachment of nerves, muscles, organs and bones" (63), she is committed to helping Becca. Serendipitously, Rebelle is rewarded when it is later revealed that Remus has a twin brother (Rom, presumably short for Romulus). The extraordinary embodiment in this tale that almost seems to perform as "freak show" is ultimately subordinated to the simple tale of Rebelle's conquest of her feelings of exclusion and loneliness out of love for her sister. Here, Hendricks vividly presents the drama of embodiment—an embodiment that is itself transgressive but that is the stage on which multiple forms of love are enacted, from Rebelle's love for Becca to the love of Remus and Becca and the implied future love of Rebelle and Rom.

The sensationalized bodies in these tales are tools for an inquiry into the limits of embodiment and intercorporeal dynamics. Neither the bodies nor the identities of the characters are static; they exist in a field of reflecting and refracting bodies that renew or reshape notions of self. Elizabeth Grosz views the extraordinary body as a test case for "the corporeal limits of subjectivity ... [and] the inputs and effects of the subject's corporeality on its identity" ("Intolerable" 55), while Rachel Adams, emphasizing the performative aspects of "freak" as an identity, describes the anomalous body as a "figure par excellence for the complex and shifting dynamics of identification, the problems of self and other" (4). These stories embed such notions of anomalous embodiment, inviting readers to scrutinize bodily anomaly not merely in a voyeuristic manner, but as the test case that Grosz describes and as an exploration of the dynamics of identification described by Adams. The bodies in these tales suggest that identity is both a function of biology and a response to it, that identity is effected in bodily exchange and renegotiated through that exchange. In confronting the spectacle of anomalous embodiment, readers are invited to see, perhaps, parts of their own humanity in the extraordinary bodies of the "other" presented here.

Zoophilia

> "You and me baby ain't nothin' but mammals,
> So let's do it like they do on the Discovery Channel."
> —The Bloodhound Gang

Some of the most vivid portraits in this collection are of bodies transgressively paired—in particular, of anomalous relationships between humans and members of other species. By destabilizing the border between human and nonhuman bodies, these pairings violate societal norms and disrupt traditional views of the position of humanity relative to other orders of animals. Ultimately, these relationships also call same-species human relationships into question by highlighting the ways in which various animals fulfill needs that are not being met by other humans. Three stories in this collection explore unusual bonding between humans and nonhuman animals: "Stormy, Mon Amour," "Cold-Blooded Lovers," and "Must Bite!"

The interspecies boundary is transgressed when protagonist Cherie mates with a dolphin (Stormy) and gives birth to a mermaid child, Mineaux (or Minny), in "Stormy, Mon Amour."[2] Cherie tries to escape her abusive husband, Roger, and start a new life with her beloved Stormy and their daughter, but her plan to release him from captivity is thwarted when

Stormy refuses to exit through the hole that she cuts in the wire mesh that imprisons him at Theater of the Sea: "For the first time I wonder if he has ever shared the hot sharp pain of love between us.... It's clear to me that he has never experienced the passionate longing I've read in his eyes" (32). She recognizes the futility of her attempt just as Roger arrives to reclaim her: "I sob into Minny's blanket, with nothing left except the painful knowledge of my lunacy" (34). In this moment, transgressive actions become secondary to simple humanity. Readers easily see in Cherie the plight of a tormented spouse who desires an appealing "other" who differs completely from his/her partner. The failure of her affair with Stormy becomes a tale not of bestiality, but of abuse and infidelity—and in this respect, it becomes intelligible to readers who recognize commonplace marital issues that are expressed in a fantastic manner. Moreover, the fantastic family of dolphin, human mother, and mermaid daughter holds its own surprisingly well against the traditional families found in other tales in this collection. As one reviewer notes, although this story includes potentially disturbing "scenes of interspecies intercourse ... when juxtaposed with similar scenes of sex between humans, they are some of the most tender passages in the book" (Philp). Indeed, Cherie shows heartfelt concern for both her daughter and her dolphin lover. "We're just like a real family," she asserts, "except there's no yelling, no hitting, and no money problems" (21).

In "Cold-Blooded Lovers," the boundaries between human and non-human, *philia* and *agape*, mental stability and psychological dysfunction become uncertain when Gregory Waxman stops taking his medication for paranoid schizophrenia after his wife, Greta, announces that she's having an affair. Estranged from Greta, Waxman develops a deepening relationship with Linguina, his iguana; he considers her his daughter, takes her shopping for fancy outfits, and converses with her. Through their bond, Waxman discovers the nature of *agape*, which he at first mistakes for *philia* (unlike Cherie, he rules out *eros* because "their bodies [are] so different as to prohibit a sexual relationship" [99]), until "Linguina ... put[s] her mouth close to his right ear, and whisper[s] that she [doesn't] think of him as her father" (98). His recognition—whether a disengagement from reality or a transcendent experience of a sublime personal reality—fills him with wonder; he understands that he feels for her an unconditional love that rarely exists between humans: "This was nothing like the love he felt for Greta, far superior, more elegant, eternal" (98). Linguina becomes not only an outlet for his feelings, but a sort of alter ego, a fantasy extension of himself. When he dresses her in extravagant clothing and takes her out, she becomes a colorful appendage that attracts attention that he does not seem to garner on his own. Waxman and Linguina together are no longer either Waxman or Linguina, but rather a new, combined embodiment. Like Cherie, though, Waxman eventually must relinquish his interspecies love; when exposed to other iguanas, Linguina is drawn to her own kind, and he faces a sad choice: "If he couldn't make the sacrifice of allowing her freedom, his *agape* had never been true" (111). His attachment to his cherished Linguina seems somehow more sincere and noble than most of the emotional bonds between humans in the tales.

Perhaps the darkest cross-species bond in this collection appears in "Must Bite!" Narrator Darlene is a dancer/erotic acrobat until she marries Rex, a primate caretaker with four spider monkeys and a chimpanzee named Big Man, who can communicate in sign language. When Rex begins to spend many nights out, resentful Darlene grows increasingly close to Big Man. The sexual aspect of their relationship begins with synchronized masturbation: "When I started to breathe hard, he began to huff.... I was almost there ... and Big Man wasn't far behind" (81). Untroubled by the grotesque parallelism of their acts of self-gratification, Darlene reflects on the kinship between Big Man and Everyman:

> Big Man would sit next to me and doze off with his head on my chest. He'd wake up drowsy and look at my face. Nice, nice! glowed in his round eyes. But the animal was always close. Sometimes he'd jump, as if I'd hit him, and his lips would curl back. Must bite! Must bite! was fighting to take over his brain.... He wasn't so different from the guys at the bar. You never knew with men [82].

Darlene's living arrangement invites a view of embodiment that diminishes species differences. Indeed, the tale demands reconsideration of what separates humanity from the rest of the animal kingdom as the narrator's bond with Big Man soon allows her to train him to kill her husband so that she can collect a million-dollar inheritance. However, what should have been a crime that only C. Auguste Dupin or Edgar Allan Poe fans could solve goes wrong when Big Man, after using his teeth to kill Rex, locks Darlene in the monkey room, slashes Rex with a knife that has Darlene's fingerprints on it, and signs to her through the window, "'Darlene kill Rex'" (89). When he finally releases her, Darlene can neither find the incriminating knife nor coax Big Man into revealing its location, so she tries a last resort: "I turned my back to him, slipped my shorts and panties down, and bent over.... I pushed my finger inside myself to be sure he got the message" (91). Big Man does indeed get the message, and much more as well, but he still will not produce the knife, and Darlene realizes that she is his slave, and he will "rape [her] whenever he please[s]" (92). This tale presents sex as a physical transaction of dominance and control, no matter who consummates the union. The transgressive merging of bodies collapses interspecies boundaries, reverses hierarchies, and raises the question of whether Darlene has sunk to Big Man's level, or he to hers. In either event, this Darwinian nightmare ends with the scales of justice perversely balanced and Darlene's recognition that "[i]t wasn't worth a million" (92).

In the conversation among these three tales, the joining of human and nonhuman bodies creates a space in which identity is transformed. Bodies united, even nonsexually, as in the case of Waxman and Linguina, can be viewed as an instance of what Gilles Deleuze calls an "assemblage," incorporating "states of things, bodies, [and] various combinations of bodies" (177), or a form of the composite body imagined by Jeffrey J. Cohen, building on the notion of the Deleuzian assemblage as "a dispersive network of identity" (xxiv). Indeed, the protagonists in this set of stories share, on some level, their narrative identities with their nonhuman companions. The crossing of species boundaries also serves as a tool for interrogating human notions of love, power, and family. While "Must Bite!" ultimately reaffirms the transgressed species boundary through Darlene's demotion and punishment, the other two tales are not as clearly conservative because the cross-species relationships, even when sexual, have positive qualities that are lacking in the human relationships to which they offer alternatives. Cherie and Gregory Waxman may be confused individuals who misdirect their affections, yet their interspecies relationships have a pathetic profundity and a bittersweetness that are rare in the same-species human relationships found throughout the collection. In contrast, Darlene's perverse exploitation of Big Man is the type of human depravity, matched only by his exploitation of her.

Conclusion

Florida Gothic Stories is a dark theater in which the spectacle of the body is played out relentlessly. Its occasional glimmers of light are nearly eclipsed by the bleakness of its focus on vices—including violence, cruelty, and greed—reminding readers that humans are, by nature, transgressive animals. Although Hendricks has suggested that her "unsympathetic characters are possibly an acquired taste, so far acquired by very few" (Smith 66), the duality of her characters allows readers to experience the provocative ambivalence of comparing themselves to transgressive individuals from whom they can feel safely distanced. Readers can freely judge these characters; they may not like, admire, or fully identify with them, but their problems and temptations are often those of common people, giving rise to a potentially unsettling sense of connection. Readers glimpse, perhaps, parts of themselves in the bullying husband, the meretricious mother, the murderous wife. To those who conduct their lives within the boundaries set by society, those who live at its fringes may seem outrageous, yet Hendricks invites readers to discover their likeness with these marginalized, desperate individuals: "ugliness is a part of life that noir uncovers, reminding readers that they may not be so far removed from at least traces of the lives Hendricks portrays" (Lipkin). By emphasizing how vulnerability and circumstances may combine to lead common people into uncommon territory, Hendricks challenges the fragile illusion of stable identity that many "ordinary" people fight to maintain.

Notes

1. Hendricks cites these authors as influences in an interview with Michele-Jessica Fievre.
2. Such a union was not a crime in Florida when Hendricks first published this story in *Tart Noir* in 2002 or when it was collected in *Florida Gothic Stories*, but it is now.

Works Cited

Adams, Rachel. *Sideshow, U.S.A.: Freaks and the American Cultural Imagination.* Chicago: University of Chicago Press, 2001. Print.
Anolik, Ruth Bienstock. "Sexual Horror: Fears of the Sexual Other." Introduction. *Horrifying Sex: Essays on Sexual Difference in Gothic Literature.* Ed. Anolik. Jefferson, NC: McFarland, 2007. 1–24. *Amazon Book Preview.* Web. 11 July 2013.
Botting, Fred. "Gothic Excess and Transgression." Introduction. *Gothic.* Ed. Botting. New York: Routledge, 1996. 1–20. Print.
Cohen, Jeffrey J. *Medieval Identity Machines.* Minneapolis: University of Minnesota Press, 2003. Print.
Dead Ringer. Dir. Paul Henreid. Warner Bros., 1964. Film.
Deleuze, Gilles. "Eight Years Later: 1980 Interview." *Two Regimes of Madness:*

Texts and Interviews, 1975–1995, revised edition. Ed. David Lapoujade. Trans. Ames Hodges and Mike Taormina. Paris: Semiotext(e), 2007. Print.

Doyle, Laura. *Bordering on the Body: The Racial Matrix of Modern Fiction and Culture*. New York: Oxford University Press, 1994. Print.

Fievre, Michele-Jessica. "*Florida Gothic Stories*: Delightfully Disturbing." *Examiner*. 9 June 2010. Web. 12 June 2013.

Grosz, Elizabeth. "Intolerable Ambiguity: Freaks as/at the Limit." *Freakery: Cultural Spectacles of the Extraordinary Body*. Ed. Rosemarie Garland Thomson. New York: New York University Press, 1996. 55–66. Print.

_____. *Volatile Bodies: Toward a Corporeal Feminism*. Bloomington: Indiana University Press, 1994. Print.

Halberstam, Judith. *Skin Shows: Gothic Horror and the Technology of Monsters*. Durham, NC: Duke University Press, 1995. Print.

Haut, Woody. *Heartbreak and Vine: The Fate of Hardboiled Writers in Hollywood*. London: Serpent's Tail, 2002. Print.

Hendricks, Vicki. *Florida Gothic Stories*. Crawfordsville, FL: Kitsune, 2010. Print.

Hurley, Kelly. *The Gothic Body: Sexuality, Materialism, and Degeneration at the Fin de Siècle*. New York: Cambridge University Press, 1996. Print. Cambridge Studies in Nineteenth-Century Lit. and Culture 8.

LeBesco, Kathleen. *Revolting Bodies? The Struggle to Redefine Fat Identity*. Amherst: U. of Massachusetts P., 2004. *Google Book Search*. Web. 19 June 2013.

Lipkin, Michael. "*Florida Gothic Stories*." *New York Journal of Books*. 10 May 2010. Web. 17 June 2013.

Massé, Michelle A. *In the Name of Love: Women, Masochism, and the Gothic*. Ithaca, NY: Cornell University Press, 1992. Print.

Philip, Geoffrey. "Book Review: *Florida Gothic Stories* by Vicki Hendricks." Web. 17 May 2013.

Poe, Edgar Allan. "The Murders in the Rue Morgue." *Complete Stories and Poems of Edgar Allan Poe*. New York: Doubleday, 2012. Print.

Schwartz, Richard B. *Nice and Noir: Contemporary American Crime Fiction*. Columbia: University of Missouri Press, 2002. Print.

Shaw, Daniel. "The Mastery of Hannibal Lecter." *Dark Thoughts: Philosophic Reflections on Cinematic Horror*. Ed. Steven Jay Schneider and Daniel Shaw. Lanham, MD: Scarecrow, 2003. 10–24. Print.

Smith, Ellen. "Vicki Hendricks, South Florida Noir Specialist." *Florida Crime Writers: 24 Interviews*. Ed. Steve Glassman. Jefferson, NC: McFarland, 2008. 64–73. *Google Book Search*. Web. 19 May 2013.

Walters, Glenn D. "Understanding the Popular Appeal of Horror Cinema: An Integrated-Interactive Model." *Journal of Media Psychology* 9.2 (2004). Web. 3 May 2013.

What Ever Happened to Baby Jane? Dir. Robert Aldrich. Perf. Bette Davis and Joan Crawford. Warner Bros., 1962. Film.

Wilt, Judith. *Ghosts of the Gothic: Austen, Eliot, and Lawrence*. Princeton, NJ: Princeton University Press, 1980. Print.

12

Mary Jane Ryals

Mary Jane Ryals, Ph.D., is a poet and novelist, who was born, raised, and still lives in Tallahassee, Florida. Her secondary and postsecondary education is Florida through and through: Tallahassee's North Florida Christian School, Tallahassee Community College, Florida State University, and Florida A&M University—as well as the University of Florida (Meredith "Have Poems, Will Travel").

Ryals is currently the fiction editor for *Apalachee Review*—where her husband, award winning writer Michael Trammell is managing editor—and she teaches writing in the College of Business at Florida State University. She has earned numerous awards for her literary work including Poet Laureate of the Big Bend of Florida from 2009–2012, and the 2006 Second Annual Yellow Jacket Press Chapbook Contest for her poetry collection, *Music in Arabic*. She is also the recipient of the Florida Arts Council Individual Artist award, and she has been involved in the Tallahassee Writers' Association Festival of Books. Her short story collection, *A Messy Job I Never Did See a Girl Do*, is available from Livingston Press, and her nonfiction book, *Getting into the Intercultural Groove: Intercultural Communication for Everyone*, was released in 2006 ("Mary Jane Ryals." *Goodreads*). She has also released another book of poetry called *The Moving Waters*. Her poetry has been called "delicious, sensory, rapturous, riveting ... a feast for the senses" ("Mary Jane Ryals." *Goodreads*). Ryals is as much a Florida girl as any of our writers, but she travels extensively, spending most of her summers teaching in Valencia, Spain. *Moving Waters* simultaneously chronicles her desire for travel and her love for home.

Her novel *Cookie and Me* won the 2010 Bronze medal from the Florida Book Awards. The book explores a 1960s relationship between two thirteen-year-old girls who are of different races. Ryals felt compelled to write the book "because so much in southern writing does not talk about race," even though the race problem is evident in southern writing (*Furious Fiction*), and she "urgently ... needed to tell [her] era's story to her daughter" (Meredith. "Meet Mary Jane Ryals"). Ryals's novel captures the turmoil of a troubled decade and a problematic friendship without oversimplifying the difficulties or anachronically imposing "twenty first century ideas about race and equality" ("Mary Jane Ryals: Poet Laureate").

Besides her teaching and writing work, Ryals performs her poetry and her friends' poetry in a group called the Black Dog Java Girls. Her co-performers are good friends Lynne Knight, Melanie Rawls, Laura Newton, and Donna Decker. It is little wonder that Ryals has also participated in the Poetry Out Loud National Recitation Competition. She is working on an environmental mystery novel set on the island of Cedar Key, Florida, which will feature a single mom/ hair stylist /detective, who tries to unravel the mysterious death of a close friend—another Ryals's story to watch for!

Works Cited

Furious Fiction: Mary Jane Ryals Interview. 28 Apr. 2012. YouTube. 14 Mar. 2014. http://www.youtube.com/watch?v=4_9dLoJVjyU

"Mary Jane Ryals." *Goodreads.* Goodreads, Inc. 2014. Web. 14 Mar. 2014. http://www.goodreads.com/author/show/391029.Mary_Jane_Ryals

"Mary Jane Ryals: Poet Laureate." *Mary Jane Ryals.* Web. 14 Mar. 2014. http://mjryals.weebly.com/about-mary-jane.html

Meredith, Donna. "Have Poems, Will Travel." *Tallahassee Magazine.* Sept.-Oct. 2008. Web. http://www.tallahasseemagazine.com/September-October–2008/Have-Poems-Will-Travel/

_____. "Meet Mary Jane Ryals, Author of Cookie and Me." *Southern Literary Review.* 2010. Web.

Author Profiles & Interviews. 13 Mar. 2014. http://southernlitreview.com/authors/meet-mary-jane-ryals-author-of-cookie-and-me.htm

Racial Progress, Not Movement, Is Evident as the Trees Slowly Walk in Mary Jane Ryals's Novel *Cookie and Me*

VALERIE E. KASPER

Toni Morrison published her essay, "A Slow Walk of Trees (as Grandmother Would Say) Hopeless (as Grandfather Would Say)," on July 4, 1976, in the *New York Times Magazine*. In it, she illustrates the perception of racial progress through three generations of her own family. Starting with her grandparents, she explains the cautious optimism of her grandmother and the constant pessimism of her grandfather, who was five-years-old when the *Emancipation Proclamation* was signed and believed his entire life that "there was no hope whatever for black people in this *country*" (Morrison 3). His wife, on the other hand, "believed that all things could be improved by faith in Jesus and an effort of the will" (4). Morrison's parents also took opposing views of white society, but instead of focusing on the chance for black Americans' conditions to improve, they disagreed on the chance for white Americans' moral fiber to improve. Her father "distrusted every word and every gesture of every white man on earth," but her mother "*believed* in them—their possibilities" (6). The women in Morrison's family would see "the slow walk of certain species of trees from the flat-lands up into the mountains, [they] would see the signs of irrevocable and permanent change" (5), yet Morrison questioned whether the walk was "progress, or merely movement" (8). She, too, saw disappointment where she thought there was permanent change between black and white relations, but she also saw the future within the children and how black children no longer grew up feeling the need to prove something to white people, and their perceptions of themselves were new and different. The children believe "they *live* here, *belong* here on this planet earth and that it is *theirs*" (14). Morrison decided "the trees *are* walking, albeit slowly and quietly" (11).

Morrison's question of racial progress is illustrated in Mary Jane Ryals's novel *Cookie and Me*. Ryals, who won the 2010 Florida Book Award for general fiction for this novel, was inspired by one of her college professors who made her realize it was her "generation in which the races were thrown together and had to work it out" ("Interviews"). With this in mind, she brings many of her own social experiences to the story, such as the bonding of best friends, the love of horses, and the inability to bring home a black friend (Meredith). In the story Ryals combines racial progress with the psychological and moral journey of a 13-year-old white girl awakened to the world of black America and the country's social values in the 1960s. Rayann Wood is emerged into the world of black America through her friendship with a 13-year-old black girl, Cookie Johnson, and Rayann's discovery of prejudice, both white and black, produces knowledge and strength that enlightens and educates her summer. Both girls learn about the inaccuracies of the commonplace knowledge within their community, and both girls use that understanding to continue to advance the slow walk of trees that is racial progress. Ryals illustrates through Rayann the "ridiculous ideas she's gotten from her culture," and how she "learns to live in a different way" (Interviews). Through their bond of friendship, the girls are able to overcome racial obstacles that might have bolstered the commonplace ideas of the time period. Instead, each girl learns about the other's culture, and this knowledge and understanding allows them to see not only fallacies within their own racial community, but to disregard those fallacies and work for the better good of a homogenized society. They are the future Morrison hopes for in her essay.

Rayann Wood narrates this tale about family, friendship, and racial recognition and understanding. The story is set in Ryals's hometown of Tallahassee, Florida during the civil rights movement of the 1960s, which was the decade before Morrison wrote her essay and the time period in which Ryals was an adolescent about the age of Rayann and Cookie. Rayann's upbringing is during the end of the Jim Crow years in the South and therefore, full of controversial commonplace rules and categories of people, such as white trash, rich people, colored, Negroes, liberals, and crackers. Her mother has been "ill" for three years, suffering from alcoholism and depression, and her father is trying to have her deemed incompetent and sent to Chattahoochee. In the meantime, he is entertaining his friends and girlfriend at their house. During this time, Rayann feels she cannot bring friends to her home, and during her loneliness, she meets and befriends Cookie, one of two Negro girls at her school. Cookie is the niece of Rayann's housekeeper, Miss Jesse, who lives down the street and whom Rayann relies on for unrecognized love and stability in her dysfunctional household. The girls meet one day on the road between their houses. They create a forbidden friendship based on the bonds they share—such as animals, music, nail polish, and boys—and they work through the obstacles and assumptions presented by the time period they inhabit. As they navigate their friendship through disconcerting and dangerous terrain, it forces them to make some difficult decisions and learn some tough lessons about their community and those they love. The girls are both products of their time period, but their friendship allows them to offset and defy the commonplaces of the racially divided and categorized environment within which they live.

Rayann's world consists of categories of people and the assumptions that are associated with those categories. For example, there are three types of black folks: colored, niggers, and Negroes. Colored people are poor blacks who Rayann considers nice people. They live down by the pond in brightly colored wooden houses on Saturday Street; whereas, niggers are those who beat up their wives and are disrespectable. Negroes are "uppity, like those people on TV such as Martin Luther King" and "they wore dapper suits" and "wanted to ride [in] the front of the bus" (Ryals 17). White people also have categories. Poor white trash are "poor like colored people, but they don't have a good excuse for it like colored people" (11), and rich people, like Rayann's mama, drive big cars, eat Sunday fried chicken dinner, run for public office, and "wanted everything to match," like towels, clothes, and baby booties (14). The liberals run the Lewis State Bank, and "only nasty Jewish men" live in The Floridian apartments (81). Rayann considers herself a regular person, which is what happens when a rich person, like her mama, marries a poor white trash person, and, she, herself, is categorized by the kids at school. They call her LRG—little rich girl—which she hates. Through this label, she realizes how being categorized feels and affects people. Rayann understands society's categories and assumes all people fit into one of them; however, she learns that these categories are far more complicated than she originally understood. Initially, everyone fell into a category and was treated accordingly, but Rayann soon realizes these categories are not only flawed, but are used to oppress certain classes of people. It is this understanding that opens up her social consciousness, changes her beliefs, and causes her to make some difficult decisions.

Like Rayann, Cookie, too, makes assumptions about race because the actions of white society in the 1960s have taught Cookie to distrust and dislike most white people. In the beginning, she, also, categorizes Rayann as LRG, and her family refers to some whites derogatorily as redneck, cracker, and hophead. Cookie resents losing her mother and father, and she blames white society. She's bitter that her Aunt Jesse has to work for the Wood family and feels the family is unappreciative and takes her aunt for granted. Like Toni Morrison's family, she and her family have prejudices against whites. Some of these prejudices are justifiable. Rayann's father, AJ, is supposed to pay Miss Jesse $15 a day, but instead, only pays her $8. AJ's friend, Red, claims to have cut off a black man's finger and kept it like one of the animal trophies hanging on his wall. However, Cookie's brother, Ivory Jones, explains how Red obtained the finger when one of his own white friends had a machete accident, thereby revealing white society's belligerence and stupidity. Both these incidents justify the black community's distrust and wariness in white society. Other incidents involving white society focus on commonplace beliefs that blacks drink and steal. Although Rayann had been told these misnomers, she has never seen Miss Jesse drink, but her father and his friends drink and get drunk frequently, and when Rayann and Cookie shop at Woolworth's the saleslady follows Cookie and wrongly accuses her of stealing, until Rayann stands up for her. While some of the assumptions the girls observe about society are assessed and rejected, others, unfortunately, are easily verified in this southern town.

Throughout their friendship, both girls find themselves making difficult decisions and changing their beliefs about these categories and assumptions concerning each other's race as they observe and scrutinize their community. When Rayann and Cookie first meet, Rayann assumes Cookie lives on Saturday Street, where all the other colored people live. Cookie boldly tells her she lives "up here" near Rayann (Ryals 29). Rayann had also been told that "black families drank a lot and fought and talked bad about girls and didn't have moms and dads around" (152). However, once she begins to frequent Miss Jesse's house, she realizes they are a typical family. They are not dirty, nor do they drink a lot. They even have a bathroom instead of an outhouse, which Rayann is thankful for. Miss Jesse's family provides a counter balance for Rayann. Like Morrison's family, Miss Jesse's family is hard working, honorable, and place importance in education. They are the opposite of the racial stereotypes Rayann has grown up hearing. For Cookie, Rayann and her mother, in addition to other whites in the community, provide the possibilities Morrison's mother spoke of. Morrison's mother "believed in [white people] – their possibilities" (Morrison 6). The possibilities for both races cause the girls to dissect their racial beliefs, understand their environment, and consider changes in their viewpoints. By doing this, they fight against the "racial vertigo" Morrison suffers from, and by the end of the book, it appears they have prevailed over their vertigo and see each other's families as human beings, not black or white (8).

Rayann recognizes that Cookie's family has problems just like her family; however, the difference is many of their problems are the result of white society. Cookie's father is in jail for manslaughter. His band was playing in a bar in Montgomery, Alabama when a fight broke out and a man was killed. Her father was convicted based on the word of another white man and did not receive a fair trial. Her mother was unable to handle the deferred dreams and oppression brought on by white society and left. Cookie, like Morrison, blames white society for the inability of black society's condition to improve and also wonders about the likelihood that white society's moral fiber will ever improve. Morrison looks at the past and realizes that the "monstrous events" that took place in her grandfather's time period were "duplicated in alarming detail" in her own (Morrison 4). Racially motivated murder, torture, and riots existed in both time periods 100 years apart.

Ten years before Morrison wrote her article, racial tensions were strong in Tallahassee, and the Rayann and Cookie must face Jim Crow, which has a strong presence in the 1960s South, despite the laws. This not only exacerbates racial tensions, but it hinders society's progress toward equality. From her first encounter with Cookie, Rayann begins to understand the inequality of Jim Crow and its impact on Cookie's family. Jim Crow laws segregated blacks from whites under *Plessy v. Ferguson's* "separate but equal" ruling. These laws were maintained in many parts of the country, and especially in the south, until 1965 when the Civil Rights Act of 1964 was passed. Under *Plessy v. Ferguson* public facilities and services were allowed to be segregated by race as long as both races had access to facilities that were equal. Equality, of course, was a subjective term. In the girls' community of

12. Mary Jane Ryals

Tallahassee, the public swimming pools have been closed because blacks are demanding equality and access to them. According to *Plessy v. Ferguson*, the town needs to provide a public swimming pool equal to that of the white pools for the black community. However, the cost of operating the pools is $20,000 a year. Instead of building and maintaining a pool of equal value for blacks, the city commission chooses to close the pools and place the blame on the town's black citizens. The city commission would rather see the pools closed than see "their kids swimming with filthy colored people" (Ryals 189). When Rayann, Cookie, Ivory Jones, and Johnny secretly sneak into the pool one night and are caught swimming in it, the word spreads, and "not twenty-four hours later" the KKK brazenly, yet under the cover of night, fills all the public pools with dirt (265). Cookie said the black community believed the KKK was just looking for an excuse to close the pools permanently. So, 100 years after the Civil War ended, racial tensions and prejudice are still firmly implanted in the South.

This theme of racial inequality doesn't go unnoticed by Rayann and is constantly brought to the forefront by Cookie and Ivory Jones. They are all part of Morrison's future. Cookie and Ivory Jones have grown up "with nothing to prove to white people" (Morrison 13). They're "the baby sisters of the sit-in generation, the sons of the neighborhood blockbusters, the nephews of jailed revolutionaries, and a huge number who have had college graduates in their families" (13). Their perceptions are different than the generation before them, which is evident in the beliefs and philosophies between Cookie and Ivory Jones and their Aunt Jesse. Aunt Jesse doesn't want to draw attention to them; she wants changes but is fearful of speaking out because of certain whites in the community. Cookie and Ivory Jones have a different attitude. They want society to change for the better, and they want to speak out. Rayann, too, wants to speak out. She comments how the soda fountain at Woolworth's is closed because blacks want to use it, and how the Top 40 records are kept separate from the Motown records. The movie theater has segregated seating, and blacks sit in the balcony, where it "was baking hot-as-the-devil ... in the summer time" (Ryals 259).

In addition, Tallahassee Memorial Hospital, where Rayann's father works, is for whites only; black society is relegated to A & M Hospital. However, it is well-known that A & M Hospital is old, and its equipment is outdated. According to Ivory Jones, who is allowed to work at the white hospital due to his athletic ability in track, the lighting at A & M is like the inside of a Coke bottle, and the "black hospital ain't worth a damn"

(Ryals 103). Inequality continues when Rayann and Cookie go into town because Tallahassee's public bus system is also segregated with blacks sitting in the back of the bus, despite the fact that Rosa Parks defied racial segregation 10 years prior in Montgomery, Alabama. Tallahassee's bus driver makes Rayann sit up front with him, and she feels that *her* freedom, too, is being taken away because she can't sit with Cookie (188). Separate but equal is not taken literally in Tallahassee in the 1960s, despite the law, and the Rayann, Cookie, and Ivory Jones realize the law doesn't mean the people in the South will abide.

The one area in town that isn't segregated is the school; however, whether this is progress or just movement has not yet been determined. In 1954 the Supreme Court ruled against *Plessy v. Ferguson's* "separate but equal" policy in regards to the school system. *Brown v. Board of Education of Topeka, Kansas* stated that schools were inherently unequal, and struck down the constitutionality of *Plessy v. Ferguson*. Therefore, Cookie and Rayann attend the same school, but as Rayann notices, no one talks to Cookie. In addition, Cookie doesn't ride the school bus because the older boys said they didn't want "no niggers riding on their bus" (Ryals 38). After the humiliation of being kicked off the bus one morning, Cookie chose not to ride it ever again, and understanding the dangers of challenging the situation, her Aunt Jesse didn't contest the issue. Rayann, however, said they had to let her ride the bus because it's the law, and Cookie replied, "the law don't mean they'll let me" (38). Rayann is starting to realize what blacks have known for decades: white society doesn't always follow the law when it comes to racial matters. Rayann also understands what the boys did is unfair and wrong, and she believes that other people know this too. However, if she speaks her mind, she also knows she will be considered a "nigger lover, which is much worse that being called LRG" (38). Rayann realizes these categories help maintain the racial divide because it keeps those who may disagree with racial inequality from challenging the current system, and it takes her until the end of the story to find the courage to speak out.

The girls realize unfairness and injustice is much easier to identify than it is to stand against it. Throughout their friendship, the girls must make decisions about when to challenge the status quo. Some of these decisions have lesser consequences than others. Cookie stands up for Rayann when other black children call her a white bitch, and Rayann stands up for Cookie in Woolworth's when the saleslady accuses her of theft, but Rayann is incapable standing up for Cookie in school when some of the white girls call her names because she lacks the confidence and strength needed. However, being called a "nigger lover" is a lesser consequence than the dangers that exist for blacks when interracial relationships are discovered. The girls know from the moment they first meet that their friendship is forbidden, and Rayann knows her father would not be happy if he caught her with a colored girl. Miss Jesse, too, is concerned about the girls' friendship but for different reasons. She understands the danger of their friendship and the risk of sheltering Rayann. She plainly states to her nephew, Ivory Jones, that she "don't want to be harboring nobody whose daddy's friends hate colored folks" because "it might be [his] finger next" that gets cut off by some white man (145), and when their pet goose Waldo is killed, the family knows it's a warning because "when [whites] visited in colored people's houses, blood started to spill" (41). Rayann and Cookie experience prejudice firsthand from both sides of the racial line, and with each act of prejudice the girls encounter, their understanding and disdain for the current racial atmosphere grows.

Nonetheless for Rayann, prejudice is not just part of society. It's part of her family, and it hits close to home as she discovers her father's bigoted beliefs. The perception of white America by the men in Morrison's family is plainly shown through Rayann's father, his friends, and many in the community. They are the reason Morrison's grandfather believed "that there was no hope for black people in this country," and her father "distrust[ed] every word and every gesture of every white man on earth" (Morrison 3, 6). AJ Wood is the administrator at Tallahassee Memorial Hospital, which only serves the white community. According to Rayann, he came from white trash, but he learned to speak correctly, and "he urged every blessed body else too" (Ryals 11). AJ hides his past from the community—his Indian heritage. Only Rayann and her mother know his real name is Antelope Jumper Wood. Everyone else calls him AJ or Allen. AJ made the choice to assimilate into white society. Instead of becoming a voice for minorities, he becomes a force against them. By oppressing another minority, it elevates his own status and deflects attention from his own heritage. AJ believes blacks aren't like whites, not acknowledging that he, himself, is not white. He never acknowledges his own people's history with the white man. Instead, he focuses on the black minority. He complains about "fighting those hospital niggers" (183) when a black woman approaches him to admit her son into Tallahassee Memorial because "the colored hospital didn't have the right medicine, and he'd already lost one leg and was about to lose the other" (132). AJ refuses. He lacks any sympathy for the woman or her son because he does not see them as human. He said she "wanted to put her son in *my* hospital" (132). He believes if society "give[s] them an inch, [then] they'll take a country mile. Put them in the schools and soon enough, they'll be wanting to eat with us" (132). Rayann slowly begins to realize how the white patriarchal men in Tallahassee maintain their power and supremacy by looking at women and blacks "like they weren't human beings" (232). These men look down on women as subservient, obedient objects, and blacks as less-than-human beings.

These men stand in stark contrast, though, to some of the other white characters in the story, including Rayann's mother, Elizabeth Wood; the Tallahassee Memorial Hospital emergency tech, Skip; and the Ellis State Bank president, Mr. Ellis. Rayann's most important role model is her mother, Liz, who transforms from the traditional upper-class woman of this time period to a stronger, more modern woman. They are the reason Morrison's grandmother "believed all things could be improved," and her mother believed in white society's possibilities and possessed an "open-mindedness in each new encounter" with them (Morrison 6, 8). In the beginning, Liz is a weak character, who is more concerned about her appearance than her child. By the end of the novel, she is strong enough not only to take ownership of her situation, but also to challenge her husband's authority. Realizing her marriage has disintegrated, Liz speaks out. She tells AJ that if he doesn't admit Cookie into Tallahassee Memorial to treat the concussion she received during the demonstration-turned-riot at the public pool, then she will make their divorce "so bad the judge would have him walk out without the shirt on his back" (Ryals 309). Another example of white progression is Skip, the medical tech who cares for Cookie outside of Tallahassee Memorial after she receives her concussion. Knowing Cookie can't be admitted to the hospital and knowing white patients are being brought to the hospital from the riot at the pool, Skip is still willing to treat Cookie. Jeopardizing his own reputation and risking possible bodily injury, Skip returns time and time again to help treat Cookie until Mrs. Wood forces her husband to admit her. Then, it is Skip who carries Cookie to the Emergency Room. The final example of white progression is Mr. Ellis, who is placed in juxtaposition with Rayann's father because Mr. Ellis is a white man of stature. He owns one of the banks in town, a bank he allows the black community to use. In addition, he also is known throughout the black community as someone who will help them. When Rayann meets him, she notices immediately he is different from her father's friends because he doesn't look at her chest; instead, he talks directly to her (274). It is Mr. Ellis who educates Rayann on the law concerning her mother's mental confinement at Tallahassee Memorial; he is the impetus for her mother's final push toward freedom from both the hospital and her husband. These white people epitomize racial progress. These are the white people who Morrison's mother *believed* in and who had possibilities. These are the white people who challenge the system, demand improved conditions for the black community, and demonstrate that white America's moral fiber can improve. These are the models of humanity whom Rayann looks upon for guidance; they provide her with the direction toward progress, not just movement.

Rayann always believed that racial problems stemmed from the fact that "colored people were a mystery" to whites (Ryals 30). Colored people thought differently, and whites didn't understand them. As Morrison points out, it isn't that colored people thought differently; history had taught them not to trust white society, and once Rayann realized this, they were no longer a mystery to her. Another more difficult problem in the community was a lack of communication because "you didn't talk about colored and white problems" (38). The girls' education about one another's race allows them to understand, communicate, and empathize with each other's situation and environment. This ability and opportunity to understand, communicate, and empathize allows them to overcome their own racial beliefs. It gives them perspective. They look at each other as human beings and not just by the color of their skin. At the end of the novel when Cookie is knocked unconscious at a demonstration-turned-riot at the public pool, Rayann overcomes her fear of being called a "nigger lover." She elicits help from the white pool maintenance man who once worked at the hospital to take her and Cookie to Tallahassee Memorial Hospital. When he refuses, she persists until he acquiesces. When they reach Tallahassee Memorial, Rayann again overcomes her fear and cries out to Skip for help. In her panic, she tells Skip that Cookie is her "friend, her best friend, and she lives across the woods," and he needs to help her (292). It is the first time she openly admits their friendship to anyone. By the end of the novel, the colored community is no longer a mystery to Rayann, and she is able to speak up in support.

Ryals felt the need to "tell [her] era's story," and she hopes her readers remember that the "surface isn't everything" and that there is depth, and society needs to remember that and approach life with an open mind (Meredith, "Interviews"). Unlike Morrison, Ryals was part of the future generation who had to work through their racial differences because they were thrown together in a society full of controversial rules and stereotypes. She shows through her characters that although the situation was "messy and difficult," it taught the girls that "people are people are people" ("Interviews"). Ryals illustrates through the novel the changing attitudes of her own generation. According to Morrison, the children and young adults in black society also have different attitudes; they believe they *belong* here on this earth and that it belongs to *them* (Morrison 14). Rayann sees the difference between Miss Jesse's attitude toward white America and that of her niece and nephew's attitude. Cookie and Ivory Jones believe America belongs to them, and as such, they should have equality. Though, at times, it may not look like racial progress; though it may look like the disappointment Morrison ponders, it is progress, not movement. Morrison points out numerous examples of progress in her essay, and Ryal's novel shows that the trees are walking slowly. Miss Jesse owns her own property, and it isn't living on Saturday Street. Ivory Jones works in a white hospital, and he helps and cares about Rayann and her mother. Mr. Ellis, the white bank owner, helps the black community in town. Cookie is the first "Negro to ever get treated at Tallahassee Memorial," a white hospital (Ryals 310). Struggles for equality are happening for access to the public swimming pool and the local soda fountain in Woolworth's. The black community is realizing its worth and place within white society, and is fighting for its place within American society. The novel may trace the psychological and moral growth of one thirteen-year-old girl in a Southern city in the 1960s, but it also shows the awakening of an entire community as the trees slowly begin to walk; though this time, they aren't so quiet.

Works Cited

"Interviews with the 2010 Award Winners." *Florida Book Awards*. Florida Book Awards, 14 July 2011. Web. 05 Dec. 2013. http://floridabookawards.lib.fsu.edu/videos/2010/interview/.

Meredith, Donna. "Meet Mary Jane Ryals, Author of Cookie and Me." *Southern Literary Review*. Southern Literary Review, 28 Aug. 2010. Web. 15 Nov. 2013. http://southernlitreview.com/authors/meet-mary-jane-ryals-author-of-cookie-and-me.htm.

Morrison, Toni. "A Slow Walk of Trees (as Grandmother Would Say) Hopeless (as Grandfather Would Say)." *What Moves at the Margin*. Jackson: University Press of Mississippi, 2008. 3–14. print.

Ryal, Mary Jane. *Cookie and Me*. Crawfordville: Kitsune Books, 2010. print.

Appendix: Interviews

BY APRIL VAN CAMP

Interview with Lynne Barrett

Why did you choose to set much of *Magpies* in a Florida landscape?

I selected the stories for *Magpies* from among a larger number of them that I'd written and published over several years. I chose ones I felt shared thematic elements, particularly how values tested by the pressures caused by opportunities or threats—both of which are, paradoxically, dangerous. The first story in the book, "Links," is set in New York and New Jersey during the dot com boom and bust, so it contains a giddy rise and rapid fall. It comes first chronologically and I also felt it set up the way storytelling itself would be of importance all through the book. The other tales are all set in various parts of Florida, a place full of promise—for a new life, safety, escape, prosperity or fame. Several characters are involved in reclaiming old things—houses or antiques, while others are developing, making new places on the map. At the same time, the state draws threats, from hurricanes to economic storms to crime. And it's a place of both fame and notoriety: One story looks at the gossip "boom" (which shows no signs of stopping), while another includes a formerly gossiped-about femme fatale.

Is there anything in your particular area of Florida—or your original home—that influenced your decision to set the character's life there?

I drew on places I know in New Jersey, where I grew up, for "Links"— and later a character from that story makes a brief cameo appearance on Miami Beach's Lincoln Road in "The Noir Boudoir." I used a number of places in South Florida, where I've lived for 25 years—but I also drew on Southwest Florida for "When, He Wondered," while a part of "One Hippopotamus" takes us to central Florida. I've also used other Florida places in stories not in this collection—for instance, "To Go," in an earlier collection, *The Secret Names of Women*, is set at old tourist attraction on Route 27, in the middle of the state. To me, character and place are deeply intertwined, each affecting the other.

I often lightly fictionalize my places, so that whether the reader has been to that place or not, I will be describing it freshly, with the aim of heightening reality. For example, I like inventing new place names, as I did for Peregrine Springs in "When, He Wondered," or Tangerine Gardens (which has neither citrus trees nor gardens) in "Cave of the Winds." Even in a real, named place, like the Upper East Side of Miami in "The Noir Boudoir," I will invent a neighborhood hangout (Cafe Nublado), or a famous old building (The Delphi), which I then can describe in a way that concentrates into them, I hope, some essence of the place. Often I sketch maps while I'm writing, so that I know what's out a window, and which way the water is.

If your protagonist is from another state, then what makes the character particularly Floridian? I am thinking particularly of characters like Ray Stout in "Noir Boudoir."

Some of my characters come from not just other states, but other countries. In this book, Jen, who grew up in Virginia, moves to South Florida for work and falls in love with Carlos, who was brought from Chile as a child to rescue him from a dangerous political situation. Florida is the crossroads where this relationship can happen and where both may grow through understanding each other, as at the culturally mixed-up Christmas in "Gift Wrap." Someone like Ray, who was a cop in New Jersey before he retired to an old deco neighborhood in Miami, is part of a group of antique dealers that includes, among others, a gay man from the North Carolina, a middle-aged woman who has watched her native Miami change, and a son of Cuban immigrants: their love for old objects, history, and lost worlds brings them together.

For me one crucial element that defines what is "Floridian" involves displacement, whether that means coming from somewhere else, through choice or necessity, or, for those who were born in Florida, feeling displaced (which can be frightening or exciting, or both) because of rapid development and the ever-changing mix of people. In "When, He Wondered," the two main characters grew up in my fictional Peregrine Springs, and they explored every inch of it, including its sinkholes, as boys. They love it, but have been part of making the town over into a place of golf villas and shops, so that they see it doubly, as it was and as it is. To me, that's Floridian: everybody is reckoning with transformation, which they may resist or find freeing, and everybody is carrying memories of some lost past, whether that was bright or dark.

From your own observations, what is distinctive about Florida women writers, and how do you fit in?

I think Florida women writers are bold: they are not bound by presumptions. In the work of Florida women writers I've read, the paradoxes of Florida's environment, its mix of beauty, danger, strangeness and fragility, extend to character. Toughness and vulnerability and desire and criminality and courage can be found in a multitude of combinations in Florida characters without regard to gender: who entices, who endangers, who rescues whom: it's not predictable.

As for me, I aspire to do what I've just described, of course. Florida's constant changes make me feel free to change, too. Living here, I feel no limit to what I'm "allowed" to do: I write stories that may be a mystery or center on family conflict, may show a grim reality or include a bit of magic or the surreal, and I can lay claim to places I've explored without having lived in them forever—and all of that, it seems to me, is Floridian.

Who is your favorite female Florida writer? Why?

I don't have a single favorite writer. I do have a favorite form, the short story. I read short stories with great pleasure, and I think that the form suits Florida, where one person may have several, disconnected, lives. A few story collections I think readers interested in Florida women's writing should read include *St. Lucy's Home for Girls Raised by Wolves* by Karen Russell, Vicki Hendricks' *Florida Gothic, Vida* by Patricia Engel, and Mary Jane Ryals' *A Messy Job I Never Did See A Girl Do*—all quite different from each other. Two other Florida books that have meant a lot to me in my own writing are the memoir *Space*, by Jesse Lee Kercheval, about growing up in the Cape Canaveral of the 60s and 70s, and Lu Vickers' *Weeki Watchee, City of Mermaids*, which offers fascinating Florida history and portrays (in writing and photos) some truly inspiring Florida women.

How have your experiences with Florida weather or climate contributed to the setting of the *Magpies* stories that use it as a backdrop?

I was affected a lot by the seasons of many storms: 2004 with Charley, Frances, Ivan, Jeanne all crossing the state, and then, topping that, the most active Atlantic hurricane season ever, 2005, which went all the way on to Epsilon and Zeta. Katrina knocked power at my house before going on do so much more damage elsewhere and Wilma hit us very hard. I found myself interested, especially, in the anxiety that followed, the desire to prepare, and the dread as we got to the point of watching the smallest possibility of a storm appear off of Africa on the satellite maps. A hurricane season is itself a kind of suspense form, I saw, and I used that in "Cave of the Winds." Our wild thunderstorms helped me find the premise for "One Hippopotamus" (where the title is a way of counting seconds between the lightning and the thunder). On the other hand, our very beautiful weather is also part of our setting: it's the allure that brings people here, the underlying premise of development. The sunlight, and the shadows it casts, plays a part in the imagery of "When, He Wonders," for instance, and the fantasy world for visitors built on top of natural beauty on South Beach come together in "Gossip and Toad."

Characters Jen and Carlos appear in three stories within the *Magpies* collection. What was it about this couple that led to your making that decision?

I first wrote what is now the middle story, "Gift Wrap," where the characters are married with a young son. For the first Christmas since the death of Jen's mother, Jen's family descends on them, wanting her to replicate the home and holiday they knew—which is, of course, impossible. I found myself, after the story was published (first in the *Sun-Sentinel*, then in two anthologies, *Irrepressible Appetites* and *A Dixie Christmas*), still thinking about the couple. How did these people from such different backgrounds find each other? So I decided to go back to when they were newly together, on a night when it could be that they would split apart or that they'd become more involved. Though I knew that outcome, they didn't, and it was exciting to write, knowing this night would have consequences beyond what they could imagine. The story, "One Hippopotamus," is told in Jen's point of view, but, after the power goes out in a storm, in the heat and dark Carlos tells her a story about his past that he might never have told her otherwise, and everything is changed by it. That story was published in *Apalachee Review*. Sometime later, I began to imagine a story about the anxiety of a hurricane season and the ways people respond to that. I realized that its focus on home as a shelter and a place of vulnerability connected to things I'd touched on in the other two Carlos & Jen stories, and that this would be a good one to tell from Carlos' point of view. From that grew "Cave of the Winds," which is set later in the marriage, and tests it.

There are two crime stories in *Magpies*, and you've published others, what is it about crime that interests you?

I'm interested in fraud, and imposture, and secrets. This shows up in both my crime and non-crime stories. The fact that my father was an insurance fraud investigator is undoubtedly relevant here, but I'm sure my fascination began earlier. For me, story requires some sort of transgression, someone crossing a line, which might be criminal, or moral, or some rule in a relationship, or tradition in a family. For that line to be crossed, a character must have some strong drive, and then doing it changes both that character and others. In some situations, transgression may be liberating, but it always has consequences. Crime, of course, immediately brings tension as well as expectations about justice (which may or may not be fulfilled). In "The Noir Boudoir," I was drawn to the idea of an old crime resurfacing and instigating a contemporary one, which happens just before the start of the story. Where we come in, a group of antique dealers are dismantling what is—though this is not yet evident—a crime scene. My former-cop antiques dealer investigates, and his voice telling the story contains echoes of classic noir; it's a story about the long reach of the past. In "When, He Wondered," I got fascinated, during the period when the economy went into free-fall, with the idea of someone who'd been prospering and riding high, who might be desperate to rescue what he could by faking his own death. There's a bravado about this, a transgressing of the line of life and death, which leads to unexpected danger, and so this became a suspense story. On the other hand, the mere threat of crime adds tension. In *Magpies* the last story, "Texaco on Biscayne," is set at a gas station late at night, where it is an island of light in the darkness and a place of possible refuge or danger.

Appendix: Interviews

What can we look forward to next, Lynne? When the next edition of Women of Florida Fiction comes out, we are certain you will be represented!

Since *Magpies* came out, I've been writing both essays and stories. Recent stories with Florida settings have appeared in *Real South* magazine (online) and an anthology, *Blue Christmas,* and new ones are coming out in *Fort Lauderdale Magazine* (April 2014) and the anthology *Fifteen Views of Miami* (Fall 2014). More fiction is in the works.

Interview with Jennine Capó Crucet

Why did you choose to set How to Leave Hialeah in a Florida landscape?

I don't know if I chose South Florida as a landscape as much as the landscape chose me. I was living in the Midwest when I first started writing the stories that would come to comprise the book, and the long, freezing winters made me so homesick that the only way I could pull myself out of the ice-induced despair was to force my imagination south—to send my imagination home for a little while every day while working on a story. Once I had enough stories that I knew I was writing a book, setting became the guiding organizational principle behind it. I guess I chose to set the stories in a South Florida landscape because I missed that landscape so much, and it felt very urgent to me that I evoke it for (and in) myself.

Is there anything in your particular area of Florida—or your original home—that influenced your decision to set the characters' lives there?

I think the heat is important: I think it adds a source of tension to the stories, to have characters literally sweating in discomfort. There's also, at least where I grew up, a tremendous amount of noise all around that I never, ever noticed when I lived there, but which now, after having lived in quieter cities, permeates everything. That sort of noise contributes to a character's sense that they are part of a bigger world, and the ways in which they ignore or embrace or push up against that noise says a lot about how they move in the world, about their personality.

If your protagonist is from another state or nation, then what makes the character particularly Floridian?

I don't know if I know, exactly, what it means to be Floridian, except that Cuban-Americans who ended up calling other parts of the U.S. home seem different from the Cuban-Americans made in Miami in big ways. I think South Florida's Cubans feel a sense of pride in having helped make the city the vibrant, productive, international city Miami has flourished into over the last fifty years, but I know not everyone feels that way. Maybe it's more simple than that: maybe it's that they love fruit? Maybe it's each character's complete inability to function in temperatures below 45 degrees?

From your own observations, what is distinctive about Florida women writers, and how do you fit in?

I think there's a boldness in the prose and in the choice and approach to subject matter. There's a palpable energy and heat to the work. I'm not sure how I fit in—that's probably a question for a critic or a scholar—but I know that I sense it and that I hope to tap into that lineage with every sentence I craft.

Who is your favorite female Florida writer? Why?

Zora Neale Hurston, whose novel *Their Eyes Were Watching God* I first encountered in high school and which made such an impression on me that it compelled me to really become a serious, intense reader (the first step to being a decent writer). It was the first thing I'd read with which I connected, and which felt very real to me. It was also the first time I felt the power a book could have. I felt a huge sense of pride at learning that Hurston called Florida home.

Why do you think Florida women writers are so underrepresented in terms of critical work?

Having lived in a few other states for long enough to make a dent in my psyche, it's clear to me Florida has a bad rap, and that from the outside, it sometimes looks like we deserve it. We're slowly creeping down the wrong lists, joining the ranks of states that don't value higher education (in the very real sense, when it comes to funding), and that makes a bad impression on a national stage. I don't know the actual numbers, but I'm not surprised to hear that Florida women writers are underrepresented when it comes to critical work—especially when *all* women writers are having a tough time getting their voices heard in that department.

Your work *How to Leave Hialeah* makes a powerful statement for Latinas, indicating they may choose their life course and break away from prescribed cultural roles. Who influenced your break from the more traditional female roles, or do you consider yourself traditional?

I'm not sure if anyone influenced me in this specific way, or if I really think about what I do in terms of "traditional" or not. I always made things with words; I found out you could do that and maybe teach other people to do it; that seemed like exactly the life I wanted, so I set myself to that with the help of my family and the right mentors at the right time in my development. I think if I *could've* been happy doing something—anything—else, I would've tried to follow that path instead.

There *is* a sort of guilt that comes with following your dream, because for me it's meant that I don't live near my parents, and I guess in the Cuban family that's not typical or traditional, but again, that guilt feeds my work. And I tell myself that everything I'm doing for my life now will eventually enrich the lives of my parents. I would've resented them forever if I hadn't felt empowered enough to follow my calling. I think my parents got out of the way of my weirdness, as they perceived it, and I'm very grateful to them for that.

Who supported and motivated you in your artistic and academic paths? What would you say to him/her now?

Aside from my parents, my grandmother was a fantastic storyteller and always the center of any party. She held court. I wanted more than anything to be like her in those moments, and learning how to tell a good story was, I thought, key to that. She was also a singer in Cuba, but the Communist revolution and family life stunted that path for her, and I think she saw my wanting to be a writer and an artist an extension of her dreams, an opportunity afforded by this country and her and my grandfather's sacrifice in leaving their homeland.

Later on, I was lucky to find an amazing mentor, the novelist Helena Maria Viramontes, when I was in college, and the fact that she existed as someone I could talk to and who took my work seriously meant the world to me. She was (and is) a tremendous example to me, someone who carved a place for herself in American literature through the sheer power of her writing. After her, the writer Charles Baxter had a huge impact on my development as an artist and as a teacher of creative writing. When it comes to craft, he really did teach me everything I know and helped me see how much I still had to learn. To both these mentors, I would say thank you for taking me and my work seriously. Thank you for your time, as every time I knocked on your doors with a new story in my hands it was time I would be taking away from your own writing, stories and novels the world needs so much.

What pressures do you feel as a Latina academic? How do you negotiate these pressures if, in fact, you think the pressures exist?

Oh, the pressure definitely exists. There are certain expectations about the work I produce, and when it's perceived (rightly or wrongly) as "divorced" from my ethnicity, people don't exactly know what to make of it. I've begun writing stories, for instance, about Floridians living in other states, and sometimes the response from editors has been, "But this isn't set in South Florida, this isn't what you, um, *do.*"—so I sometimes feel the pressure to "perform" a certain version of my own work (or their vision for my work), which is dangerous and which I'm trying to push past with every new thing I write.

Also, as far as academia, it seems like I'm on a short list of go-to people for any "initiative" connected to diversity, which sort of makes me feels as if my role as a faculty member is more limited than it should/could be. I also think the nature of the questions I get asked about my work tend to focus heavily on some aspect of my heritage or my ethnicity. I'm not sure why this happens so often, but I'd be just as eager to answer questions about fiction craft and technique, about my teaching philosophy, about my approach to workshop—the kinds of questions I imagine other writers and teachers of creative writing tend to get.

How do you keep your heritage alive and part of your academic world?

I go to as many student-initiated events/forums/panels on campus as I can manage—anything that builds community and helps students feel like their professors are approachable and engaged. I teach Latino lit courses and take on student research projects that come out of that course even when I probably shouldn't (I'm still working toward tenure, and my own research should come first: perhaps this response on my part is just a re-visioning of the "traditional" role for a Latina brought up in the earlier question, a new Academy-friendly one?). I listen to Power96 (a cheesy Miami party-music station) via live-streaming in my campus office and

Appendix: Interviews

refuse to be embarrassed by it. And I go down to Miami as often as I can, to recharge my batteries.

Interview with Vicki Hendricks

Why did you choose to set your Gothic stories in a Florida landscape?

Arriving in Florida at the age of twenty-one, I grew up here, so it's the only place I know well enough to write about, but I couldn't have chosen any better. I learned scuba, sailing, skydiving, and birding in Florida, and lived in Key West for several months. Most likely, the steamy settings, insane characters, and adventure here have forced me to exude fiction as a brain release. Where else do you have ancient carnivores and poisonous snakes roaming free in the suburbs? There's that alluring tropical sheen complicated by hidden danger.

In addition, except for certain urban areas, Florida is the South and shares a Gothic soul. The state is rich in the grotesque, that feature of twisted psychology or physical abnormality defined by Southern Gothic literature. It's all asking to be explored.

If the character is a northern transplant, then what makes the character particularly Floridian?

Especially in the greater Miami area, we've always had an influx of new dreamers, refugees not only from other countries, but fleeing icy temperatures, past failures, and creditors up North. "Normal" people who lead happy lives don't tend to risk everything to move to this state of wild, often negative, reputation. Now, unlike in the seventies, when I was not acquainted with any native Floridians, people have families here. But we still get the dissatisfied, the adventurers, the ones not afraid to lose—or with nothing to lose. Obviously, my kind of people. I think of Cherie in "Stormy" and Mouse in "Boozanne, Lemme Be," both inspired by real people and events that begged for expansion. I brought their natural tendencies to the state of Florida to be fertilized and encouraged to bloom.

How do you fit into the group of Florida women writers?

Actually, I can barely wedge myself in anywhere, not just in Florida. In my noir novels all the protagonists are murderers, which is uncommon, and the amount and explicit nature of the sex scenes are outside the boundaries for mystery and crime. My offbeat short stories, again because of graphic sexual content and much plot, are neither literary or mainstream. However, I like the idea of sidling up to Heidi Boehringer in noir, sharing a strangeness with Karen Russell, and claiming the Gothic South with Connie May Fowler. Regardless of the uncomfortable fit, I'm thrilled to have my work featured among all of the unique Florida writers in the book and look forward to finding further connections.

Who is your favorite female Florida writer? Why?

I would have to say Lynne Barrett. Her particular understanding of human nature and the ability to encapsulate moments of contemporary life resonate for me. Her style is intelligent, yet tough, textured like expensive suede. Lynne is sought by journals and collections for her literary stories, but she dabbles in crime, and with one such dabbling won an Edgar Award for her story "Elvis Lives." Lynne makes it all seem possible to reach perfection in structure and style.

I have more insight than most, since Lynne Barrett was my instructor and mentor for my MFA in Creative Writing at Florida International University, and I still pick her brain whenever I get the chance. Having graduated in 1992, I missed out on brilliant lectures on plotting that she has developed over the past several years, so I follow her wherever she speaks. Her latest collection, *Magpies,* holds my favorite recent story "Gossip and Toad," a combination of fantasy with gritty real life with her brilliant sparkle.

Why do you think Florida women writers are so underrepresented in terms of critical work?

They're not in New York—that's a joke. However, we are missing the clout of *The New York Times*, and I believe the reputation of Florida plays a part. As a vacation state, considered low-ranking in education and high in vice, I suspect we're overlooked sometimes. Also, many Florida women write in the crime genre, which is traditionally underrepresented in terms of academic criticism. Often considered a popular and lesser genre due to the importance of pacing and plot, crime is in a different sphere. Sometimes it does pay, however.

In an interview with Stacey Cochran, you talk about "the fantasy you never had." After reading some of your work, I find it hard to imagine a fantasy you have not had! I truly say this with humility and admiration. Where do you get your ideas? What do you think about to imagine your characters in their situations?

That's a little scary, thinking that my stories grow from personal fantasies, but I guess that's one way of looking at it! Thank you for the compliment, nevertheless. I wish imagination was always available, but that's my major stress in writing. I take Robert Olen Butler's advice in keeping my "dream space," a place and time for writing, but it's not foolproof. I can tell you that since I have quit writing short stories over the past few years, I haven't had any new ideas. I think most of my inspiration comes from being open to weird quirks of human nature and unusual events or turns of phrase. When I'm looking for fodder, some tiny detail will strike me as amusing or incredible, and the rest of the story eventually slides into focus.

For example, the story "ReBecca" suggested itself to me as I walked past the TV where twins conjoined at the head were being interviewed. One of the women had dyed her hair red, and there was a line of demarcation against her twin's natural brown. I started imagining all the everyday complications and, of course, wondering what they did about sex. The story practically boiled out on its own with so many directions to go. It was a matter of choosing, instead of straining for scenes. I cautioned myself to stay far away from cliché, but the territory was mostly wide open. Since I don't have many serious convictions or knowledge that I trust, I feel free when I'm on a subject where few people can contradict me.

Your work certainly crosses boundaries, but as Dr. Angela Tenga suggests in her *Women of Florida Fiction* essay on *Florida Gothic Stories*, your work also addresses issues of love and power. Do you see these two states—raw, human, and animal—as central to your work? If so, then why and how? If not, then what do you see as central to your work?

I can't wait to read the essay, but without knowing more, I can say yes—I've certainly focused on those issues for my characters. That's what the drama of life is about, especially concerning sex. From *Miami Purity* onward, I've nurtured the influence of James M. Cain, whether I'm writing crime, erotica, or uncategorized fiction. The animal nature of Cain's characters, often regarding sex, is what first drew me to him.

Also, *animal* means *innocence*. Cain's desperate characters are thrown into a world they never chose, without the power to save themselves, and all they know is to fight, tooth and nail. Take out the murder and you have Nineteenth Century Naturalism, characters trapped by their heredity and environment. But they won't settle for it. Their lower economic and educational levels produce a rawness. They're struggling individuals, stripped down by their needs, unable to hide the earthy truths. My new novel *Fur People* has been referred to as *proletariat*. I see that I've been in working class territory throughout my writing career. Cain, Bukowski, and Carver characters have always fascinated me, and lately I've found Willy Vlautin.

Please talk to us about *Fur People*. The book's cover is as alluring as its title!

The more animals the better. The dogs and cats on the cover represent some of the starring non-humans in the novel. They live on the bus and around it, and Pancho and Rufus have their own slightly anthropomorphized viewpoints. Depending on the reader's beliefs concerning animal communication and UFOs, there could be science fiction involved. Not surprising, the protagonist has an obsessive, passionate personality similar to characters in my noir novels. She's an outsider. Her extreme love of animals, life of poverty, and a refusal to live by society's rules force her into the woods with her fur family of thirteen dogs, six cats, a couple of ferrets and rabbits, and more litters on the way. Nature and the setting of Central Florida are key to her struggle, and the lives of other people, as well as animals, are negatively affected as she draws them in against their better judgment.

It's a darker book than I expected to write. I had told myself not to write another novel about a crazy person battling normal society since readers relate to sane people pitted against a world of insanity. But now I realize that my definition of *crazy* differs from most people's. I didn't know that Sunny was a clinical case until I was far into her. I agree with her motivations and principles and admire her strength and perseverance. She's extreme, whereas I'm not, but if I had her courage, I might be. Eventually, I went all the way and dropped a bi-polar, homeless man into the mix. He's my favorite. I'm not interested in writing about normal people. I might as well face it.

What can we look forward to next, Vicki? When the next edition of *Women of Florida Fiction* comes out, we are certain you will be represented!

I have an idea for more animal-based fiction that I'm eager to try, another clinical case, but with doing publicity for *Fur People* and teaching my classes, I haven't been writing any fiction for the last few months. It might just keep fermenting in my brain until I retire in two years—or explode.

Interview with Angela Hunt

Why did you choose to set *Five Miles South of Peculiar* in a Florida landscape?

I've set several of my books in Florida—*The Elevator, The Note, Unspoken*, and probably more I can't remember right now—because it's a unique environment and I know it well. I was born and raised in Central Florida, and who doesn't like to write about their hometown?

Is there anything in your particular area of Florida—or your original home—that influenced your decision to set the character's life there?

I live in Pinellas County, so I set *The Elevator, The Note*, and *Unspoken* here because I'm so familiar with the area—and it's beautiful. *Five Miles South of Peculiar* is actually set in north Florida, closer to Georgia, because that area is much more "southern" than central Florida. I wanted a relaxed southern lifestyle for that small town story, and there aren't many small towns in the Tampa Bay region.

If your protagonist is from another state or nation, then what makes the character particularly Floridian? I am thinking particularly of your pastor in *Five Miles*.

I don't think the pastor was Floridian ... he was a transplant, if memory serves, and nearly all of my real-life neighbors are transplants from someplace else. Florida natives are particularly rare, especially if you go back a generation or so. I'm convinced that the hordes didn't move to Florida until after the invention of central air conditioning! But as to what makes a typical Floridian, I think it's a relaxed attitude and a welcoming air. Florida is a true melting pot.

From your own observations, what is distinctive about Florida women writers, and how do you fit in?

I don't actually know many other women writers in Florida, but I can't help thinking of Marjorie Kinnan Rawlings ... perhaps we appreciate nature more than most. Native Florida, with its palmettos, mosquitos, and spindly pines, is not stereotypically beautiful, but it holds a unique charm. And who can forget our beautiful beaches? I grew up on the East Coast, and now make my home on the West.

Who is your favorite female Florida writer? Why?

Marjorie Kinnan Rawlings—because she wrote about ordinary people and their foibles, but placed them in natural Florida. I think my stories are about universal human problems, but I often chose Florida as a location purely for reasons stemming from my affection for the state.

Why do you think Florida women writers are so underrepresented in terms of critical work?

Perhaps we are not writing for a "critical" audience? I write for my readers, not for the literary crowd. I write books that my book club would like to read (though I'm not in the habit of offering them my own work!).

Your work in *Five Miles* and many of your books makes a powerful statement concerning Christianity, showing faith as a primary consideration in your characters' decisions. Do you think notions of faith are particularly female? Why does faith play such a significant role in your work? What pressures do you feel as a Christian, academic female author? How do you negotiate these pressures if, in fact, you think the pressures exist?

I am aware of a strong prejudice against those whose works are often labeled as "Christian fiction," probably because many academics consider Christians to be bellicose, belligerent, and bigoted. I would point out that prejudice is prejudice, no matter who does the prejudging.

I consider myself a writer who happens to be Christian, and most of my books are written to the world at large, not only to a Christian audience. Yet an element of faith almost always shines through because the Christian faith is an integral part of my world view. Every writer exposes his or her world view in their writing, and many novelists expose their existentialism or atheism without any comment from literary critics except praise for their intellectualism.

I suppose faith is often mocked because it is what it is—a strong belief that often appears to defy evidence to the contrary. But the Christian faith is not baseless—it is grounded in historical fact, a sound biblical record, and respect for an intellect higher than mankind's. I don't see Christian faith as inherently female because it is founded in orthodoxy and complex reasoning, not emotion (despite the histrionics of some contemporary groups—those run counter to Scripture, which commands us to conduct ourselves "decently and in order").

How do I negotiate these pressures? For the most part, I ignore them. Long ago I learned that if someone did not care for my work, they simply were not my ideal reader. And trust me—I probably receive more criticism from Christians than from any other group. But I write for people who enjoy my kind of unexpected story, no matter what their belief system.

Who supported and motivated you in your artistic and academic paths? What would you say to him/her now?

I would first have to mention Janet Williams, who taught several English classes at Rockledge High School in Brevard County. I sat under her for several semesters, and while I never felt particularly talented in writing at that age, she did teach me more about writing—and teaching—than any professor before or since. By the time she passed away, I had sent her several of my books and received the most affirming words I can imagine: "I would have read from this in class."

Second I would have to thank Derric Johnson, director of the musical ensemble with which I traveled the country for a year. On an all-night drive from one city to another, he asked what I wanted to do for the next year … and then told me that singers were a dime a dozen, but I ought to consider writing because I had a way with words.

I took his words as spiritual advice, and if not for that conversation, I probably wouldn't be writing today. Many times I have told him how he influenced my life, but not only mine, but thousands of others as well. He is a pastor in every sense of the word.

In your book, *Five Miles South of Peculiar*, you include a number of romances, but the narrative is much more layered than a typical romance book. How would you describe the genre where this book fits?

Definitely women's fiction. A romance is a story in which the romance is the principal plot, and I don't think I've ever written a true romance. I appreciate love—I've been happily married for 33 years—but I find other issues much more fascinating. Women's fiction is the genre I'd define as "stories about mature women and their problems."

In some of your other novels located in Florida, the settings are real cities, but in your latest novel, you choose to create the imaginary town of Peculiar. Is there a specific reason for this?

Yes—I wanted to create a small town with a distinctly Southern feel, and there aren't too many towns like that in central or south Florida. We have been too heavily influenced by transplants from other states, Cuba, Haiti, and a thousand other places.

And I really wanted to use *Five Miles South of Peculiar* as a title. The title popped into my head one day while I was boarding a plane, but at the time I was working on another book. Yet I loved the title, so, just for fun, I wrote a scene where my protagonist was reading a book called *Five Miles South of Peculiar.*

A few months after that book released, I received a letter from a woman who said she'd searched hi and low on the Internet trying to find the book *Five Miles South of Peculiar*. After that, I knew I had to write a book with that title ... so I had to have a Florida town with that name.

Tammy Powley sees your writing in the tradition of Jane Austen—a pretty high compliment from where I sit! Do you see your work aligned with any of the classic authors?

Wow. I'm honored by the compliment. I haven't really thought about how I might fit with other classic authors, but I grew up reading novels by Margaret Mitchell, Charlotte Bronte, and Louisa May Alcott. Maybe a little of their style rubbed off on me?

Of course I read all sorts of authors, too, which may explain why my books tend to be so diverse. Except for my series, none of my books are linked and few are even similar. Which is why my motto is "expect the unexpected."

Or, to echo Forrest Gump, my books are like a box of chocolates. You never know what you're gonna get.

About the Contributors

Camila **Alvarez** is an assistant professor at Indian River State College teaching rhetoric and composition. She is a first generation college graduate and American citizen. Her parents immigrated to America in 1952 from Cuba moving to Florida in 1972. Her interests include pedagogy, digital media, imagery, gaming in the classroom, networking learning, feminist media, and transcontinental literacy.

Lori **Cornelius** was raised in the foothills of the Arkansas Ozarks in a family of storytellers. She received an M.A. in creative writing from Vermont College, then a part of Norwich University, and has published poetry, short stories, and nonfiction. She teaches writing and literature at Florida Gulf Coast University, and lives in Naples, Florida.

Wendy **Dwyer** teaches developmental English at Indian River State College. She has been an award-winning freelance writer and columnist for newspapers and magazines in New York and Florida. She is a graduate of Ithaca College and Concordia University. She is also a founding member of the Van Duzer Foundation, a not-for-profit organization designed to help families in St. Lucie County, Florida, facing severe hardships.

Jane Anderson **Jones** is a professor of literature and humanities at State College of Florida, Manatee and Sarasota. She is the co-editor of *Florida in Poetry: A History of the Imagination* and author of a biography of the artist Frida Kahlo. Born in western New York, she has been a resident of Sarasota, Florida, for over 30 years and considers herself a transplanted Floridian.

About the Contributors

Jill C. **Jones** is a professor of English at Rollins College. She has published articles on Harriet E. Wilson, Toni Morrison, Marjorie Kinnan Rawlings, James Weldon Johnson, and Jerry Springer. As a researcher, she is particularly interested in how American history and literature influence contemporary American culture.

Valerie E. **Kasper** earned a bachelor's degree from the University of Florida in journalism, an M.A. in mass communications from the University of South Florida, and she is working on a Ph.D. in the Text and Technology program at the University of Central Florida. She teaches composition, literature, and journalism classes in the English Department at Saint Leo University.

Sarah M. **Mallonee** earned a Ph.D. from the University of Florida, where she studied British and Irish literature of the nineteenth and twentieth century. Her scholarly interests include Anglo-Irish literature, women's literature, and Florida studies. She coauthored an essay on Florida's snowbirds entitled "Snowbirds Seek Solar Solace," which appeared in *Florida in the Popular Imagination.*

Maxine Lavon **Montgomery** is a professor of English at Florida State University where she teaches courses in African diaspora, American multiethnic, and women's literature. Her books include *The Apocalypse in African American Fiction, Conversations with Gloria Naylor* and *Contested Boundaries: New Critical Essays on the Fiction of Toni Morrison.* She is also writing on the specular presence in Toni Morrison's *Home.*

Lisa K. **Perdigao** has a Ph.D. from Northeastern University, and she is an associate professor of English at the Florida Institute of Technology. She is the author of *From Modernist Entombment to Postmodernist Exhumation* and co-editor, with Mark Pizzato, of *Death in American Texts and Performances.* She has also published essays in collections on Adrienne Rich's poetry, Toni Morrison's fiction and prose, William Faulkner's *As I Lay Dying,* and Caribbean women's writing.

Tammy **Powley** is an associate professor of English at Indian River State College in Ft. Pierce, Florida. She earned a Ph.D. in texts and technology as well as an M.A. in literature at the University of Central Florida. Her academic research interests include women's literature, southern literature, narrative, and domestic technology. Her publications include academic works as well as commercial "how-to" books and articles for digital media companies.

About the Contributors

Beate **Rodewald** completed her undergraduate work at the University of Freiburg, Germany, and earned an M.A. in English from Slippery Rock University of Pennsylvania and a Ph.D. in English from Kent State University, Ohio. She is on the faculty of Palm Beach Atlantic University and researches comparative and interdisciplinary subjects, with special interest in utopian studies, and teaches classes on literature and the arts and literary theory.

Claudia **S. Slate** is a professor of English at Florida Southern College in Lakeland, Florida. She has published articles and presented on Florida literature and history and has edited four volumes of *Florida Studies*, the annual proceedings of the Florida College English Association.

Angela **Tenga** earned a Ph.D. from Purdue University, where she specialized in Old and Middle English language and literature. She teaches courses that focus on literature, history, and popular culture at Florida Institute of Technology. Her research interests include early English literature, the literary monstrous, and serial violence in fiction.

April **Van Camp** is a professor of English at Indian River State College in Fort Pierce, Florida. She has a Ph.D. in texts and technology and an M.A. in literature, both from the University of Central Florida. Her research interests include narrative and memoir, women's literature, photographic and cultural theory and Florida literature. She has published several essays, a chapter in *Florida Crime Writers* anthology, and was editor for the 2008 edition of *Florida Proceedings*.

Index

abandonment 43, 47, 110, 114
aberrance 173
abuse 70–71, 74, 95–98, 100, 110, 172, 175–177, 181
alignment 172
alligator 11, 13–17, 20, 22, 24, 26–28, 30, 32–33, 35–36, 44, 86, 111–112, 119, 174
Alvarez, Camila 8, 66, 219
Alvarez, Julia 64
Alzheimer's disease 48
ambiguity 115, 35, 171
ambivalence 172, 184
animal 17, 31, 33, 45, 98, 109, 122, 170, 174, 180, 182, 184, 191–192, 212–214
anthropology 101
Aristotle 41–42, 46, 49
Army Corps of Engineers 31, 34
artist 78, 107, 157, 166, 174, 187, 208–209, 216, 219
As I Lay Dying 220
Asperger's Syndrome 42–43, 46–48
Atlantic 11, 39, 115, 155, 169, 204, 221
"Ava Wrestles the Alligator" 22
Austen, Jane 6–7, 123–132, 217

Barrett, Lynne 8, 51–56, 58, 60–61, 170, 201, 211
"Baseball Dreams" 161
Baxter, Charles 209
beach 22–24, 58, 81, 109, 112, 115–116, 118–119, 145, 147, 150, 161, 165, 201, 204, 215, 221
Before Women Had Wings 78
Bigtree, Ava 12, 15–19, 22, 24, 27–36

Bigtree, Chief 15, 26
Bigtree, Hilola 26, 29
Bigtree, Kiwi 27, 29–30, 36
Bigtree, Osceola 15, 27
Bigtree tribe 26–27, 36
Bird Man 16, 27, 30–35
Bishop, Elizabeth 3, 7
boat 19–20, 23, 27, 34, 44, 59, 150
Boehringer, Heidi 8, 109–120, 211
book clubs 6, 121, 215
"Boozanne, Lemme Be" 178
boundaries 112–113, 118, 126, 136, 138, 171–174, 176–177, 180–181, 183–184, 211–212, 220
"The Boy Who Fell from Heaven" 166
"The Boy Who Was Rescued by Fish" 165
"The Boy's Triumphant Return" 165
Brevard County 16, 216
Broward County 112, 115–116
Brown v. Board of Education 195
Butler, Robert Olen 212

Cain, James M. 51, 174, 212–213
Caldwell 124, 128–129, 135, 137–140, 142–144, 169
cancer 26, 40, 47–48, 114–115, 127
Capó Crucet, Jennine 7, 8, 63–64, 66–70, 72–75, 206
Caribbean 164, 220
Carnival Darwinism 30, 36
Carpentier, Alejo 164
Carr: Five Years of Rape and Murder 145
Cassadaga, Florida 45
Castro, Fidel 158, 160–161
Catholicism 81–84

223

Index

Catts 91, 93–94, 96–98, 100
"Cave of the Winds" 53, 56, 58, 202, 204–205
character 1, 7, 12, 14–15, 17, 19, 20–24, 27, 29, 30, 33, 36, 42–44, 46, 53–54, 56, 61–62, 64, 67, 69, 73, 79–83, 85, 88, 91, 94–95, 100, 103, 105–107, 110, 112–114, 124–126, 128–131, 133–138, 142–144, 147–148, 150, 152–153, 158–159, 163, 166, 169–173, 175, 177, 179, 184, 197, 199, 201–207, 210, 212–215
Chasing Jordan 109, 113, 119
childhood 12, 17, 21, 34, 36, 74, 77, 82, 94–95, 98, 159–160, 163
Christianity 69, 81–84, 5, 121–122, 124, 187, 215–216
"The City of Shells" 15, 17–18, 22
civil rights 93, 105, 190, 193
Cocoon 12, 133, 138
"Cojimar" 165
The Color Purple 82
comedy 41–46, 48–49
conceal 136–137
"Confusing the Saints" 162, 165
conversational retellings 45
The Corpse Had a Familiar Face 145, 147, 154
courage 43–44, 93, 99, 115, 195, 203, 213
crime 15, 21–23, 60, 145, 146–149, 151–153, 169–170, 172–174, 182, 201, 205, 211–212, 221
Crossing the Dark 109, 111, 117–119
crossroads 202
Cruel Poetry 169
Cuba 63, 66, 68–69, 72–73, 116, 147, 155, 157–167, 202, 207–208, 217, 219
The Cult of True Womanhood 113
culture 63–64, 67–68, 70–72, 75, 80, 92, 94, 96, 102–103, 105–106, 113, 119, 155, 178, 190, 220–221
cypress 80

Dangerous Sex: Three Stories 169
Darcy 126–128
dark humor 3–40
Dead Man's Daughter 146
death 6–7, 19, 26, 30, 42–44, 47–48, 54, 60–61, 79–86, 89, 94, 109, 111, 114–116, 128–129, 137–138, 145, 148–151, 153, 164, 188, 204–205, 220
Deen, Paula 104
dementia 47, 164
deviance 171
Dexter 133, 173

diaspora 7, 220
Disney World 133
displacement 83, 157, 162, 167, 202
dispositional 172
Dominicans 158
Domino Park 159
dredge 27, 30, 32–33, 36
DuFresne, John 170
Dust Tracks on a Road 79, 87, 89
dysfunction 43, 46, 93–94, 96, 99, 181

economic storms 201
elderly 17, 40, 42, 174
The Elevator 122, 214
embodiment 31, 115, 117, 171, 175, 178–180, 182
empowerment 64, 80, 100, 118, 131, 178, 208
Engel, Patricia 203
environment 78, 188
Epic Laws of Folk Narrative 29
escape 7, 18, 34–35, 44, 59, 74, 77, 97, 110, 113–115, 118, 151, 157, 159, 162, 164, 166, 180, 201
ethnicity 102, 209
Everglades 12, 27, 30, 111, 119, 150, 153
excess 60, 115, 133, 171, 173–175
exile 157–159, 161–162
exotic 31–32, 160, 174

fairy tales 31
faith 80, 87, 89, 128, 142, 156, 165, 189, 215–216
fame 128, 148, 201
family 5, 11–12, 14–16, 18, 20, 21–23, 26–33, 36, 40, 42–43, 46–50, 56–57, 64, 70, 72, 75, 78, 91–103, 114, 117, 126–127, 134–140, 142–143, 151–153, 155, 161–163, 173, 176, 181, 183, 189–190, 192–193, 196, 203–205, 208, 213, 219
Faulkner, William 100, 220
feminism 6, 111–113, 117–118, 219
fiction 3, 5–9, 11–12, 26, 39–41, 46, 51–53, 63–65, 71, 78, 82–83, 92, 94–95, 101, 106–107, 111–115, 117–119, 121, 123–126, 128, 131–135, 139, 142, 145, 147–148, 153, 155, 158, 163, 168, 171–174, 187, 190, 202–203, 206, 209–210, 212–217, 219–221
The First Paper Girl in Red Oak, Iowa, and Other Stories 39
Five Miles South of Peculiar 122–123, 128, 130, 134–135, 137, 139, 142–144, 214, 216–217

Florida 1–3, 5–9, 12–21, 23–24, 26–27, 31–32, 39–40, 42–43, 45–46, 51–54, 56–58, 61–64, 66–67, 72, 73, 77–86, 88–89, 91–93, 95–96, 101–109, 111–113, 115–117, 119, 122–127, 129, 121–135, 137–139, 142–155, 159, 162, 164, 167, 169–174, 176–178, 183, 187–188, 190, 201–204, 206–207, 209–212, 214–215, 217, 219–221

Florida Gothic Stories 169, 171–172, 174, 177, 183, 212

folk tales 28, 31–32

forbidden 8, 111, 113, 172, 191, 196

forests 31

Fowler, Connie Mae 6, 8, 77–88, 112, 211

fraud 205

freedom 93–94, 98, 100, 118, 165–166, 182, 195, 198

Freud, Sigmund 94, 135–136

friendship 2, 5, 12, 14, 17, 22–23, 33–34, 45–46, 49, 55–57, 70–71, 73–74, 77, 80–84, 87, 94–95, 103, 105, 126–127, 129–130, 136, 140, 148, 152–153, 158–162, 175, 188, 190–192, 195–196, 198, 209

Fur People 169, 213–214

Gatorland 16–18

gators 11, 13–20, 22, 24, 26–28, 30, 32, 33–36, 44–45, 86, 111–112, 119, 174, 192, 205

gender 7, 6, 70–72, 95, 113–114, 117, 203

ghost 12, 15, 19–21, 24, 27, 29–30, 33–34, 92, 98, 101–103, 105–106, 108, 115, 117, 142–143

"Gift Wrap" 202, 204

González, Elián 165

"A Good Man Is Hard to Find" 83

"Gossip and Toad" 53, 58, 204, 211

Gothic 7, 12, 80, 93–96, 98–100, 169, 171–177, 179, 183, 203, 210–212

grace 79–87, 90

"Greenleaf" 83

grief 13, 19, 46–48, 78, 84–85, 91, 109, 128, 147, 162

Grotesque 94, 95, 96, 97, 100, 171, 174, 182, 210

guilt 19, 48, 61, 84, 109, 110, 114, 117, 118, 119, 130, 148, 166, 172, 177, 208

"Haunting Olivia" 11, 15, 19, 20, 22, 25

Havana 155, 158, 167

heat 64, 104, 107, 127, 148, 149, 151, 152, 204, 206, 207

Hendricks, Vicki 8, 169, 170, 171, 172, 173, 174, 175, 177, 178, 179, 184, 185, 203, 210

"Her Mother's House" 163

Hiaasen, Carl 2, 3, 134, 142, 144

home 1, 2, 5, 8, 11, 13, 14, 15, 17, 19, 24–27, 29, 30, 35, 40, 44, 46, 53, 57, 60, 61, 64, 71, 73, 74, 79, 80, 82, 85–87, 89, 92, 95, 96, 98, 99, 101, 102, 107, 109, 112, 115, 117–119, 121, 122, 126–130, 134, 135, 137–140, 143, 144, 149, 151, 152, 154, 156–158, 163, 164, 166, 167, 174, 178, 187, 190, 191, 196, 201, 203–208, 213–215, 220

horror 94, 97, 98, 115, 147, 172, 179, 184, 185

How to Leave Hialeah 63–67, 71, 74, 75, 206, 208

human 1, 15, 16, 23, 32, 41, 42, 44, 46, 48, 49, 61, 73, 78, 81, 84, 85, 87, 94, 97, 111, 148, 149, 151, 170, 171, 180–183, 193, 197, 198, 211, 212, 213, 215, 219

Hunt, Angela 7, 8, 34, 102, 121–124, 126–144, 214

hurricane(s) 53, 56, 57, 59, 122, 148, 162, 174, 176, 201, 204, 205

Hurston, Zora Neale 2, 6, 7, 79, 80, 82, 85–87, 89, 90, 112, 142, 143, 207

identity 27, 29, 36, 64, 66, 68, 70, 72, 76, 86, 87, 95, 104, 105, 107, 108, 113, 116–119, 131, 135, 142, 143, 157, 159, 163, 175–177, 179, 180, 183–185

imposture 205

In Cuba I Was a German Shepherd 155, 157–159, 163, 167

"Interview with a Moron" 39

invasive species 27, 32

island 12, 15, 16, 18–24, 26–29, 31, 32, 34, 51, 82, 121, 144, 188, 205

isolation 16, 19, 29, 110, 114

Johnson, Derric 216

Jones, Jane Anderson 8, 157, 219

Jones, Jill C. 7, 79, 220

Kasper, Valerie E. 8, 189, 220

Kelsey, Angela 53, 62

Kercheval, Jesse Lee 203

Kindness Project 77

King, Martin Luther 104, 191

KKK 194

landscapes 5, 94, 138, 174
"The Last Rescue" 162
The Last War 156, 157, 163, 167
Latina 63, 208, 209
"Links" 201
Little Havana 158
loss 7, 13, 14, 26, 27, 31, 35, 43, 61, 64, 78, 95, 110, 114, 133, 134, 137, 142, 143, 159, 162, 167
love 1, 13–15, 17, 30, 36, 39, 40, 42, 43, 45, 46, 49, 54, 55, 56, 60, 71, 73, 78, 80, 81, 82, 85, 86, 88, 89, 94–101, 106, 110, 114–116, 119–120, 123, 124, 126–132, 136, 140, 141, 146, 148, 149, 151, 153, 161, 162, 166, 171, 179–183, 185, 187, 190, 191, 195, 196, 198, 202, 203, 207, 212, 213, 217
Lydenberg, Robin 135, 136, 144

magic 12, 13, 18, 19, 21–23, 34, 52, 53, 58, 64, 69, 79, 91, 106, 163, 170, 203
Magpies 51–53, 59, 62, 201, 204–206, 211
Mallonee, Sarah M. 7, 93, 220
marriage 46, 47, 58, 60, 77, 92, 109, 114, 117, 124, 125, 130, 131, 137, 160, 162, 163, 197, 205
Martin, Treyvon 104
McLane, Maureen 55, 62
Melaleuca 31, 32
memory 33, 45–47, 49, 50, 70, 84, 89, 99, 106–108, 148, 158–160, 214
Menéndez, Ana 8, 155–159, 161–167
mermaid 39, 42–46, 50, 180, 181, 203
A Messy Job I Never Did See a Girl Do 187, 203
Miami 12, 20, 56, 59, 61, 63, 64, 66, 72, 73, 76, 101, 109, 133, 145–151, 154, 155, 157–162, 165, 166, 178, 201, 202, 206, 207, 209, 210, 212
Miccosukee 17, 28
modernization 134, 138, 141
Montero, Britt 146–150
Montgomery, Maxine Lavon 8, 111, 220
Montgomery, AL 193, 195
Mormino, Gary 133–135, 138, 139, 142, 144
Morrison, Toni 8, 114, 115, 117, 120, 171, 174, 189, 190, 192–194, 196–199, 220
Mother Nature 18, 24, 148
The Moving Water 187
"Mudlavia" 39
murder 46–48, 60, 61, 88, 115, 118, 119, 145–147, 151, 153, 172, 173, 175–177, 184, 185, 193, 210, 213

Music in Arabic 187
myth 7, 8, 27, 43, 56, 58, 91, 96, 133, 144

Navakas, Michele Currie 134, 139, 143, 144
Necee, Regis 60, 62
Never Let Them See You Cry 145
Nip/Tuck 133
noir 53, 59, 60, 62, 118, 120, 169, 170, 172, 173, 184, 185, 201, 202, 205, 210, 211, 213
noise 260
nostalgia 17, 159, 161, 167
notoriety 201

Obama, Barack 104, 108
O'Connor, Flannery 7, 40, 79–83, 85, 89, 90, 169, 174
Olrik, Axel 29, 30, 37
Olshan, Joseph 55, 62
"One Hippopotamus" 53, 56, 60, 202, 204
oral tradition 28, 36
ordinary 49, 121, 163, 170, 173, 177, 179, 180, 184, 185, 215
Owens, Janis 8, 91–93, 95–103, 105, 107, 108

parks 14, 32, 112, 134, 174
Parks, Rosa 195
"The Party" 161
past 5, 13, 14, 17, 18, 29, 36, 44, 47, 52, 55, 59, 60, 94, 99, 101, 102, 105–107, 110, 115, 135–137, 139, 141–144, 148, 159–161, 163, 164, 193, 196, 203–205, 209–212, 214
peculiarity 43, 67, 117, 122, 123, 128, 130, 132, 134–139, 142–144, 159, 170, 214, 216, 217
Peregrine Springs 202, 203
"The Perfect Fruit" 159
The Plutonium Files: America's Secret Medical Experiments in the Cold War 40
Poetics 41
politics 46, 50, 72, 96, 107, 108, 142, 179
Powley, Tammy 1, 7, 8, 13, 123, 217, 220
prejudice 72, 99, 105, 125–127, 132, 190, 192, 194, 196, 215
The Problem with Murmur Lee 78–82, 85, 88–90
Pycior, Casey 56, 57, 62

race 7, 60, 68, 75, 101–104, 107, 108, 188, 190, 192, 193, 198

Index

Radcliffe, Ann 94, 124
rape 16, 32, 34, 70, 84, 114, 118, 145, 176, 183
Rawlings, Marjorie Kinnan 2, 3, 7, 79, 80, 85, 90, 215, 220
relationships 2, 41, 43, 56, 70, 71, 129, 135, 137, 138, 140, 158, 162, 175, 180, 183, 196
retirement 5, 22, 42, 46, 59, 60, 145, 158, 202
The Revenge of the Radioactive Lady 39, 40, 42, 46, 49, 50
romance 7, 71, 101, 121, 123–125, 127, 128, 131, 132, 179, 216
Russell, Karen 1–3, 8, 11–19, 21–37, 203, 211
Ryals, Mary Jane 8, 187–192, 194–199, 203

St. Augustine, Florida 77, 79, 80–85
St. Lucy's Home for Girls Raised by Wolves 1, 2, 11, 13, 15, 25, 203
saw grass 17, 20, 28
The Secret Names of Women 202
secrets 91, 94, 160, 177
Seminole 28
settings 1, 2, 7, 8, 12–15, 17, 19–22, 24, 39, 48, 52, 53, 56, 64, 87, 96, 109, 112, 113, 115, 117, 135, 142, 147, 148, 151, 170, 174, 204, 206, 210, 213, 217
sex 23, 33, 47, 48, 54, 66, 67, 70, 75, 95, 103, 112, 114, 116, 118, 120, 129, 169, 171–176, 178, 179, 181–185, 211, 212
shell 13–15, 17–20, 22, 25
Showalter, Elaine 112, 120
Slate, Claudia 8, 53, 221
slavery 102, 106–108, 115
space 24, 53, 55–57, 69, 95, 99, 112–114, 116, 119, 136–138, 143, 164, 171, 176, 178, 183, 203, 212
Standiford, Les 170
"The Star-Gazer's Log of Summer-Time Crime" 15, 21, 22, 25
stereotype 8, 42, 105, 172, 193, 199
storm 18, 46, 53–55, 57, 68, 148, 151, 162, 169, 180, 181, 201, 204, 210
"Story of a Parrot" 159, 160
storytelling 8, 28, 29, 53, 54, 56, 58, 59, 61, 74, 91, 101, 154, 163, 201
Stuckey-French, Elizabeth 7, 8, 39–48, 50
suffer 14, 47, 48, 78, 79, 93, 95, 97, 100, 110, 114, 118, 157, 162, 191, 193
swamp 12, 15, 16, 22, 26–28, 30–33, 35, 35, 80, 102, 105, 106, 152

Swamplandia 1, 11, 12, 15–17, 24–30, 36, 37
Sycamores 124, 134, 135, 137, 144
symbol 7, 8, 18, 73, 112, 119, 135, 141, 144, 153, 158

Tallahassee 40, 46, 139, 143, 187, 188, 190, 193–199
Tangerine Gardens 202
Ten Thousand Islands 20, 26, 32
Tenga, Angela 7, 171, 212, 221
"Texaco on Biscayne" 205
Thanksgiving, Louis 27, 30, 33
Their Eyes Were Watching God 82, 87, 90, 207
Thoreau, Henry David 80, 85
"Three Betrayals" 166
"To Go" 202
tradition 6, 7, 17, 27–29, 36, 43, 63, 71, 72, 74, 80, 91, 92–95, 103, 112, 116, 117, 119, 123, 124, 131, 132, 138, 141, 164, 173, 174, 177, 180, 181, 197, 205, 208, 209, 211, 217
tragedy 20, 41, 45, 49, 135
transcendence 47
transformation 50, 105, 203
transgression 171, 173, 174–177, 184, 205
transplants 5, 42, 139, 214, 217
twins 128, 135, 139–141, 176, 179, 212

unspoken 94, 105, 136, 214

The Vagina Monologues 78
values 6, 58, 61, 102, 117, 131, 190, 201
Van Camp, April 2, 5, 41, 221
Vergangenheitsbewältigung 107, 108
Vickers, Lu 203
violence 77, 78, 90, 94, 95, 99, 102, 172–174, 183, 221
Viramontes, Helena Maria 208

Walker, Alice 82, 89
Weeki Watchee 203
"When, He Wondered" 202, 203, 205
"Why We Left" 162
Williams, Janet 216
Woolworth 192, 194, 195, 199
World of Darkness 26, 30, 31
Wuthering Heights 14, 129

Zoophilia 180

www.ingramcontent.com/pod-product-compliance
Ingram Content Group UK Ltd.
Pitfield, Milton Keynes, MK11 3LW, UK
UKHW041950140426
5217IPUK00014B/735